SENATOR Dennis DeConcini

SENATOR Dennis DeConcini

FROM THE CENTER OF THE AISLE

Dennis DeConcini and Jack L. August Jr.

The University of Arizona Press | Tucson

Frontispiece: Senator DeConcini testifying before the Senate Foreign Relations Committee, 1977.

The University of Arizona Press
www.uapress.arizona.edu

First paperback edition 2015

Printed in the United States of America
20 19 18 17 16 15 7 6 5 4 3 2

ISBN-13: 978-0-8165-2569-0 (cloth)
ISBN-13: 978-0-8165-3207-0 (paper)

Cover designed by Carrie House, HOUSEdesign, llc
Cover photo: Senator DeConcini testifying before the Senate Foreign Relations Committee, 1977.

All photographs in this book are used with permission of the University of Arizona, Special Collections, Dennis DeConcini Congressional Papers Collection.

LIBRARY OF CONGRESS CATALOGING-IN-PUBLICATION DATA
DeConcini, Dennis.
Senator Dennis DeConcini : from the center of the aisle / Dennis DeConcini and Jack L. August, Jr.
p. cm.
Includes bibliographical references and index.
ISBN-13: 978-0-8165-2569-0 (hardcover : alk. paper)
ISBN-10: 0-8165-2569-2 (hardcover : alk. paper)
1. DeConcini, Dennis. 2. Legislators—United States—Biography. 3. United States. Congress. Senate—Biography. 4. United States—Politics and government—1945–1989. 5. United States—Politics and government—1989– 6. DeConcini, Dennis—Philosophy. I. August, Jack L. II. Title.
E840.8.D44A3 2006
328.73092—dc22
2006006352

♾ This paper meets the requirements of ANSI/NISO Z39.48-1992 (Permanence of Paper).

To Saint Jude Thaddeus and my family

CONTENTS

FOREWORD

I first saw Dennis DeConcini at St. Gregory's Church in Phoenix. His parents, Evo and Ora, watched proudly as the pious little boy walked up the aisle for Holy Communion. At the time, Evo was on the Arizona Supreme Court, establishing the long history of dedication to community service that has characterized the DeConcini family.

Since that time, with pride and pleasure I have watched Dennis grow. His life and career rose steadily: a teenage volunteer for Ernest McFarland in the 1950s; legal counsel and administrative assistant to Governor Sam Goddard in the 1960s; Pima County attorney in the 1970s; and finally U.S. senator from 1977 to 1995.

During his tenure in the U.S. Senate, he served the people of Arizona faithfully and well. His firm stands on effective law enforcement and drug control sent a clear message: the bad guys will go to jail, and law-abiding citizens will feel safe. This dedication extended well beyond Arizona's borders. Dennis used his knowledge and expertise for the benefit of the nation and the world, and he became widely regarded as an expert on the appropriations and budget process in Congress.

Dennis was a vigilant centrist who could get results by his ability to form friendships and working coalitions with members of both political parties. He never let party affiliation get in the way of administrative appointments. On many issues, he confounded Democratic Party regulars, as in his Judiciary Committee vote to send to the Senate floor the nomination of Clarence Thomas to the Supreme Court. Similarly, his swing vote in 1993 to support President Bill Clinton's tax bill raised the hackles of mainstream Republicans in Arizona. Dennis was independent, an attribute in Arizona politics.

On a personal note, I always treasure the encouragement and camaraderie from Dennis and his family. The impeachment of Governor Evan Mecham was one of the most traumatic events in Arizona's history. Dennis offered advice, support, and friendship as I sought to bring calm to the state. Even now he reaches out, maintains close ties, and offers sound guidance.

Several years ago it was my good fortune to introduce Dennis at an event in Tucson. When I arrived dressed as the Flying Nun, his delight at my presence was truly genuine. His intelligence, grace, sense of humor, and ability to laugh at himself have made him one of Arizona's most important public servants. I only wish that Evo and Ora could see him now. His outstanding successes, along with those of his entire family, would have made them so happy. I'm sure they're in heaven, smiles beaming down, pleased with and proud of their little boy.

The Honorable Rose Mofford
Governor of Arizona, 1988–1991

ACKNOWLEDGMENTS

When one is not a professional author and attempts to craft an autobiography or memoir, the challenge is daunting. Raised by wonderful and supportive parents, Evo and Ora DeConcini, I was taught not to promote or boast about my accomplishments. Others, they admonished, should praise your successes. Yet I wanted to write a book that reflected my perspective on the most significant aspects of my public career and at the same time acknowledge those who helped me in so many ways.

My parents, of course, gave their four children love, attention, direction, education, values, and financial opportunities. My brothers, Dino and David, and my sister, Danielle, are friends as well as brothers and sister. Their wives and husbands are friends as well as in-laws, and they have enriched my life. Steve Thu, my brother-in-law, an F-16 pilot, along with his friends Don Shepard, who became a two-star general and headed the National Guard Bureau of the Department of Defense, and Bud Sittig, a Delta Airlines pilot, flew me around Arizona for much of my tenure in the Senate. Cousins, aunts, and uncles encouraged me in this work and helped me keep my focus on important values.

Ron Ober—who ran all of my campaigns, served as my first Arizona state director, and organized my Washington, D.C., office—is truly a good friend, as is his wife, Gail. I am indebted to him for so many contributions—political, professional, and personal. His help in organizing this manuscript was crucial to the overall project. Gene Karp, my longtime friend and my lawyer and chief of staff in Washington, as well as his family and his in-laws, the Silvers, have always been helpful and deserve special mention. Some of my dearest friends and supporters reach back to grammar school and high school days: Dirk Broekema, Andy Cracchiolo, Bill Polson, Bob King, and Joe Ceasar, to name a few. I grew up with these friends and developed personal bonds that remain meaningful to me. Political differences notwithstanding, they have always been there to support me, and many times they urged me to write a memoir about my service in the U.S. Senate.

I am grateful to so many other friends that I dare not mention for fear of offending some that I have accidentally excluded. With three offices in Arizona and one in Washington, D.C., as well as numerous committee and subcommittee staff offices, I was blessed to have many able people around me. They understood my priorities, values, strengths, and weaknesses. My staff was unquestionably loyal and helpful with political and public-policy successes. They also helped immensely with this manuscript. In addition to those people already mentioned, I am grateful to Rip Wilson, Ken Ballen, Mary Hawkins, Dennis Burke, Tim Carlsgaard, Irene Hamburger, Judy Leiby, Bob Maynes, Pat Moran, Margo Myers, Romano Romani, Tim Roemer, Karen Robb, Ed Baxter, Laurie Sedlmayr, David Steele, Bobby Shore, and Nancy Suter.[1] Cele Swensen, Cybele Daley, Jane Fisher, June Tracy, Jeanette White, Chip Walgren, and Marilyn Washington worked diligently in my office and contributed, in part, to this manuscript. I am also indebted to Jim Fasco and John Libonati.

Bonnie Fricks and Avis Jackovich, who ran my Tucson office with great efficiency, and Mary Jane Perry, who likewise held forth in the Mesa office, contributed to the overall successes we experienced while in office. Barry Dill worked with me in many ways and remains a friend, advisor, and first-rate political strategist. The oral history interviews with him contributed much to the contents of this memoir. Michael Crusa and Judy Abrams gave extra effort on behalf of government service and to me personally and professionally. Their labors, especially early in my electoral career, were crucial to any campaign success I achieved.

I appreciate the efforts of Virginia Turner, who worked in my Phoenix office and met historian Dr. Jack L. August Jr. She discussed my project with him and helped schedule our initial meeting in Tucson. Dr. August, a well-known historian of the American West who serves as director of the Arizona Historical Foundation at the Hayden Library at Arizona State University, is unfailingly personable and one of the leading authorities on water resource development issues at this time. A brilliant writer, he took notes, interviewed scores of people, and helped me frame my writings into a readable manuscript.

Guy Inzalaco, Don Moon, Tony Gabaldon, Oscar Duarte, Sally Isaly, and Nancy Wolicki helped raise money, sharpened political strategies, and scheduled meetings throughout Arizona during my tenure in the Senate. They, too, assisted in the crafting of this manuscript.

Professor Toni Massaro, dean of the College of Law at the University of Arizona, provided the institutional framework for securing grant funds for this project. She and the College of Law provided assistance and support that enabled me to complete research, oral histories, and revisions of the manuscript. Ninth Circuit judge Michael Hawkins was indispensable as a campaign strategist and supporter throughout my career, and his service on the federal judiciary has been exemplary.

I would be remiss if I did not mention Earl Katz, a dear friend for many years, who helped raise money for me. The late Sam Sneller was also a strong supporter and fund-raiser. And I will never forget my cousins and friends in Graham County, who took up their Pima County relative's cause and gave unyielding support for our political efforts.

Four term state congressman Ed Pastor, one of the state's key Hispanic leaders from Arizona's Fourth District, provided invaluable political support in my first primary campaign for the Senate. When he decided to run for the House of Representatives, I supported him against some formidable Tucson-area Democrats. He continues to be a friend, and I will not forget his assistance early in my electoral career.

Still others—including Mary Mahoney, Carolyn Kapla-Bass, Bob Fiedler, Bobby Mills, Shirley Wilson, Marie Grijalva, Lynda Melton, Judy Tyre, Mary Rose Wilcox, Ramon Valadez, and Joann Piccolo—were always there for me in Arizona and Washington. Two other friends who worked tirelessly and volunteered their time were Bob Kohn and his wife, Karen. In a two-decade period and on numerous occasions, Bob piloted the plane that flew me throughout the region, and Karen always accompanied us. They remain dear friends today.

Dr. Morris Martin, who married my mother about three years after my father died, has been a profound influence on our family. He was an eighty-year-old widower, and my mother was eighty-three when they married. Morris brought joy, friendship, and intellectual stimulation to my mother and all the family. A native of the United Kingdom, he received a Ph.D. from Oxford University and taught and wrote on European history. He traveled the world and speaks six languages, and he and my mother had a wonderful love for each other. He was kind, gentle, and attentive during their fifteen years of marriage.[2]

A number of clergy also played a significant part in my political career. Catholic priests, Protestant ministers, Jewish rabbis, and Evangelists offered counsel during both my formative years and my professional and political career. They fostered deep moral standards, passion, and commitment to help those less fortunate. I thank them.

Of course, the most important people who helped advance my life and career were members of my family. My children—Denise, Christine, and Patrick—and later their families tolerated my political and professional ambitions. I am supremely proud of my children. One is a pediatrician, and two are lawyers. One even serves in the military as an F-22 fighter pilot. Of course, my seven grandchildren are perfect. Though I do not get to see my children and grandchildren often, I am deeply committed to them and have deep love for them. Their mother, Susie, was a tremendous support in my political advancement. I have always wanted to express in writing the pride and honor my children have brought to me, not only for their professional successes, but also for their values and their family lives. Their mother contributed immensely to this wonderful outcome.

My wife, Patty, who served on my staff and eventually worked for Senator Robert Byrd, has brought me joy and happiness in my retirement. She has been and continues to be a support and an inspiration.

—DWD

SENATOR Dennis DeConcini

1 First Days

On January 5, 1977, I walked into my new office, empty, silent, without life. For the previous twelve years an Arizona stalwart, U.S. senator Paul Fannin (R) had served his state and nation with dignity, and he had inhabited this space in the Dirksen Senate Office Building across from the majesty of the U.S. Capitol. His desk and swivel chair remained; I turned on the light, assessed the bare walls and vacant space, and glanced again at this spare remnant of my predecessor's twelve years in office. This would be my office until my senior colleagues in the Senate would consult traditions and assign a permanent office space—the location of which would be influenced significantly by my proximity near the bottom of the U.S. Senate food chain.

In a few hours, Vice President Nelson Rockefeller would swear me into office as the new freshman senator from Arizona. I approached the desk and sat down in the swivel chair. There was nothing on the desk—no briefcase, no files, nothing. I rolled around in the chair and stared out the window. I pinched myself and thought, "What are you doing here? Do you realize that you are going to be sworn in as a U.S. senator?" In an almost reflexive Catholic response to the situation, I crossed myself and thanked God. I was thirty-nine years old.

Family and friends had arrived for one of the most prideful days of my life. The late-morning swearing-in ceremony, an especially lengthy affair because there were eighteen newly elected senators, would be one of the high points of my career. We went over to the Senate in the underground train at about 11:00 A.M., and freshmen mingled with the old-timers. At the appointed time, Barry Goldwater (R), Arizona's political legend and senior senator, escorted me down the aisle. We lined up according to seniority; I was ninety-eighth. Orrin Hatch (R–Utah) and Malcolm Wallop (R–Wyoming) were behind me. Senators are sworn in four at a time, and it took at least an hour to complete the ceremony. As we walked across the floor, a smiling and waving Goldwater acknowledged my family and took special note of my mother-in-law, Peggy Hurley, a longtime Republican Party activist. We walked down before the presiding officer, Vice President Rockefeller. The Senate sergeant at arms announced, "Mr. President, I present to you the following senators duly elected by their states to be sworn in . . . raise your right hand." It was exciting. I never thought I would meet Nelson Rockefeller, who graciously posed for pictures with my wife and me in the old Senate chambers. As the day progressed, I was still overwhelmed. I would soon serve with Russell Long (D–Louisiana), Edward "Ted" Kennedy (D–Massachusetts), Robert Byrd (D–West Virginia), and Barry Goldwater—Senate icons.

We ate lunch at the Monocle—a legendary Capitol Hill restaurant replete with tradition and history. My three children, wrenched from friends, schools, and familiar surroundings in Tucson, grasped for ways to process the profound changes in their lives. Earlier, as they had stepped off the plane from sunny southern Arizona and entered the frigid twenty-degree Washington, D.C., winter, they had looked at me and seemed to ask, "Why in the world did you do this to us?" One daughter especially resisted this transition and asked to stay in Tucson with friends. Watching my children eat, I realized how difficult all of this was for them. In these early days, my wife, Susie, helped plan everything: searching for a home in Virginia, scrutinizing the schools, and arranging travel plans for family and friends. My parents, Evo and Ora, were enormously proud, and in many ways my election was validation of my father's years of political, legal, and business leadership in Arizona. Indeed, he had played a significant role in influencing me to run for office, and I know he enjoyed this day as much as I.[1]

That afternoon a Democratic caucus met. Committee assignments were at stake, and I had already received calls from Robert Byrd, Hubert Humphrey (D–Minnesota), and Ernest "Fritz" Hollings (D–South Carolina), among others, asking how I was doing and treating me as though they had known me for years. Hollings, in fact, had called me shortly after the election, while I was convalescing at home after a car accident had placed me in the hospital during the final days of the campaign. I even received a check from his political action committee (PAC). With sixty-four Democratic senators and a newly elected Democratic president, Jimmy Carter, leadership positions were sharply contested, and I knew I had to consider carefully whom I supported for these slots.

Indeed, on my first day of service in the Senate, the maneuvering commenced in earnest, and I knew I had a great deal to learn in a very short time. That first night, after dinner at an Italian restaurant in northern Virginia, I spoke to my wife and commented that I thought I knew a lot about government, but after one day on the job I realized that I had no comprehension about how Washington operated. I was hungry to learn everything I could as quickly as possible. I thought to myself, "My God, this is quite a challenge. You've got a lot to learn; there are a lot of smart people here, and the Panama Canal is coming at us."

The first order of business, which started even before I arrived in Washington, was choosing the Senate leadership. The race for Senate majority leader was hotly contested. Shortly after the election and while I was recovering from my injuries, my twenty-three-year-old campaign manager Ron Ober began a series of trips to Washington to begin the process of organizing my Senate office staff and to extend my greetings to my new colleagues. He faced several daunting tasks, especially interviewing applicants for various crucial positions: legislative aides, constituent service personnel, and office manager. Plus, I asked him to pay my respects to the three serious majority leader candidates—Hollings, Humphrey, and Byrd. As Ron informed me upon his return to Arizona from Washington, Hollings was exceedingly gracious, and Humphrey left him in awe, but his meeting with Robert Byrd was memorable.

The West Virginia senator was a formal, southern gentleman who possessed little in common with my young chief of staff from Tucson. The first part of the meeting was awkward. As Ron told me later, "Senator Byrd didn't know what to do with me, so he walked over to his closet, pulled out his fiddle and played for me . . . then said, 'You go tell your Senator DeConcini that I played the fiddle for you.'" That was my introduction to Robert Byrd, and the interesting thing was that after this initial meeting with Ron, he could never remember Ron's name.

Ron, however, would never forget Byrd's secretary's name—Miss Love. For the first two years of my service in the senate, whenever Senator Byrd saw Ron walking in the hallway, he would greet him with the salutation: "Miss Love says hello."

During my early days in the Senate, I became good friends with Edward Zorinsky (D–Nebraska), a conservative Democrat from Nebraska. Our wives also got along well, which made this transition a bit more tolerable. Byrd, who was majority whip and had won a close election against Ted Kennedy for that position four years earlier, wooed Zorinsky and me. I voted for Byrd—although his considerable musical talents played little in my analysis of the situation. He won by a slim margin. I made the right choice. During the campaign for majority leader, I asked Byrd to assign me to the Appropriations and Judiciary Committees—an unheard of proposition from a freshman senator. Byrd hesitated and told me that he had committed to another freshman senator for Appropriations, James Sasser (D–Tennessee), but that I was free to try to secure an appointment on that committee. After some maneuvering and lobbying of colleagues later in the session—especially with strong help from Senator James Eastland (D) of Mississippi—Byrd did help me gain assignments to the Appropriations and Judiciary Committees. In effect, he delivered on his commitment to support me for these two committees.[2]

Ron Ober and Gene Karp, a Tucson attorney who also helped orchestrate my election to the Senate, navigated the transition from Arizona to Washington in several ways. Although their knowledge of the subtleties and nuances of Washington folkways and decorum was limited, their sound political instincts served me well during these crucial, early days at the Capitol. In the first set of interviews for staff positions, they targeted Dr. Romano Romani, who had worked with outgoing senator Vance Hartke (D–Indiana) on legislative matters; Carolyn Kapla-Bass, an experienced office manager; and Joanne Picolo, a veteran Capitol Hill staffer who became our first director of constituent service.[3] This combination of sound political instincts and luck helped in creating a model office staff at the outset of my first term. More important, most of my key hires stayed on staff for many years, working together and adding cohesion and continuity to the office.

Ron also helped me with some of the practical considerations surrounding the move from Arizona to Washington. In order to make the transition for my children less traumatic, I took each of them to Washington with me during late November and December 1976. One night Ron, who was on Capitol Hill interviewing staff applicants, asked my wife and my daughter Denise if they wanted to have dinner. He had yet to learn the Capitol's dining landscape and erred when he asked my daughter if she knew of a good place to eat. "I went to this place in Georgetown with my dad . . . Rive Gauche." Ron dutifully made the reservations. As the party of three entered the elaborately appointed restaurant, he grew nervous. His credit card, with a modest limit, might not cover the bill. He told me shortly after the episode, "The minute the menu came, I got sticker shock; it was the most expensive meal I had in my life!" This cultural phenomenon doubtlessly confronts many Washington newcomers, but Ron, after paying the bill with his credit card, fortunately survived that particularly costly evening.

Freshman senators, like anyone assuming a new job, have papers to fill out and forms to sign. All new senators have to go almost immediately to the secretary of the Senate's office to sign their names on forms for their franking signature on government envelopes. My handwriting and signature, distinctive with its rough edges to the letters, was legible, but generated gentle kidding among my staff, who looked at me quizzically as the secretary of the Senate office staff watched me sign my name. I informed them that I was still having a little trouble writing because of my accident. But soon thereafter I learned that my penmanship had spurred a running joke among them: "How many people does it take to sign Dennis's name? Five. One to hold the pen and four to shake the table." My unique signature and penmanship notwithstanding, Ron, Gene, and my family helped make the move more tolerable.

Some Senate old-timers also contributed to my good fortune during those first days. Former Arizona senator Ernest McFarland (D), a majority leader during his two terms (1941–53), called old friends Senators Eastland, Herman Talmadge (D–Georgia), and Warren Magnuson (D–Washington) and informed them that "some guy with a funny-sounding name is coming from Arizona . . . you take care of him and treat him right." I went to see them right away, and Senator Eastland recommended that I serve on the Steering Committee. I went to Majority Leader Byrd and said I wanted to be appointed to the Steering

Committee, but was forced to wait. He made no commitment, but in time he put me on this committee along with another freshman, Sasser. That appointment during my first two weeks in the Senate was, I learned later, of profound importance. Those senators who wanted to move from, say, Finance to Armed Services, had to go through the Steering Committee. I heard some fascinating debates, gained insight into the subtlety and nuances of the Senate committee system, and appreciated the power of this particular committee.

My appointment to the Senate Appropriations Committee mirrored the early good fortunes I experienced with my support of Byrd and my appointment to the Steering Committee. Senator Russell Long, through a series of unusual maneuvers and political compromise, helped me secure a slot on Appropriations, where one of my distinguished predecessors, Arizona senator Carl Hayden (D), had served as chairman (1954–69) so effectively for many years. In a curious way, I ended up being the last person to get on the committee that year. Long had promised Sasser an appointment, but Eastland had placed my name ahead of Sasser's. With a larger population, Sasser's state posed potential problems for me in terms of seniority, but a remarkable compromise was struck. Though Long favored another southerner on the committee, he realized that my name had been placed before the committee earlier than Sasser's, and he wrestled with this dicey parliamentary issue. He arrived at a creative solution, asking to enlarge the committee from twenty-seven to twenty-nine members. The Republicans agreed. Still, according to the rules, I was technically ahead of Sasser, so I spoke up and voluntarily let him gain appointment ahead of me. Long was shocked, almost overwhelmed. As he put it, "I never saw anybody give up seniority around this place."

As the new junior senator from Arizona, I regularly met with my senior colleague Barry Goldwater. He was so direct that oftentimes people would misinterpret him, but I appreciated his candid responses to my questions. One of our earliest conversations in Washington concerned the 1976 Senate Republican primary campaign that pitted John Conlan against Sam Steiger. Goldwater congratulated me on my win in the general election and complimented me on my campaign platform. He liked that many of my views coincided with his conservative values, regarding methods to deal with inflation, welfare reform, drug enforcement at our nation's borders, local government as the best problem solver, and the return of more power to local and state governments through federal tax cuts and revenue sharing. Although I was a Democrat, Goldwater agreed with much of what I wanted to do as I "spoke to Washington for Arizona, [rather than] . . . speak[ing] in Arizona for Washington."[4]

Though Goldwater had supported Steiger in the 1976 Republican primary and general elections, he had some surprising observations, and his comments convinced me that he was not unhappy that I won the election. "Denny," as he called me throughout our tenure, "Steiger was obnoxious, and if Conlan didn't have that right-wing religious group behind him, he might be a good public servant." Goldwater, in fact, refused to meet with Conlan after the election when the former candidate wanted to discuss Goldwater's endorsement of Steiger. I appreciated Goldwater's forthright demeanor and sensed that he believed the better candidate won the general election in 1976.[5]

My first Senate campaign, in fact, had almost turned out to be a campaign for the House of Representatives. Arizona's popular congressman Morris Udall (D), who undertook a strong and memorable campaign for the presidency in 1976, also had his eye on the open U.S. Senate seat being vacated by Republican Paul Fannin. As I gauged the emerging political landscape in 1975–76, I reasoned that if Udall wanted to run for the Senate, I would declare for his vacant seat in the House of Representatives. As Udall's presidential campaign gained traction through the early months of 1976, however, I recalibrated my strategy. I was willing to wait on Mo as long as I could, but after conferring with my campaign staff, I decided to take a proactive stance and make a decision after the Wisconsin presidential primary. Communications between Udall's staff and my staff grew less frequent, and after Mo's strong second-place finish in the Wisconsin primary, I took action. On March 9, 1976, at a luncheon reception attended by six hundred persons at the Hotel Westward Ho in downtown Phoenix, I declared my candidacy for the Senate, thus preempting Udall's plans for a safety valve Senate candidacy. In fact, the next day Udall held a press conference announcing that he would not run for the U.S. Senate.[6]

Earlier that spring I sought out the aid of Michael Hawkins, a politically active Phoenix-based attorney who hailed from the northern Arizona community of Winslow. In my initial entreaty, I approached the receptionist in his Phoenix law office. I nervously introduced myself, and I remember her saying, "There's a guy out here named 'De'-something; he says he's running for the Senate and wants to talk with you." Hawkins later admitted that he sensed it was I and that it had already been rumored that I was running for the U.S. Senate. Our initial political parlay was not one of my more impressive showings. Hawkins, now serving on the Ninth Circuit Court of Appeals, recalled that I was not Giorgio Armani. I was decked out in a polyester suit, a checked tie over a striped shirt, pockets bulging with an assortment of notes, pens, and more. I was focused on the task at hand. Fortunately for me, Hawkins saw beyond his initial sartorial impressions and believed I was, as he put it, "the real deal." He supported me wholeheartedly, and in fact he agreed to serve as campaign chairman and was at the Westward Ho for my announcement with campaign manager Ron Ober, close advisor Gene Karp, a host of other supporters, and, most important, my family.

At the announcement, I laid out the framework for my campaign. A corresponding press release that was provided to newspapers, radio stations, and television outlets statewide summarized my plans. I emphasized my background in law enforcement as Pima County attorney and cited inflation, unemployment, crime, and federal government interference in the lives of Americans as the major issues that must be confronted. I informed the public that shortly after my election to the county attorney's post in 1972, I had established the Consumer Protection Office, had played an instrumental role in creating the widely praised Border Counties Strike Force, and in the previous year had been named by Arizona governor Raul Castro as head of the Arizona Drug Control District. I wanted to stake out a centrist position as a moderate Democrat who had spent his public career protecting the rights of citizens, upholding the law, fighting organized crime, and ridding the streets of illegal drugs.[7]

I faced two able opponents in the Democratic primary, scheduled for September 7, 1976; Arizona superintendent of public instruction Carolyn Warner and former Arizona attorney general Wade Church. Both were fine candidates, and to this day I consider Carolyn Warner a good friend.[8] She proved the more formidable opponent, and during the primary, especially in July and August of 1976, when it became clear that

I was the front runner and had received the endorsement of organized labor, she took the offensive. In several speeches and joint appearances, she raised the issue that seventy of the one hundred members of the U.S. Senate were attorneys. Arizonans, she allowed, should send a nonlawyer to Washington. I responded to this criticism in an address to the Mesa Rotary Club at Dobson Ranch on August 17, stating that perhaps some of these legally trained senators served special interests, but that I was a prosecutor. I wanted to declare war on organized crime, to encourage a dialogue with the Mexican president on drug issues, and to tighten Congress's fiscal belt. I blamed members of my own party for overspending and fiscal irresponsibility and declared that I would "take on the establishment Democrats."[9]

As the campaign heated up, Warner turned her attention to me and my public record. She made some aggressive political moves. At a joint appearance before the Paradise Valley Teachers Association, for example, a group favorably disposed toward her, she cast herself as the moderate candidate and me as the left-leaning liberal who experimented with the most fashionable legal bromides rather than taking a tough law-and-order stance. She criticized my leadership on the Border Counties Strike Force and the Arizona Drug Control District. I responded the next day in Lake Havasu City: "Mrs. Warner's charge is a bold misstatement. It's a shame that Mrs. Warner stoops so low for publicity. My record stands nationally as a fighter against . . . drugs."[10] The attempt to paint me in a liberal corner did not work effectively; I was well known for my moderate-to-conservative positions on many issues within the party, and my anti-abortion views conflicted with those of many Democratic Party activists.

With two weeks to go before the primary balloting, Warner tried to undermine my credibility. She virtually ignored Church, dismissing him as little, if any, political threat. At a speech to the Camelback Kiwanis Club at the Beefeater's Restaurant, she continued to paint me with a liberal brush. "My Democratic opponent believes the way you solve all problems of this country is by throwing more and more money at them, creating more bureaucracies. Whether it is Humphrey-Hawkins, national health insurance, or organized crime, the answer always seems to be more and more federal involvement in the private lives of our citizens. I am opposed to this on philosophical grounds, and I am opposed to this on the common sense of a businessperson committed to a balanced budget. . . . The real problem is the $76 billion deficit."[11] Indeed, as the campaign headed toward a conclusion, Warner seemed to borrow lines from my political playbook and, ironically, used them against me.

Church, however, ignored the parry and thrust of the campaign and chose to address some of the broader international topics of the day. He spoke often of nuclear power as a central issue. He told his supporters that "nuclear reactors, which are sold to foreign countries for peaceful purposes, are being used to produce nuclear weapons." At a talk to a group of voters at a private residence, he was quoted in the press as saying, "India produced its first nuclear bomb in 1974 by extracting plutonium from reactor by-products." Church walked to a different drummer throughout the primary, and though he had his core supporters, he never posed a serious challenge.[12]

Our campaign received a pleasant surprise when on August 19 the Arizona political action committee (AZPAC) of the Arizona Education Association (AEA)—held a vote and cast fourteen ballots for DeConcini, twelve for Warner, and four for Church. This outcome reflected somewhat negatively on Warner and positively on me. Tom Beauchamp, AEA governmental director, told *Arizona Republic* reporter Don Harris that the AZPAC vote was a statement "on Mrs. Warner's performance as state schools superintendent." He added that the vote demonstrated that Warner was popular in Maricopa County, but that "DeConcini is popular around the state."[13]

Ron Warner, Carolyn's husband and campaign manager, later stated to the press that he believed the AZPAC vote had tilted in my favor because my staff had outworked his. He added, "We just weren't that well organized."[14] I expressed my gratitude for the result but realized that I needed 60 percent of the votes to win the teachers' official endorsement. The AEA therefore withheld an endorsement and any campaign contributions it could have awarded the victor. But Warner's core constituency was neutralized, and victory on September 7 seemed within reach for me.

I was convinced also that Warner's refusal to quit as state superintendent of public instruction during the campaign cost her key votes among teachers. Instead of writing off the teachers—there were twenty-five thousand teachers in Arizona at the time—I went school district to school district, and Warner and I often crossed paths. In my pledge to Arizona educators, I called for collective bargaining for all public employees, including teachers. I also advocated an increased role for classroom teachers in formulating education policy and told them that I would seek federal funds and improved retirement benefits. My effort to pursue teachers' votes, in spite of Warner's powerful position within that critical Democratic voting bloc, was a key to my overall strategy in the primary campaign.[15]

In the days prior to the September 7 primary, I crisscrossed the state, sometimes appearing jointly with Warner and Church, and at other times making solo appearances. We debated the pros and cons of the various versions of the Humphrey-Hawkins bills, refined our stances on agricultural policy, scrutinized my anti-abortion views and how discordant they were with the national party platform, and called for funding of the Central Arizona Project (CAP) to bring more Colorado River water to the state. During this period, I predictably experienced more negative attacks, but at a higher decibel level; I was accused of being such a weak, one-issue candidate that the Republican nominee would win if I received the party nomination.[16] I was prepared for these types of attacks, though they were unpleasant. I remained on message and countered only the most outrageous charges.

On August 25, 1976, I received the endorsement of the state's largest and most influential newspaper, the *Arizona Republic*. "With Arizona's primary elections less than two weeks away," the editorial began, "attention is focusing on the race for party nominations for the U.S. Senate. . . . We think Dennis DeConcini is best qualified for the Democratic nomination. He is a brilliant young man from a noted Arizona family. His father, Evo DeConcini, was attorney general and a member of the Supreme Court." The *Republic* continued, "Dennis DeConcini has served as special counsel to Governor Samuel Goddard, and four years as county attorney of Pima County. He has been particularly active in the continuing campaign against the illegal importation and sale of drugs in Arizona." Although I would not receive the endorsement of this conservative newspaper in the general election, its support in the primary boosted my steadily growing name recognition throughout the state and added to my political viability.

My campaign staff grew confident as the primary-election day approached, but I remained cautious. They and my family had campaigned indefatigably, and on election night we were rewarded with a nearly two-to-one victory over Warner, with Church receiving only nominal support. The press described the results as "decisive": I received 121,433 votes to Warner's 71,612 and Church's 34,266. I won every county in the state, including voter-rich Maricopa County (where Phoenix is located), Warner's home base. I issued a victory statement shortly before midnight: "This victory really belongs to many people. My name was on the ballot, but the campaign was waged by friends, helpers, volunteers in the hundreds. The victory belongs to them. It also belongs to hundreds of thousands of Arizona people who went to the polls today. . . . It's the greatest system in the world, and the voters make it work. I thank them all." I thanked Susie, who had accompanied me to most of my campaign appearances, and my children for tolerating a relentless schedule of speeches and travel. I concluded my brief primary victory speech with a reference to the upcoming eight weeks: "There is no warmer feeling in the world than this. I am among friends, and finally we have won the first round. . . . The general election starts tomorrow."[17]

The next morning I opened the *Arizona Republic* and read the editorial page, which featured a piece entitled "What a Climax!" The editors suggested that my "runaway" victory made two points: the so-called "women's vote" did not materialize for Warner, and the Phoenix metropolitan area was now politically mature enough to support a "political sibling" from customarily rival Tucson. The latter point may have been more significant as I turned my attention to the general election.

The Warner campaign was gracious in defeat, and Carolyn campaigned for me in the general election. "DeConcini won it going away. I congratulate him on a well-run, well-orchestrated campaign. He won because his strategy was better, he was better financed, he was better organized, he was in the campaign early enough to build that organization, and he did an excellent job."[18] I was thankful for her elegant concession statement, which contrasted sharply with the end of the Republican primary election, one of the most tempestuous, interesting, and strangely complicated campaigns at any level in Arizona's history, drawing even Senator Goldwater into the debate.

In the spring of 1976, two sitting Republican members of the U.S.

House of Representatives declared their candidacy for the U.S. Senate. Arizona congressman Sam Steiger of the Third District, an irascible, blunt-speaking rancher from Prescott, had served in the House for five terms and in his humorous and inimitable way claimed to be a fiscal conservative who would guard the taxpayers' wallets. His opponent, John Conlan from the Fourth District, son of famed major league baseball umpire Jocko Conlan, was also a five-term Arizona congressman who championed a host of causes espoused on the religious right wing of his political party. His zealotry offended some, including Republican Party regulars, but his supporters were true believers. Conlan's candidacy in 1976 symbolized the increasingly significant role of religion in twentieth-century American politics. Moreover, Steiger and Conlan detested one another personally, and the race grew ugly very early in the primary season. This contentiousness threatened to divide the Arizona Republican Party into two warring factions, and the negative aspects of this campaign drew national attention.

Early in the Republican contest, a note pasted together from newspaper clippings was slipped under the door of Steiger's Tucson campaign office. It took aim at the fact that Steiger was Jewish, and its message injected an anti-Semitic dimension into the Republican primary. The note stated in part, "Quit working for that Jew because it doesn't take long to score runs. Remember you have been warned."[19] The national press, including the *New York Times*, the *Washington Post*, and the *Washington Times*, picked up on the growing controversy, and *Newsweek* published a feature on the two Arizona congressmen entitled "Politics from the Pulpit: Meat Ax versus Scalpel." One of Conlan's aides revealed that the congressman often referred to Steiger as "that New York Jew." Indeed, at the time of "born-again" Baptist Jimmy Carter's emergence as a leader in the national Democratic Party in the summer of 1976, a group of right-wing Protestant clergy and businessmen launched a major movement to organize the nation's evangelical Christians into a political force. According to *Newsweek*, "Republican Congressman John Conlan of Arizona and evangelist Bill Bright, head of the Campaign for Christ Crusade International" were spearheading a movement that used local prayer groups, Bible study meetings, and the Sunday-school lecture circuit to create a grassroots constituency for what supporters hoped would become "a third political party of real Christians only." Indeed,

Bright boasted that Conlan was "the only man I know who has a plan to bring Christians into politics."[20] Thus, the problematic mix of religion and politics, coupled with the suggestion of Conlan's anti-Semitism, diverted voters' attention away from more cogent issues.

Conlan supporters sent a letter to eight hundred Arizona clergymen urging his election to the Senate because "it would be nice to have a man with a clear testimony to Jesus Christ representing Arizona and America." The letters were signed by Ralph H. Eaton and Elmer Bradley, former chairmen of Arizona Billy Graham Crusades. Worse for Conlan, however, was the fact that the letters were mailed in official U.S. House of Representative envelopes containing the legend "public document" and "official business" in the upper left-hand corner. The letters contained a plea for these clergymen to urge Republicans, "including members of your congregation," to vote for Conlan in the September 7 primary.[21] Some religious leaders who received the mailing were sharply critical of the tactic, claiming it was an unpatriotic attempt to use religion for political gain. The Reverend Dr. Culver H. Nelson, senior minister at the Church of the Beatitudes and a founder and leader of the North Phoenix Corporate Ministry, said, "I am appalled by the way in which Mr. Conlan and his people have inserted sectarian religion into the campaign at every turn. . . . I am angered that this mailing came in a government printed envelope labeled 'public document, official business.'"

Then, in a reference to Senator Goldwater's not so subtle expressions of displeasure with Conlan's tactics, Nelson continued, "I am astonished by a sectarian appeal of such blatant proportions. Senator Goldwater may be right. This is a veiled but evident form of anti-Semitism calling for us to support him [Conlan] because of his Christian faith." Other religious leaders joined Nelson in his criticism. "God forbid that the intent of our Founding Fathers should ever be subverted so that sectarian appeal will take precedence over decency and honor and capability," another Protestant minister wrote. "From Conlan's initial partisan mailing piece in which he boasts a photo of Billy Graham—a photo he included without Graham's knowledge, permission, or endorsement—until this most recent episode, he has sought to 'use' the clergy, 'use' the church, 'use' religious people toward wholly partisan and personal ends. This is unconscionable."[22] The mailing backfired, and Conlan retreated into silence as the press tried to confront him on the issue.

Things grew worse for the Republicans, and I sensed that this situation would play to my advantage in the general election. Barry Goldwater, who maintained a self-proclaimed policy of not endorsing any candidates in a Republican primary, grew so frustrated with Conlan's repeated transgressions that he placed himself squarely in the center of the Conlan-Steiger primary fracas. He accused Conlan of injecting religion and anti-Semitism into the campaign and issued a formal statement from his offices in Washington, D.C. "In all my years as a Republican I have never endorsed a person running for state office in the primary. This year I am breaking my long-standing rule and announcing my support of Congressman Sam Steiger for the office of U.S. senator from Arizona." Goldwater said he had been following the campaign and had grown deeply concerned over the injection of religion into what he called "a struggle." "My comments," he continued, "have obviously gone unheeded by Mr. Conlan because I continue to read and get reports from Arizona of not only the continued injection of politics in the form of a particular new Christian movement, but also of anti-Semitism."[23] Goldwater's release included the statement that as a half-Jewish person, he might condone the new Christian movement, but not the anti-Semitism. Steiger naturally expressed his pleasure at receiving Goldwater's backing.

Conlan's response to Goldwater's August 24 endorsement of Steiger fueled the Republican conflagration to unprecedented levels: "Goldwater has claimed neutrality before in other Republican primaries and most recently the presidential race where he violated his pledge to stay neutral. . . . Goldwater has never discussed my Senate race with me at any time. He has neither given me advice nor criticism." The angry tone revealed his bitter disappointment at the content and timing of Goldwater's message, but Conlan continued to fan the flames, and he did not stop with this recalcitrant response.[24]

In the presence of the Washington press corps, Conlan uttered, "I don't know what it is with Barry. Maybe it's the pain (from a hip operation), maybe it's the drinking he's been doing." An enraged Goldwater, when he received word of Conlan's public statement, said, "I could never work with Conlan if the man was elected." Two days later, at a fund-raising dinner in Newport Beach, California, Goldwater was forced to issue a denial of a "drinking problem." "I've had all I can take from this guy. . . . I'd hate to serve in the U.S. Senate with a man who makes continued use of religion in politics." Even outgoing senior senator Paul Fannin, an unusually discreet politician, called *Arizona Republic* political commentator Bernie Wynn and offered his opinion on the controversy. He told Wynn that before Conlan had arrived in Washington, the Arizona congressional delegation was always tightly knit. Conlan, Fannin offered, had been a disruptive force. "I have the greatest respect for Barry," Fannin continued, "[and] I was concerned about the damage Congressman Conlan's statements have done to the GOP and to the whole state."[25] Conlan stumbled and never really regained his footing as the primaries drew to a close. With both of Arizona's sitting senators denouncing Conlan in unequivocal fashion, I sensed that Congressman Steiger would win the Republican nomination.

Still, Steiger could not get too comfortable. An almost comical yet bizarre incident just outside the Wishing Well bar in Chino Valley nine months prior to the primary election somehow drew press attention throughout the Republican primary and in the waning days of the general-election campaign. On the night of October 9, 1975, Congressman Steiger had shot and killed two tame burros owned by the Stan Tanner Youth Foundation. Tanner tried twice to sue Steiger over the incident. Steiger claimed that the animals had attacked him, and he had fired in "self-defense," though Yavapai County investigators concluded that the animals were shot from behind. After a full investigation, the Yavapai County Attorney's Office asserted that the congressman had reacted "out of fear." He had committed no crime. Tanner filed a lawsuit against Steiger for $76,200 just four days before the primary election. Steiger claimed that the suit was an attempt to keep the burro killing in the public's eye in an effort—presumably by Conlan backers—to short-circuit his bid to win the Republican nomination.[26] The Republican primary came to an unusual ending, with religion and burro killing dominating the headlines.

Burros, dirty tricks, religion, and whispers of anti-Semitism notwithstanding, many thought the election would be close. Steiger defeated Conlan for the Republican nomination for the U.S. Senate by nearly

9,800 votes, a narrow, yet comfortable margin. Conlan's defeat by his archenemy not only was a humiliation for the better mobilized and more fervent Conlan organization, but also derailed his other political ambitions—control of the state Republican Party and his eventual rise to the presidency. Shortly after the results were announced, I realized that Conlan's undoing was tied to his unbridled political ambition. He ridiculed, ignored, and insulted the party's senior leaders, littered his campaign talks with religious insinuations, and tried to turn the political lectern into a pulpit. And he made no effort to conceal his haste to reach national prominence. In the end, he made voters feel uncomfortable.

I thus faced off against the colorful and inimitable five-term congressman Sam Steiger of Prescott.[27] He emerged from the brutal Republican primary a bloodied and wounded candidate, and I knew that I had some advantages heading into the general election, including a unified Democratic Party and a campaign staff that had been tested under fire. Steiger, I knew, burned the candle at both ends, personally and professionally, and was experienced with rhetorical play. Republicans were divided, and on many issues I knew that I could persuade disaffected Republicans to cross over and vote for me. Steiger was a formidable candidate. His humor and charming demeanor were personal qualities that endeared him to a wide range of people. With two decades of Republican Party registration gains behind him, as well as Senator Goldwater's almost rock star status and long political coattails, I knew I had little, if any, room for error.

On Wednesday, September 8, the morning after our primary victories, Steiger called my home to discuss the possibility of debating specific issues during the general-election campaign. I was amenable to this idea, and when reporters contacted me about it, I said, "I am available for any kind of joint appearance. I make my living practicing law, which is debating in a courtroom." In the eight weeks between the primary and general elections, Sam and I held joint appearances thirty-one times; many were debates. One reporter from the *Arizona Republic* noted that "there were days when the two candidates met on the same forum as many as five times." We crossed paths on the campaign trail frequently, and we grew to know one another during this intense eight-week period.[28]

Meanwhile, the political hubris of the Republican primary affected my opponent. At a press conference at Republican Party Headquarters shortly after the primary results were made official, Jim Colter, the state Republican Party chairman, announced that "John Conlan will support Sam Steiger" in the race for the U.S. Senate. But when asked to issue a statement of support, Conlan remained silent.[29]

Our joint appearances contributed greatly to the integrity of our campaign, and although some of our encounters and debates were heated, most were civil. As the November 2, 1976, general election approached, I grew increasingly confident. Sam arrived at joint appearances unprepared and somewhat out of sorts, which redounded to my benefit. My family worked tirelessly, traveling throughout the state beyond our base in Tucson. My father's enduring reputation; my strong antidrug, anticrime record in the Pima County Attorney's Office; and the organizing skills of Ron Ober, Gene Karp, and others, including Michael Hawkins and my brother Dino, came together in almost synchronized fashion. I remained on message in the eight weeks before the election and held my ground during our one-on-one debates.

From the outset, Sam attacked, and I hit back. The most frequently discussed issue and the most popular topic debated during the campaign was the role of organized labor in elections. On September 21, for example, in one of our first joint appearances, we appeared at a luncheon function at the Glendale Chamber of Commerce. The debate began pleasantly enough with a friendly handshake. I drew the long straw, so I addressed the audience first and described myself as "an issue candidate" who would make Arizonans proud. Steiger then took the floor and launched immediately into a negative attack. "There would be no dealing in personalities," he began, and he went on to "the most important issue in the campaign; big labor's stranglehold on Congress." In textbook fashion, he moved in: DeConcini is controlled by organized labor because he has received the endorsement of the Arizona branch of the American Federation of Labor/Committee of Industrial Organizations (AFL-CIO) in the primary. He poked fun at my campaign slogan, "Arizona's Answer to Washington's Problems," and finished his opening salvo by reiterating the point that "big labor owns its candidates, including DeConcini, . . . body and soul."

I could not wait to get back to the microphone. Turning toward Sam and looking directly at him, I said, "I consider it an insult to say that I am controlled by big labor. I am not controlled by big labor." Then, in answer to an audience question, I stated, "Seventeen thousand of the $250,000 I spent in the primary came from union members." I noted also that Steiger had appeared before the AFL-CIO Committee on Political Education five weeks earlier in an effort to gain their endorsement. "Get the facts straight," I snapped. I elaborated on my views on organized labor, indicating that I was concerned about labor's influence in Congress, that I did not follow the dictates of union leaders, and that I opposed repeal of Section 14b of the Taft-Hartley Act that enabled states to enact right-to-work laws.

Taken aback, Sam offered a transparent rejoinder: "Good try, Dennis. You bet I went to the AFL-CIO. I didn't expect to get their support, and I told them I wouldn't want their support. I just feel it's important to keep the lines of communication open with organized labor." I took to the offense: "I expect Mr. Steiger will accuse me next of being anti-Semitic. That's the way he campaigns." Under the rules, Sam had the last word, and he remained on script. He said he was sorry that I had taken his charge about being under labor's control personally, but "if that's the case, you're going to be offended for the next seven weeks." My staff prepared me well, and I considered this encounter an outstanding engagement. I gained insight into the nature and style of Steiger's debating tactics.[30]

At every turn, I focused attention on Steiger's voting record in Congress. As a congressman, Steiger frequently voted "no" on issues of importance to many groups in Arizona. He said he voted against federal aid bills because they called for the expending of more money than was in the budget. I countered that "just to be against something is not enough." Indeed, this negative approach summed up Sam's tactical errors in the campaign; he did not advocate a strong conservative philosophical approach to public policy and instead relied on humor and showmanship to mask a "glass is half empty" approach that at this time did not appeal to the electorate.

My first campaign for the U.S. Senate ended with me in a hospital bed. On October 29, just four days before the general election, I was in an automobile accident at a busy intersection in east Phoenix. I suffered facial cuts and three broken ribs. After the campaign, reporters asked if I had any regrets, and I said, "Yes, going through the intersection at

44th and Van Buren." But the election results did much to ease my pain as I recovered at St. Joseph's Hospital.[31]

When the votes were tallied, I won rather handily, garnering 400,334 to Steiger's 321,236. I lost only two counties: Yavapai County, Sam's home base, and Mohave County, a strong conservative region in northwestern Arizona. I even won Republican stronghold and voter-rich Maricopa County, 206,481 to 200,395. I issued statements from St. Joseph's, crediting my victory to "a very good Democratic turnout and to those Republicans who crossed over and put the person before party loyalty." I praised my wife, Susie, who was a remarkably effective campaigner.

Steiger's concession statement was unique. On the morning after the election, he called me. I answered the phone, and on the other end of the line was Steiger, who, discarding phone etiquette, greeted me with the salutation, "Luckyyyy, Luckyyyy!" In many ways, this amusing concession call captured the essence of Sam's personality. He remained in political life, serving briefly in Governor Evan Mecham's ill-starred administration and later as mayor of Prescott. Despite my relatively easy general-election campaign, I did in fact feel lucky to have won.[32]

As I began my service in Washington, two hundred years after the Declaration of Independence was issued, I felt I was blessed with divine good fortune. My family, wrenched from a comfortable life in Tucson, was supportive of my endeavor; my campaign staff orchestrated a smooth and efficient transition to Washington; and my swearing in as a U.S. senator was one of the most memorable days in my life. Reflecting on this overwhelming set of circumstances, I thought back to my childhood and my parents, without whom none of this could have transpired. It was truly an American story of ancestors and immigrants that stretched from northern Italy to southeastern Arizona.

2 And We Danced for Fifty Years

The Webster family farmhouse, where my mother was born and raised, still stands in Thatcher, Arizona. It was there that I spent some of my most memorable childhood days, riding tractors, working and playing at harvesting crops, and gaining exposure to a set of ethics and values that characterized the pioneer farm families of Graham County. It differed markedly from my home environment in Tucson, then a small city, but increasingly urban and busy. In the summer of 1945, my parents decided that my health, plagued by food allergies among other things, could somehow improve with a diet of organic vegetables, farm-fresh produce, and country living. I was eight years old; World War II was winding down, and for the next five summers Aunt Zola, my mother's oldest sister, and her husband, Marc Claridge, taught me the rudimentary facts of life on a working farm. Though the prime reason for my initial summer sojourn was quickly forgotten—Aunt Zola and Uncle Marc let me eat ice cream and anything else I wanted—I came away from this summer and four subsequent ones with something vivid, enduring, and useful.

I was blissfully unaware of the Webster Farm's local historical significance. I may have known vaguely that my mother had descended from Mormon pioneers, but at the time I was more interested in discovering the farm's secrets and sources of excitement. My maternal grandparents' families migrated to Graham County in 1883 as part of what western historian Walter Nugent calls the second generation of Mormon colonization. In many ways, my mother's parents, Oscar Webster and

Ollie Damron Webster, were among the vanguard of pioneer Mormon settlement in the Gila Valley of southeastern Arizona Territory. In the generation after Brigham Young led the Mormons to the Great Salt Lake, Latter Day Saints usually stayed where they settled, and populations were stable by American standards. Religious commitment doubtlessly encouraged this unusual degree of frontier stability. Some settlements were the result of "calls" by church leaders, but most were not, and Mormons of the late nineteenth century preferred to keep to their own communities. Whether the Gila Valley migration, which included my maternal grandparents, was the result of a "call" or of collective decision by several Mormon families, the result was that my mother's parents were soon to meet in the Gila Valley.[1]

The two migrating families left either three days apart or one year apart; accounts vary. The Damrons, however, preceded the Websters. In Kanosh, Utah, William T. Damron and his family loaded covered wagons, rounded up animals and livestock, and set forth for the Gila Valley in August 1883. His nine children accompanied him, including my grandmother, Ollie, then eleven years old. She rode bareback and took care of the loose stock that followed the wagons. The journey, long and arduous, saw the Damron party forge rivers at flood stage, prompting the men to affix logs to the sides of the wagons and float them down the rivers as the horses swam alongside. They arrived in the area called Pima on November 25, 1883, and thus commenced their residence in Arizona Territory. In that first winter, the Damron family lived in tents, but soon thereafter William built an adobe house in the small settlement of Central, where my mother was born.[2]

The Websters lived in Chicken Creek near the southern Utah hamlet of Levan and were led south by family patriarch Thomas George Webster. They settled near the Damrons, and Oscar, who, like Ollie, was eleven years old at the time of the migration, arrived in the Gila Valley with similar tales of hardship and adventure. Their families forged an agriculture-based existence as successive waves of pioneers, Mormon and non-Mormon, migrated to the fertile Gila Valley and reinvented themselves on the far southwestern frontier.[3] Oscar and his brothers helped their father clear the land that they patented, known later as Webster Farm, and located today on Webster Lane about one mile west of the Eastern Arizona College campus in Thatcher.[4]

By his late teens, Oscar could claim ranching and freighting as steady vocations. Besides engaging in irrigated agriculture below the recently completed Union Canal, which abutted the family's land, he owned and operated a freighting company for which he used strong, heavy freight wagons that required several spans of horses to pull the heavy loads of ore from the mines at Globe and Miami over to Bowie—the closest connection to the Southern Pacific Railroad. On return trips, the wagons were loaded with flour, sugar, beans, cloth, and other provisions.

Ollie helped her father in the mercantile store that he opened in Thatcher soon after consolidating his holdings, securing land and a home, and moving the family to that nearby town. She also helped her father run the post office that took delivery of mail and payroll from armed Wells Fargo drivers, who protected and delivered mail and passengers throughout the territory. In time, William became a much-beloved civic leader, called "Uncle Billie" by those he served in a variety of guises: schoolteacher, postmaster, store owner, and, later, county school superintendent. Fellow settlers elected him county treasurer in 1888 and again in 1890. Likewise, in 1892 and 1896, he was elected probate judge, and, according to contemporary accounts, he conducted his affairs with dignity and decorum. My grandmother clearly benefited from her father's public stewardship, and as the nineteenth century blended into the twentieth, the Damrons emerged as civic leaders in Graham County.[5]

In the context of carving an existence out of the remote yet verdant Gila Valley, Oscar and Ollie married on January 30, 1894. They had known each other for ten years; they were socially and culturally bound by their church, and the almost predictable ceremony took place at the Damron home with another Mormon pioneer, Samuel Claridge, officiating. The newlyweds took no honeymoon; Oscar departed on a freighting venture the next day. Ollie did not see him until two weeks later, when he returned from his trip.

Indeed, freighting was Oscar's primary business, and he spent many days traversing Apache land, facing danger from attack. Most settlers had developed a healthy respect for Geronimo and his followers during the 1880s, but, incredibly, Oscar never carried a gun while working his route. Apaches on horseback often rode to his camp at night and searched his wagons. In all his years, however, they never stole property or harmed anyone in his freighting parties. Only once, when an angry young trespasser kicked sand in the campfire and upset dinner plates in disgust over finding nothing desirable to pilfer, did Oscar suffer any kind of mishap. He maintained a sunny disposition and smiling face, never carried liquor or firearms for sale, and thus apparently avoided harm.

In a few years, however, the Arizona Eastern Railroad completed the track from Bowie to Globe, and this new form of transportation eliminated the need for freighting. Oscar, like so many of his contemporaries, became involved in many enterprises, and the loss of the freighting business allowed him to entertain other ventures. He partnered, for example, with five friends, one of whom was his brother-in-law, William Damron Jr., and built a big store in Thatcher appropriately named the "Big Six." In time, he farmed and invested in ranches with large herds of angora goats, cattle, horses, mules, and burros. In fact, he gained much notoriety in the Angora goat business. Known as the Goat King of the World, he owned eighteen thousand goats, the largest herd in the world at the time. During this period, from the turn of the century until his untimely death in an automobile accident on June 21, 1933, he served as a mohair buyer for Ryder and Brown of Boston, Massachusetts, one of the largest mohair brokers in the United States.[6]

Oscar and Ollie had eight children, but only four survived: Zola, Jessie, Raleigh, and Ora, my mother, who was born on March 19, 1907, in Central, Arizona, a little town between Safford and Pima. She was the youngest and the only child delivered with the assistance of a physician, Dr. William Platt. She grew up among a large, extended family, with sisters, brothers, and cousins living in close proximity. They shared all aspects of daily life; they were constant playmates, attended the little grammar school together, and remained close at school and play. Domestic life included helping her elder sisters clean and manage the house, milking the cows, and at times aiding Oscar and Ollie with any number of daily activities. Significantly, as Ora grew older, her parents admonished her to get a good education before she married.

My mother excelled in school. She went to grammar school in Central and then attended high school at the Gila Academy in Thatcher, graduating in 1925.[7] Toward the end of her sophomore year, the instructor for her shorthand and typing class took ill. School administrators, in a bind, turned to Ora and asked that she keep the class together. As she recalled, "I started assigning work, and we just sort of did the work together."[8] The class and my mother made it through the semester—she was a natural in the classroom—and as a result of this trial by fire the teachers asked if she could attend summer school and take over the shorthand and typing class. So, at age seventeen, Ora traveled to Los Angeles with her sister, attended Woodbury Business College, and, following that first summer, signed a contract to teach shorthand and typing. For two years, while she finished high school and took beginning college units, she taught shorthand at Gila Academy and served as secretary to the president of the college.[9]

Ora looked to new horizons after high school and business school, working as a court reporter as well as finding a good job in the Bank of Safford. She enjoyed the banking community but contemplated further education. In fact, her father urged her to continue, but the agricultural economy in the Gila Valley during the 1920s already manifested the telltale signs of the Great Depression, and my mother felt compelled to keep her job. One day, however, her father came to see her at the bank, and before she had time to greet him, the bank president preempted her with, "Mr. Webster, where are we going to send this girl to school?" The question was framed not as "Are we going to send her to school?" but "Where?" Oscar replied, "Wherever she wants to go." Ora wondered how the family would find the money, but the following year she attended Brigham Young University.[10]

"It was a very small, very Mormon school at that time," Ora recalled, and she spent a lonely year there. By Christmas, she was contemplating returning to Arizona, and the following year found her at the University of Arizona in Tucson, where she was able to transfer a surprising number of units from Brigham Young and continue her education. She finished with a double major in finance and accounting; plus she had the foresight to take all of her electives in education. So when she graduated in 1930, at the beginning of the Depression, she was a certified teacher as well as having a degree in finance and accounting. She was twenty-three years old.

Indeed, her pragmatic notion of taking education credits paid dividends. A friend from school, Rose Bush, told my mother that the Tucson Unified School District was starting the six-three-six plan for a new group of junior high schools. She rushed down to the offices and applied for Tucson openings, though she had already sent in her résumé to other school districts around the state. She soon received offers from Round Valley, Willcox, and other places, but she wanted to stay in Tucson. As she put it much later, "My better judgment told me that Evo [her future husband] was not going to be there—I had not met Evo, but . . . Round Valley was not the place for a girl of my age to go to teach; that was going to be kind of a dead end."[11]

She took the initiative to apply to the superintendent of the Tucson School District, C. E. Rose, in person, informing him that she had other offers, but that she preferred to stay in Tucson. The following Monday she received in the mail a teaching contract from the Tucson School District. She learned later that her audacious job-searching methods were unprecedented and that she was not supposed to approach the superintendent directly. But she was pleased at the outcome. "It wasn't pressure," she remembered, "it was just asking was he going to give me a job."[12]

Her priorities lay with her family in Graham County. When my mother learned that her father had borrowed money to keep her in school, she obliged herself to repay him. After paying her debts, she realized that she needed to purchase a car. Buses did not run from Tucson to Safford or Thatcher, and she wanted to visit her parents on a regular basis. The circuitous train route—from Tucson to Bowie, then a change to the Arizona Eastern Railroad, which went to Globe and finally to Thatcher—took too long. As Ora settled her school debts and commenced teaching in Tucson School District 1, she purchased a car that enabled her to travel home on weekends and holidays. In a short time, however, she met my father on a blind date, and her teaching career and the need for her car came to an abrupt and happy end.

My father, Evo Anton DeConcini, was born in Iron Mountain, Michigan, where his parents, who had emigrated from Italy, owned a restaurant and hotel. His father, Giuseppe, was seventeen when he immigrated to the United States in 1893. He was born in the town of Casez, in the Tyrolean Alps, in the beautiful Val di Non area, which at the time was part of Austria. The legendary Father Francisco Eusebio Kino (Eusebio Chini) was born in nearby Segno. This distinction, however, brought little fame or fortune to my grandfather, though he grew up speaking German and Italian, like Kino. Soon after his arrival in the United States, he learned English and abandoned his previous vocation as a farmer. He took a job as coal miner in Hazelton, Pennsylvania, for $1.03 per hour. He worked ten hours a day. While he was working under a hanging wall one day, a portion fell and killed a fellow worker. A piece of coal pierced my grandfather's right thumb, and he took the scar to his grave. The next day he walked off the job and headed West, vowing never to work underground again.

My grandfather was a musician—he played the concertina—and his favorite songs were "I Want What I Want When I Want It" and "I Don't Know Why I Love You But I Do, Do, Do." This talent afforded him safe passage and a seat in the caboose—apart from the less desirables. Although he never intended to settle in the north woods of Michigan, he arrived and began his life as a merchant, musician, and, eventually, family man.[13]

My paternal grandmother, Ida Tremontin, was born in Udine, north of Venice, near Trieste, on September 11, 1880. She made the crossing in 1891, when she was eleven. My father's parents met by accident in Iron Mountain, which reinforced his belief that besides love being made in heaven, geography played a role as well. The newlyweds moved to Duluth, then north of the border to Canada, where my grandfather pursued a music career, and my aunt Alice was born on April 7, 1899. After a little more than a year, they returned to Iron Mountain in 1901, and my father, Evo, was born on March 25, 1901.

My father's childhood on the "North Side" was lively and multicultural—the Italians, the Irish, and the French all had their own parishes—and he learned the hostelry business from his parents. As my father recalled in his autobiography, "My mother was a frugal person, and any virtue such as thrift and saving must have come from her. (My father was the opposite. He was a free spender; any freewheeling I have comes from him.)" In any event, he remembered Iron Mountain fondly: "my hometown didn't have a wrong side of the tracks. . . . There was good and bad, rich and poor, on both sides." There were two railroads in Iron Mountain, and, incredibly, my grandparents lived between the tracks. Every church in this cultural cross-section of America rang on Sunday; they were part and parcel of Iron Mountain. When Evo turned nine, my grandfather set him up in a shoeshine business. He purchased a shoeshine stand and four brushes. As soon as he started to make money, he purchased his own clothes. The shoeshine stand perhaps first demonstrated the entrepreneurial skills that eventually made him a success in business. While in high school, for example, he expanded the business during the summer, branching out with a chain of stands operated by other boys. He had saved more than $700 when he moved on to other ventures at age seventeen. In fact, Evo argued that he could have made more money, but his father, who considered barbershops questionable social settings, declared them off-limits.[14]

Evo last saw his father on Halloween night in 1920. His parents had spent three years in Florence, Wisconsin, where the business climate appeared better, but recently had returned to Iron Mountain. They departed from the Chicago, Milwaukee, and St. Paul Railroad Station on a planned trip to the West. My grandfather wanted to move to a more salubrious climate because the Spanish influenza, which reached epidemic proportions in 1918 and 1919, had victimized him, and he hoped to avoid future illness. A friend praised the climate of Roswell, New Mexico. They went there, but it proceeded to rain for three weeks, so they tried El Paso, Texas. It was too windy and very unfriendly. At Douglas, Arizona, the sun shone, and the smelter belched smoke. When they reached Tucson, on Thanksgiving Day 1920, my grandfather, after experiencing two days of the Old Pueblo's weather, declared it his new home. In less than three months, however, he was killed in an automobile accident on the road from Nogales to Tucson. My father received a telegram in Iron Mountain, from an unknown person, stating, "Prepare for the worst." His father was dead, and his mother injured. Before my grandfather died in February 1921, however, he had purchased three pieces of property in Tucson: the Goldring Apartments at 502 S. Fifth Avenue, the American Hotel at the corner of Toole and Pennington, and a vacant lot next door to the hotel property. On April 2, 1921, after organizing the funeral and then taking care of business in Iron Mountain, my father returned to Tucson with his mother and sister, where the DeConcinis claimed a new home. The vacant lot my grandfather purchased remained in the family until 2005.[15]

My father was nineteen, Alice twenty-one, and my grandmother forty at the time; the only people they knew were the neighbor and an undertaker named John Reilly. Evo operated the hotel with his mother and sister, and for the next ten years he oversaw a variety of enterprises and completed his undergraduate and law degrees at the University of Arizona. Although real estate eventually demanded the majority of his attention and proved his most successful business activity, he tried his hand at other vocations during the 1920s.

In the context of the nationwide recession of 1919–21, he somehow befriended the owners of a candy store, the Cactus Sweet Shop, and watched the business for six months. He concluded that it was "a winner" and entered into a business partnership. All of them decided to relocate to a fashionable part of Los Angeles to open an upscale cactus candy store, modeled after the Tucson enterprise. The venture, according to my father, took nine months to fold. His partner, trying to save a failing marriage, spent the majority of time with his wife and soon disappeared from the scene. My father's sister, Alice, assisted valiantly, but reality sank in, and Evo looked for other ways to earn a living. Still in Los Angeles, he sold adding machines and town lots for a time, but finally decided to return to Tucson when the purchasers of the hotel could no longer make payments and he had to repossess the property. At this time, in the mid-1920s, he worked at a service station and began taking classes at the University of Arizona.

Meanwhile, my father looked carefully at the developing real estate market and its relationship to the inexorable growth and development in the American Southwest. With a $3,000 loan from his mother, he purchased a forty-acre tract on East Broadway and developed the Country Club Heights Subdivision. He continued apace—attending classes, overseeing various small businesses, and developing nine subdivisions. He also purchased and operated two suburban water companies. In addition, he bought a property at 1301 East Speedway, where he, my aunt, and grandmother lived until the University of Arizona purchased it in the 1970s.

Education became a significant part of my father's dizzying schedule. From the mid-1920s onward, he attended school and took a variety of courses. Many who got to know him, especially through real estate transactions, said that he "ought to be a lawyer." At age twenty-nine, he commenced this process—completing some undergraduate courses and graduating from the University of Arizona College of Law in 1932.[16]

Toward the end of his undergraduate and law school career, in February 1932, my father asked a friend of my mother's, Julia Schendel, for a date. Julia said she was engaged, but that she had a friend, Ora Webster, who might be interested. "So our meeting was on a blind date," my father wrote fifty years later, "but who needs to see when the mixture is right?" They went to the annual Rodeo Saturday Night Dance at the Women's Club and hit it off immediately. My mother's recollection of this first meeting corresponded with my father's account. According to her, they met on a blind date at "the Arizona Women's Club, down on Granada when it used to be down in Snob Hollow. And we danced. And we danced for fifty years."[17] The courtship was swift, and they were married on December 24, 1932.

Because my mother was Mormon and my father Catholic, they compromised and were married in the Episcopalian Church at Stone and Third in Tucson. It was a small wedding, and my mother's family failed to attend. It wasn't that they did not like my father; it was, as he put it later, "just because." Two weeks later, however, religious issues were placed aside, and on the way home from the honeymoon in San Francisco they stopped in Bell, California, a suburb of Los Angeles, and the entire family gathered for a postwedding reunion. I grew up never knowing of this early religious tension, which in the end amounted to nothing of significance.[18]

I was born May 8, 1937, and my older brother Dino taught me much as our boyhood trials, travails, and companionship helped shape a happy childhood. My parents were always there for all of us, including my two younger siblings, David and Danielle. We had the best education possible, traveled, and spent time with relatives outside our daily routine in Tucson. As I noted at the outset of this chapter, I recall vividly my time at the family farm in Graham County. My aunt Zola and uncle Marc taught me a great deal and provided me with memories that have endured to this day. When we took the six-mile ride into Thatcher, whether to purchase a hay baler, gas, tires, wire, or seed, nothing was written down about these transactions; they were completed based on a person's word. At the end of the month, my aunt or uncle would ask a merchant, "What do I owe you?" Then they would pay the bill. There were no questions and no paper to exchange. I marveled at this set of business ethics. Compared to living in Tucson, where I knew my parents had to retain an invoice or receipt, this practice was refreshing and noteworthy.

My uncle Marc also taught Dino and me how to fire shotguns and other weapons. I recall learning to take aim and fire behind the barn at the main farm. Sometimes Dino and I would shoot birds, but more often we plunked tin cans on a fence several hundred feet away. Uncle Marc was a wonderful teacher and gave us steady counsel and advice. He taught us rules of safety and how to maintain our weapons. Dino and I became fairly good marksmen, and in time Uncle Marc allowed us a degree of flexibility with our firearms. One day, while Dino and I were left unsupervised with our shotguns, we noticed that several quail had flown into the barn and settled upon the rafters. Like an anxious hunter, I pointed my shotgun toward the birds and proceeded to fire a round. It blew a ten-inch hole through the roof, and Dino and I could see blue sky. I was petrified, and I cannot recall if we killed the birds or not, but we went back outside and continued firing, hoping that Uncle Marc would not notice the hole in the barn roof. Fortunately for me, there were other holes, and I rationalized that it was a tin roof in need of repairs. Nothing was ever said about the incident.[19]

The Mormon ethic of taking care of the family extended to the Mexican laborers and the Apache farm laborers from the nearby San Carlos Reservation. Aunt Zola used to take food and medicines to those who needed these items. When one of the workers cut his foot badly, she hauled the injured man in the family Hudson coupe all the way to Globe hospital. My aunt and uncle had a great deal of compassion, and that memory has remained with me.

While I learned these forms of farm ethics, my uncle Marc, a great "cowboy dad," taught me another lesson about country culture. One day he called me into the barn to watch him shoe a horse. As he began the task, the horse grew jittery and moved back and forth. Suddenly my uncle hauled off and began hitting the horse with terrific force. I began to cry and asked him what he was doing. He shot back, "Just sit there." Scared, I sat on a truck and observed that the horse did not move throughout the remainder of the horse-shoeing process. I recovered from the trauma to realize that was how things were done; I rode that horse around the farm for the next several summers and enjoyed every minute.

I have heard I was a good kid and a wonderful child, but at the end of first grade at St. Peter and Paul School, I could neither read nor spell.

My mother, blaming the teachers, decided to enroll me at Sam Hughes, a public school, to repeat first grade. I was perplexed and a bit humiliated because at my new school I was bigger than the other kids. In fact, I had a learning disability, undetected at the time, that created a host of challenges throughout my grammar and high school years. Unaware of the problem, I compensated in various ways, usually by memorizing everything. But to this day I am a terrible speller.

My parents took drastic measures after Sam Hughes, which was not much of an improvement over St. Peter and Paul. For the third year of school, I was tutored at home. This concerted effort helped make up lost ground, and I spent fourth grade at All Saints, though this new school also posed problems. All Saints was situated in one of the marginal areas of town, and I began getting into fights. With that, my father and mother shipped me off to St. John's Military Academy in Los Angeles. Dino went, too, and his status as an eighth grader—a big shot—enabled him to flourish in the military school environment. He immediately became an officer. As a fifth grader, I was one of the grunts, and the bigger boys beat me up and visited upon me the traditional hazing that younger students experienced. I cried myself to sleep many nights and, predictably, returned to Tucson and Sam Hughes for the next school year. A very attentive teacher helped me with my reading that year, working with me in ways that others had not, so I progressed significantly in school.

Yet sixth grade brought another minor problem: I kissed a girl. I received six swats for this rule violation, and I was held back from recess. My parents, to their enormous credit, worked with me, tried to find the right school environment, and responded to every circumstance. By the junior high school years, I was beginning to compensate for my learning disability, getting more out of school, but also misbehaving just enough to keep everyone on their toes.

Then my father's legal career, which took him from the Pima County Superior Court in Tucson to attorney general of Arizona in 1948 and then to the Arizona Supreme Court from 1949 to 1952, caused the family to relocate to fast-growing Phoenix. My younger sister, Danielle, had just been born, bringing the household to three boys and one girl, and the move brought new schools and new friends. At first, we lived on Manor Drive near the Phoenix Country Club, and my father soon learned that state salaries were difficult to stretch with a growing family and expenses. For ethical reasons tied to his role in judicial leadership, he decided to stop all land business at this time. As a result of this belt tightening, we moved to a more modest home at Flower Circle near Phoenix College. I attended eight schools in eight years: seventh grade at Emerson at 1817 North Seventh Street and eighth grade at St. Gregory's School on Fifteenth Avenue and Osborn. The latter had recently opened, and the nuns and sisters, I recall, were enthusiastic teachers. I developed an abiding interest in geography, history, and some of the related social sciences.

At St. Gregory's, I became a big shot of sorts. I excelled at sports and served as head of the school patrol, where my helmet and uniform provided me with a degree of authority that I embraced with alacrity. I was an average to good student, though I had to work hard for my grades. All seemed to progress smoothly, when a mature-looking, very cute Italian girl drew my attention. I kissed her at a football game in front of the rectory. Someone, perhaps a rival suitor, reported the apparent transgression, and I was called in the next day and suspended from school. My father was furious, and it was one of two times I remember his inflicting corporal punishment. I spent a long week at home, and upon my return to school I completed a variety of demeaning tasks, in addition to sitting with the third-grade class for a week or two. I lost my patrol position, thc uniform, and thc hclmct.

Other significant developments occurred during these years in Phoenix. At one point, in eighth grade or my first year in high school—I attended newly completed West High School—my class took a school outing at the State Capitol. I recall my father had something to do with the tour. I was proud of him and began to seek him out more often while he was at work. He would take us to court, and I would sit and enjoy the attorneys' verbal jousting and arguments. He encouraged us to go to his chambers, when possible, and I enjoyed the interplay of his law clerks. My father spent much time talking with them, and as I observed this fascinating aspect of the legal profession, I grew increasingly interested in it. I developed friendships with some of his law clerks and later in my career was able to appoint a few of them to various judicial positions, including the federal bench. In fact, Dino and I developed an abiding interest in the law at this time, and my father, sensing this interest might become a future vocational direction, took the time to tutor me in spelling, reading, and especially math. He put it this way: "You have to learn to read and write, and I'm going to teach you this math." He did not press Dino or me into pursuing law, but by the end of my freshman year in high school, I knew I wanted to be a lawyer.

That first year of high school benefited me because I found a journalism teacher who helped me with writing, composition, and critical thinking. I made great strides and looked forward to improving my grades at West High, but my father, always concerned about four growing children, looming college costs, and much more, could no longer afford to be a judge. He returned to the private sector in Tucson, where he could pursue a private legal career and reenter the real-estate market. Thus, I began three great years—some of the best years of my life—at Tucson High School.

I continued to make fair grades, chased girls, and drank beer—an almost traditional rite of passage for adolescent boys. I ran for my first office as a junior and thought that my popularity with the girls and my father's prominent name in Tucson and throughout Arizona would assure my victory as a senior high school councilman. I attended no debates and did not campaign. I was not elected. This woeful lack of effort served as a critical reminder throughout my later political career.

I had some great teachers at Tucson High; Danny Romero was among the most memorable. He was advisor to the senior class, knew my mother from the University of Arizona, and could relate to me. He toned me down, yet reassured me that I was doing a good job in school. He became a valued friend and kept me focused on what was important in high school. But here, too, I ran into a bit of trouble. The senior class always put on senior follies, a series of skits for the entire student body. In my role, I imitated the boozy songster Dean Martin. The follies ran for three nights, and on the third night the production crew used real alcohol in the prop drink. Mr. Romero sipped it, found out it was alcohol, and kicked me out of the remainder of the follies. Our friendship withstood this test, and he remained an important influence during my college years.

At best, I was a B student in high school. Dino, in contrast, excelled and later attended Georgetown University. I performed relatively well in geography, history, and biology and somehow survived math (thanks to my father's efforts). I liked Spanish, but overall I could have done better in most classes. I graduated from Tucson High with great memories and one of the largest classes in history; more than one thousand graduates marched in 1955.

Travel was an important dimension of our rearing and education. We traveled to Safford and Thatcher often and would visit San Diego during the hot summer months. My father took us on road trips—to Yosemite, Canada, Maine, and elsewhere. We would eat meals cooked on a Coleman stove and check into a modest hotel at night. We thought it was great fun, though my father would make us study and write about the places we had visited, reinforcing his admonition that education was the key to a full and successful life. He said, "You might not want to do this, but this is what it's all about." So when we traveled, my father made us read and write something about the places we visited—a kind of travel journal designed to make us think and write critically about our experiences. As a teenager forced to write these travel journals, I naturally preferred to get away or to look out the window. Later I appreciated the importance of this activity.

When I was seventeen, my family visited Italy, seeking out our relatives. My mother was so enthralled that when we returned to Tucson, she took a course in Italian at the university. Shortly thereafter, she went to Florence, where she and my younger sister spent months touring and learning about the Renaissance, architecture, and Italian cuisine. My mother's Italian was soon equal to my father's, and my family maintains an enduring fascination with Italy and our personal history there.

We also visited London and Paris. We stayed at a nice hotel in Paris, and my parents purchased tickets to the opera. Somehow I was able to excuse myself during the evening and found the Lido, where a false identification enabled me to view the showgirls, purchase drinks, and take part in this fabled Parisian cultural attraction. Dino, when he learned of this side trip, was extremely envious, and for once my parents did not find out about my objectionable activity. Travel provided me with another important element in my overall education. I grew to appreciate the enormity and complexity of the United States and Europe, while at the same time becoming familiar with my state and region.

Like so many eighteen-year-olds, I wanted to get out of the house—away from my parents—to attend college. I applied to the University of Hawaii and was accepted. I also gained acceptance at the University of Oregon, the University of Santa Clara, and the University of San Francisco (USF). At the time, San Francisco seemed the best place for me—cosmopolitan, urbane, sophisticated. I wanted good times. School, however, was difficult, and I did not want to work that hard. Worse, there were no girls; it was not a coeducational university in 1956. Bill Russell was powering the basketball team to new heights, but I was more concerned with finding new forms of distraction. I quickly acquired a false identification. The law students, who were older than I and worked as the residence hall monitors, became my friends. These wizened veterans of academia were knowledgeable about San Francisco and its environs. Soon I was out after the 11:00 P.M. curfew, drinking and carousing. Not surprisingly, my academic performance fell far short of expectations. In brief, after one semester at USF, I asked my parents about the possibility of transferring to another school. They greeted this entreaty with a profound rejection. I had embarrassed the family with my antics, and I had to await permission to transfer. Meanwhile, Dino went to Mexico to take a Georgetown University course during the summer semester. I tagged along and took a Georgetown freshman English course—an effort to escape the rigors of USF freshman English. As it turned out, I received an A, and when I transferred to the University of Arizona in 1957, the credits for this course transferred. My humble return home engendered a more serious tone for my education, and the influences of the family doubtlessly helped me to develop a renewed commitment to higher education. My father's repeated admonitions that education and public service were noble pursuits formed a foundation for my next series of challenges.

3 Gaining Political Literacy

I attended high school and college in the 1950s, went to law school in the early 1960s, and held political office from the 1970s until 1995. Committed to community service, my parents raised their children with a spirit of involvement, both through political and public service. Into our adult years, my brother Dino and I would sit at the table and listen to my father talk about state or federal politics. He would emphasize that public service was most honorable. My first serious contact with political life came in high school, when then-governor Ernest McFarland, who had previously served twelve years in the U.S. Senate, called my father during dinner to solicit his advice on a variety of issues.[1] In fact, McFarland's election as governor of Arizona in 1954 prompted another dinnertime call asking my father to serve as state chairman of the Democratic Party. My father complied with the request.

Mac, as he was popularly known, was a friendly farmer-lawyer who went to Washington in 1940 and became Senate majority leader in 1950. I recall vividly the 1952 general-election campaign for the U.S. Senate. He ran unopposed in the Democratic Party primary, so his election to a third term in 1952 seemed assured, and his Republican challenger, Barry Goldwater, a nice young man who was heir to the Goldwater department store and a Phoenix city councilman, appeared to pose little threat to the majority leader of the U.S. Senate. In fact, few people, including the political punditry, gave Goldwater a chance. The DeConcinis concurred with the general consensus that McFarland would win an easy reelection.

Yet this election took place amidst a revolutionary change in Arizona politics. In 1947, on the heels of a political coup that swept corrupt Phoenix-area politicians from their jobs, the local business and political elite spearheaded an effort to reform local government. At issue were payoffs from pimps, madams, gamblers, and drug dealers, which, according to many, were responsible for a series of unlawful acts and a general disregard for the law. These leaders sponsored a successful drive to revise the city charter and allow a city manager to run local government. Two years later the same group formed the Charter Government Committee (CGC) and succeeded in electing its designated set of candidates to the Phoenix city council. Civic leaders such as Frank Snell, Walter Bimson, and Sherman Hazeltine led this group along with the support of conservative newspaper publisher Eugene Pulliam, who had purchased the *Arizona Republic* and *Phoenix Gazette* in 1946. One of the first CGC council members was Goldwater, and in many ways he symbolized the new image that Phoenix wanted to convey. Most members, according to historian Thomas Sheridan, "were white, male upper-middle-class businessmen and lawyers, and even though Arizona was a predominantly Democratic state, most CGC members were conservative Republicans." They tended to live in north Phoenix and belonged to the exclusive Phoenix Country Club. A number of future female politicians also gained traction in this changing political context; Sandra Day O'Connor and Margaret Hance, who began their public careers in the mid- to late 1960s benefited from this conservative shift. Indeed, Goldwater, Harry Rosenzweig, and Pulliam led a Republican insurgence that germinated in populous and geographically centered Maricopa County and that eventually spread to the rest of the state.[2]

The 1952 senate campaign was my first meaningful political experience, and although only a high school student, I attended meetings wherein Mac and my father would discuss strategy. McFarland was a two-term senator, one of the authors of the GI Bill, and the Senate's Democratic majority leader. He laid claim to incumbency and possessed both a national reputation and a distinguished political record that dated back to the early 1920s. Moreover, voter-registration figures in Arizona favored McFarland. Goldwater was indeed the underdog. As a fifteen-year-old, eager to learn and spend time with my father and his political friends, I was greatly attracted to this opportunity to work with the campaign.

Upon reflection, however, it is clear that the revolution in Arizona was not so unusual; there was widespread disaffection with President Harry Truman and twenty years of Democratic Party rule. Pressure for change was evident nationally as Truman administration scandals, the Korean War, and fears of communist infiltration fueled these sentiments. Moreover, Truman's decision not to seek reelection in 1952 and the Democratic Party's nomination of Illinois governor Adlai Stevenson further stimulated Republican campaign rhetoric. In General Dwight David Eisenhower, the Republicans believed they had found a candidate who could wrest the White House from the Democrats. Throughout the country, they campaigned on the slogan "K1C2"—Korea, corruption, and communism—and hammered home the notion that Americans had to choose between "Liberty or Socialism."

I remember the devastating negative campaigning conducted during the election, with the Goldwater campaign accusing McFarland of having ties to the Communist Party—an Arizona version of McCarthyism. The absurd allegations, perpetrated through anonymous fliers and distributed to churches and other organizations, tainted this historic election. According to the press, the fliers, distributed the weekend before the Tuesday general election, helped Goldwater significantly and aided in his defeat of McFarland. Goldwater and his close advisor Harry Rosenzweig denied direct involvement, but the allegations and their impact were crucial in determining the outcome of the election.

These tricks were not confined to those who supported the upstart Republican candidate. The AFL-CIO PAC distributed handbills full of misinformation about Goldwater, claiming he was a right-wing radical who would steer the federal government away from its international involvement with the North Atlantic Treaty Organization (NATO) and other international defense agreements. Worse, they hinted that he planned to blur the lines between church and state by putting prayer in our schools. These allegations were absurd. Goldwater was a very conservative senator and grew more so as he advanced toward the 1964 presidential election, but he was far from today's right-wing religious advocates.

The Arizona press, especially *Arizona Republic* owner and publisher

Eugene Pulliam, supported Goldwater, and the Republican candidate benefited mightily from the groundswell of popular support for General Eisenhower, whose enormous popularity carried him to the Republican presidential nomination in 1952. Heir apparent to the nomination, Senator Robert Taft (R–Ohio), had little chance against the hero of World War II.

As I licked envelopes and placed handbills in conspicuous spots around Tucson, I was aware how Goldwater was served well by the national mood and Eisenhower's popularity, but he nevertheless campaigned in an innovative fashion. I recall distinctly that Goldwater, in contrast to others, ran the first professional media-oriented campaign in Arizona. He hired Stephen Shadegg to serve as campaign manager. Shadegg was an experienced and shrewd publicist who had orchestrated Senator Carl Hayden's reelection in 1950.[3] (Shadegg's son, John, currently serves as a member of the U.S. House of Representatives from Arizona and has gained a fine reputation.) In addition, Goldwater stood at the head of a united Republican Party in Arizona. Unlike its counterparts in other states, the Arizona Republican Party avoided intraparty struggles between Taft and Eisenhower supporters at the national convention. Goldwater was a "Taft man," but he demonstrated leadership by crafting a compromise whereby Eisenhower maintained representation at the convention. This foresight portended well for the upcoming elections.

The seeds for the electoral upset of Senator McFarland were palpably evident in the formal opening of Goldwater's general-election campaign on September 18, 1952. In an inspired political maneuver, he held his official announcement in Prescott, the Goldwater family's pioneer home. With the state's rugged territorial past so close and celebrated, this location was a powerful reminder of Goldwater's deep Arizona roots. Shadegg made sure that the candidate's message echoed beyond the small-town central Arizona community by arranging television and radio hookups that broadcast his address throughout the state.

The message was simple and powerful. Goldwater tied the incumbent senator to President Truman, depicting how this duo represented all that was wrong with the country. This theme, first articulated on the steps of the Yavapai County Courthouse and repeated with almost monotonous regularity during the two-month general-election campaign, was presented on television, on the radio, and in newspapers throughout the state. These messages affected me, and I marveled at their impact on the electorate.

Goldwater was "disgusted with the Truman administration's appalling record of waste, inefficiency, dishonesty, and failure at home and abroad." If elected, he pledged to stop the "expanding government bureaucracy and government-created inflation, and . . . the highest taxes ever extracted from the American citizen."[4] During the primary, he had called the Fair Deal a "devilish plan to eventually socialize the country," but in the general-election campaign he moderated his rhetoric, retreating toward the political center, reassuring voters that no responsible Republican would abolish federal programs such as the Federal Deposit Insurance Corporation, Social Security, unemployment insurance, the Federal Housing Authority, or the Security and Exchange Commission. His position on these issues assured moderate Democrats that he was not too far to the right.

In the international realm, he tied McFarland directly to the unpopular military stalemate in Korea. Brilliantly and out of context, he "quoted" McFarland as suggesting that the Korean conflict was a "cheap war" because of the kill ratio of nine Chinese soldiers for every American combat fatality. He turned this point to his advantage when he challenged McFarland "to find anywhere within these borders of these United States a single mother or father who counts their casualties as cheap." Though Truman's name was not on the ballot, Goldwater assured Arizonans that they could express their outrage by voting against his "personal spokesman" Ernest McFarland.[5]

I learned much from McFarland's ill-fated campaign for reelection, especially about the power of the press in shaping public opinion and influencing the electorate. The *Arizona Republic* and the *Phoenix Gazette* gave Goldwater's opening general-election speech extended coverage and ran editorials reiterating his message. The *Republic,* in fact, became Goldwater's greatest supporter, rejecting McFarland as an "administrative mouthpiece" and giving credence to the "cheap war" charge. In fact, the phraseology was damning: McFarland's comment was a dangerous rubber stamping of the Truman administration's timid and cynical forfeiture of lives in a war that could have been prevented and that was dragging on at terrific cost. Five days after the Prescott speech the

Republic endorsed Goldwater's candidacy and commenced merging the Eisenhower and Goldwater campaigns.[6]

Goldwater unseated McFarland, who ran a well-funded and for the most part traditional campaign. Eisenhower swept the country, including Arizona. Meanwhile, in the Arizona election for a spot in the House of Representatives, political newcomer John Rhodes, from the rapidly growing eastern portion of Maricopa County, upset incumbent Democrat John Murdock, thus further transforming the state's political representation in Congress. Many thought Goldwater brought about Arizona's sudden transformation from a Democratic to a Republican state, but I would suggest that it was Dwight Eisenhower who contributed significantly in bringing about the beginnings of a strong Republican political patina to Arizona. In the minds of both the press and the general public, however, a tectonic shift in the political landscape took place in 1952.[7]

In spite of his electoral defeat, McFarland remained a potent political force in Arizona, running successfully for governor in 1954 and winning reelection in 1956, two elections in which my father played a major role. He then challenged Goldwater for the Senate again in 1958. At this time, I was at the University of Arizona, and I volunteered at the McFarland campaign headquarters. My father's good friend and fellow attorney James Murphy served as McFarland's Pima County chairman. He was charming, shrewd, and knowledgeable about recruiting effective campaign staffers. I watched, listened, and learned. By this time, I had some experience in local elections and, at my father's behest, had learned the importance of political organization and getting out the vote in heavily Democratic areas.

In the 1958 McFarland campaign, I worked at the telephone bank—four phones at the back of Pima County headquarters that were designated for calling voters. I learned the power of personal contact with voters, particularly the impression and influence that a person leaves by making the effort to establish direct connections in a citizen's neighborhood. My father's admonitions once again played a significant role in my early political education. He said to be sure never to place oneself above another person. In short, be humble. Indeed, as I observed my father interact with those around him, I discerned his uncanny ability to remain humble while at the same time distinguishing himself by the power and persuasiveness of his ideas. Moreover, he was able to achieve this influence among his contemporaries without intimidation. In time, I attempted to incorporate this subtle but influential political skill into my warehouse of personal qualities. If I had any future political aspirations, my father's skill at being an "uncommon common man" would serve as a useful model.

My father still served as the state Democratic Party chairman in 1958, and he chaired McFarland's campaign. He spent considerable time in Phoenix working with the state party organization, educating and informing voters and, of course, getting the vote out for McFarland. As a University of Arizona student, I remained in Tucson, and when I was not in the fraternity socializing or studying, I spent nights and weekends at the headquarters with the political organization. This growing preoccupation raised eyebrows among my fraternity brothers, and they doubtlessly grew to view me as a bit "different," but I enjoyed my time at the campaign office.[8]

Whereas my friends were for the most part indifferent to politics, one of my political science professors, Dr. Neil Houghton, participated in the campaign. A longtime friend and supporter of Arizona's invincible senior senator Carl Hayden, Professor Houghton encouraged political activism and rewarded students with better grades for their participation in the political process. As a student who needed all the extra credit help possible, I tried to persuade Houghton that my volunteerism deserved consideration—especially as it pertained to grades. In the end, I had no proof that my work for McFarland influenced Houghton, but I received good grades in his courses. More important, I recall that Professor Houghton required students who received As or Bs to read a certain number of books. Upon completion of each special reading, the student had to take a test of six to eight questions. My first attempt resulted in a poor performance; I really had not read the book. Thereafter, I read a dozen or more books and passed these tests. Not surprisingly, the books emphasized the liberal tradition in American political culture, and I am convinced that they played a role in the development of my political philosophy. My father's more conservative political philosophy conflicted somewhat with what I was learning, and I recall that this dimension of my university education led to some lively dinner table discussions.[9]

Democrats expected to make gains in the 1958 elections. A sharp recession, rising unemployment, administration scandals, and federal intervention to enforce school desegregation in Little Rock had eroded President Eisenhower's standing in public-opinion polls and sapped Republican support nationwide. In foreign policy, the situation looked equally troublesome; crises in the Middle East and Asia as well as Russia's successful orbiting of Sputnik heightened voters' concerns about peace and further raised questions about Republican chances. To make matters worse, Republican candidates antagonized organized labor by shaping their candidacies into referenda on the right-to-work issue. Goldwater had leveled tough criticisms at organized labor during his first term in the Senate, thus making himself a political target when he sought reelection.

The situation seemed to work to the advantage of Arizona governor Ernest McFarland, anxious for a rematch against Goldwater and confident of victory. In his attempt to regain his lost seat, McFarland ran a spirited campaign, but Goldwater, with an improved media effort and effective use of the incumbency, maintained distinct advantages. McFarland, for his part, did not have to contend with the Truman albatross or Eisenhower's coattails. Moreover, in Arizona, Democrat registration outnumbered Republican two to one, though the Republicans had made modest gains in the previous five years and, as I experienced, would continue to do so for the next thirty years.

McFarland, fresh from a resounding primary victory, stumped Arizona as "Mr. Democrat" under the slogan "Send Mac Back." Indeed, Goldwater, though he had raised his name recognition during his first term, was vulnerable.[10] At the outset of the campaign, pollsters had McFarland in the lead. Goldwater could not run on his legislative accomplishments or claim insider status in the Eisenhower administration, yet he still held political capital. The nationwide recession had not reached Arizona, and the state economy was booming. Goldwater had no primary, and he stood at the helm of a united party. In contrast, McFarland had antagonized some key Democrats and had ignored the advice of others. He had also strayed to the far left of the political spectrum during his two terms as governor and faced a conservative Democrat, Steven Langmade, in the primary. This opponent claimed McFarland had taken Teamster money for secret commitments, thus providing Republicans with a potent general-election issue. Conservative Democrats were enticed by the Goldwater campaign, as they had been in 1952. Although McFarland had little trouble dispatching Langmade by a vote of 107,373 to 40,799 in the primary, money poured into Republican coffers, with Texas oilman H. L. Hunt and archconservative Robert Welch contributing more than $200,000. More important, perhaps, Goldwater presented the figure of an imagined Arizona past: blunt, unaffected, and tough-minded.

I observed the Republican campaign with a critical eye as Goldwater and his campaign manager, Shadegg, fought to reverse the early poll numbers, which had them lagging far behind. The influential Pulliam newspapers, which could make or break a candidate, were eager to provide support, and Shadegg packaged Goldwater as the "underdog, capitalizing on the drama of the lone knight on the white charger . . . this was a man of action, a man of decision, a man of courage, and a man who is dedicated to the service of the individual."[11] Indeed, the *Arizona Republic* had retooled its Goldwater propaganda machine, selling Goldwater as a new breed of senator who had his feet on the ground and as a dedicated soldier in the fight to stop the federal government from dominating our lives.

Reprising his campaign kickoff of 1952, Goldwater inaugurated his reelection campaign from the steps of the Yavapai County Courthouse in Prescott on September 10, 1958, with a speech that was carried through out Arizona on a twenty-station radio net. Again he used historical imagery and the state's pioneer heritage to great effect. His message for this campaign was as simple as the message in 1952, but he modified it to emphasize the themes of less government and individualism. He advocated reestablishing personal responsibility, reducing and limiting the concentration of power in the central government, and recapturing individuals' right to self-determination.

Goldwater's growing stature attracted the national media to the campaign. What was striking was the slanted coverage. More than one year before the election, *Newsweek* columnist Ray Moley, who wintered in Arizona, hinted at Goldwater's 1958 campaign plan, declaring it a contest between "traditional conservatism and the collectivist aim of the political machine of the big unions." Moley's reporting mirrored that of the Pulliam press, which proclaimed Goldwater a "statesman" with "rare courage," contrasting him with the Democrats, who were "mere figureheads." One writer for a national publication described Goldwater: "In his flying clothes he could pass for a character in a Steve Canyon comic strip . . . As a man's man he also appeals to women." According to historian Robert Alan Goldberg, "during the 1958 election even more than the 1952 race, the *Arizona Republic* and *Phoenix Gazette* transformed themselves into the public-relations department of the Republican party."[12]

Much to my father's and my chagrin, glowing accounts of Goldwater's attributes contrasted sharply with negative portrayals of McFarland. The Arizona governor, according to Paul Healy of the *Saturday Evening Post,* "was the red-faced, sixty-four-year-old governor who looks and acts like a farmer." Healy characterized him as "bumbling," "slow speaking," and "burning with ambition to regain his senate seat." *Time* mimicked the less than flattering accounts, dismissing the governor as "Homespun Ernie . . . who never missed a ribbon cutting." The *New York Times* joined in, describing McFarland as "portly, bucolic, and benign."[13] The press, I recall, created a huge obstacle for my candidate. Knowing McFarland as a legally trained and experienced political leader, I chafed against these portrayals. Still, I held hope for victory, keeping in mind that McFarland's name recognition remained high and that he had served with distinction in his two terms as governor.[14]

Two more aspects of the campaign left indelible impressions on me and at the same time sealed McFarland's fate. First, the Pulliam press painted him with an organized labor brush, claiming that Jimmy Hoffa and his henchmen contributed hundreds of thousands of dollars to the McFarland campaign. In fact, false accusations and inflamed rhetoric dominated the final month of the 1958 campaign. McFarland could not recover, and his early lead in the polls quickly vanished.

As a cruel and puzzling exclamation point to the campaign, the actions of two machinist union members one week before the election further damaged McFarland. In an act that still stirs debate among political observers and historians, two machinists, Earl Anderson and Frank Goldberg, distributed thousands of handbills depicting a winking Joseph Stalin smoking a pipe with the caption, "Why not vote for Goldwater?" It was referring to a favorable reception Goldwater had received before the communist-leaning Mine, Mill, and Smelter Workers Union and implied that Goldwater was sympathetic to communist ideology. When news of this handbill reached Tucson and hit the *Arizona Daily Star* (Tucson) and other southern Arizona newspapers, I realized that chances for victory had diminished significantly.

My father and the Democratic leadership attempted to refute the charges and counter the patently absurd political stunt. But rather than waste any time scrutinizing or interpreting the handbill, the *Republic* turned it to Goldwater's advantage. "Mac in Tears about Smears: What Does He Say of This?" ran the headline. Goldwater's advisors played it to their advantage. "This operation has been planned a long time," Goldwater announced, "deliberately planned, diabolically planned by those outside forces who have to get Goldwater, and this is their last desperate attempt." The *Republic* and the *Gazette* fanned the flames, repeating the story daily until the election. A stunned McFarland denied any involvement, but no one cared to listen.[15]

In the back of my mind during the 1958 election, I hoped secretly that I might earn an internship position if McFarland won. I asked my father about a possible internship in Senator Hayden's office, but he told me that he had made inquiries with Hayden's administrative assistant, Roy Elson, and was rebuffed without much explanation.[16] That disappointment notwithstanding, it was clear the weekend before the election that Goldwater would win reelection, but as a campaign worker I maintained hope of an upset. I had worked hard, learned much, walked the streets of south and west Tucson, and kept a statewide perspective as I talked with my father during the campaign.

Election night ended early for us in the McFarland campaign of 1958. It seemed to me that Steve Shadegg's organizational efforts, Goldwater's charisma, and Pulliam's war on Democrats and organized labor had produced a 56 percent majority for the Republican candidate. As I analyzed the election results in following weeks, I noticed that Goldwater had won a huge victory in Maricopa County, garnering 60 percent of the vote. Moreover, he possessed appeal to moderate and conservative Democrats, wresting one-third of their votes from McFarland. He won ten of the state's fourteen counties. In addition, Goldwater ran well with new residents—white-collar and technical workers taking advantage of the new economy emerging in fast-growing Phoenix. The results also revealed that he appealed to copper miners and union workers, demonstrated best by his carrying the copper-mining districts in Cochise County. I reflected on this crossover appeal and realized that Arizona marched to a different political drummer than the rest of the country. Eighteen years later I would turn this independent strain of the Arizona electorate on its head and have it work to my benefit, but in 1958 I could never have imagined that I would later not only run for the U.S. Senate, but also serve with Barry Goldwater, whom I had worked so hard to defeat.

In fact, that 1958 election had more than local significance and was important for reasons other than the curious role played by organized labor. Goldwater's triumph over my candidate, McFarland, had taken place in the context of a national rout of Republicans. In that year, of the ten Republicans running for Senate seats west of the Mississippi River, Goldwater was the lone victor. In fact, it was the worst Republican drubbing nationwide since 1936. In surviving the Democratic wave of 1958, Goldwater enhanced his status with rank-and-file Republicans and, more important, could now claim leadership of his party's conservative wing. All of this took place in a state with an almost two-to-one Democratic Party registration edge. I would make this defeat a learning experience, realizing that Arizona was embracing a new conservative political agenda that needed to be understood and interpreted correctly.

I knew also that I wanted to become involved more directly in electoral politics, and I commenced thinking in earnest about the best ways to achieve that goal. In fact, in the next few years my long-range focus was on politics and political activism. I almost made a false start, but with my father's guidance I was able to make the right choices at this early and critical period of my political education. At least, during the 1950s I gained a degree of political literacy that would serve me well as I embarked on the early professional and political stage of my career.

4 Road to the Senate

Over the next few years, my life changed dramatically: I completed my undergraduate degree; joined the U.S Army through ROTC; and married Susan Hurley of Phoenix, whose family, ironically, were active in Republican politics. I had matured since my ill-fated college experience in San Francisco, and my academic focus sharpened. Like many young people in their early twenties, I developed a seriousness of purpose and an inchoate ambition to do something with my life. Mirroring my father's experience of the late 1920s and early 1930s, I entered the University of Arizona Law School in 1960 and at the same time submerged myself in political activity. At twenty-two, I became a precinct committeeman, and in my third year of law school I was elected vice-chairman of the Democratic Party of Pima County. I continued to look at opportunities to run for political office.

In fact, during my second year of law school a state representative from our district died in office. In this situation, the state constitution requires that there be a special election to replace the deceased lawmaker. I impulsively began the petition process that would place my name on the Democratic primary ballot. As I organized and sought signatures, I called upon my father for advice. He counseled that I should not run for political office at this time; instead, he urged me to complete my law degree, arguing that if I were to win election and serve in the legislature, I would probably have to drop out of law school because of the demands of the job—constituent service, committee hearings, political bargaining, and more—which might limit me in the long run. Fortunately, I listened to his advice, helped the deceased lawmaker's widow get elected, and gained much goodwill for my efforts on her behalf.

In 1963, I graduated from law school; my wife, parents, and extended family took great pride in this accomplishment. As I prepared for the next rite of passage, the state bar exam, I remained determined to enter public service and appreciated again my father's good advice about not running for the state legislature. As I looked toward the future, however, I lost sight of the task at hand.

I took the bar exam and was stunned at the results: I failed it by three-quarters of one percent. I was devastated. I thought seriously about leaving the state and discarding my political ambitions. I experienced a range of emotions and even considered suing the Arizona Supreme Court, which was the ultimate arbiter on who gained admittance to the bar. Chester Smith, the University of Arizona Law School professor who taught the bar review course, encouraged me to bring suit, and he found an issue that might work for me.

The potential lawsuit was based on the fact that the bar association published a list of subjects that would be covered on the exam, and I had taken each course focusing on subjects on this list. The area in which I had scored worst on the bar exam, "Negotiable Instruments," failed to appear on the list. Professor Smith concluded that an injustice had been committed and backed his views with an offer of $5,000 toward litigation. At the time, I agreed with this reasoning, and I wanted to sue because I believed a principle had been violated. In my view, these bastions of the protection of the legal system were not playing by the rules, and someone had to bring this violation to their attention and force them into line. I prepared for litigation.

Once again, however, my father injected some profound wisdom into the process. He urged me to reconsider the time, energy, and political capital that would be expended in suing the Arizona Supreme Court. My initial reaction to this admonishment was disappointment: How could my family not support me like Professor Smith did? As I reflected on the possibility of my sitting as the plaintiff against the state bar and the Arizona Supreme Court, however, I realized that my father was correct and his advice helpful. The lawyers who sit on the bar admissions committee were senior practitioners who wielded profound influence in the field. My father pointed out to me that they would have much at stake and would fight my lawsuit with vigor and purpose. Moreover, the Supreme Court would decide the case. Although I thought I was justified and my case based on the merits, my father steered me in the proper direction and helped me avoid a potentially embarrassing legal and professional blunder at the outset of my career.

I refocused my energies on studying for the next bar exam and abstained from politics for six months. Yet I found time to visit each member of the bar association admissions committee and pointed out the wrong that had been perpetrated upon me and others who had been surprised by the content area of the previous exam. These lawyers, many of whom were contemporaries of my father's, were polite but unimpressed. I remember Henry Merchant and Bill Kimball, in particular, looking at me as though they were thinking, "Ah, to be young and full of idealism." Frank Snell, the prominent Phoenix lawyer, listened to me, then began talking about my father and what great friends they were. Getting past these brush-offs, I studied long hours, worked closely with my brother Dino, who had recently taken and passed the exam, and was successful in my second attempt the following February.

Law school and my subsequent trials and tribulations with the bar exam took place against the backdrop of the presidency of John F. Kennedy and its heady idealism. At the same time, in Arizona the incremental political shift to the right gained ground, as was vividly manifested in the 1962 election for the U.S. Senate, which pitted the legendary and seemingly unbeatable Senator Carl Hayden, a longtime friend and political ally of my father's, against Evan Mecham, a one-term state senator and archconservative. A second-year law student at the time, I watched this election with a degree of trepidation as the eighty-four-year-old Hayden, his health and mental acuity questioned by many, squared off against upset Republican primary winner Mecham, whose mercurial political career would mark Arizona in unprecedented ways.

By 1962, Hayden had attained institutional status in Arizona politics and in Congress. Unquestionably the most striking feature of Hayden's political career was its longevity. Overall, the Arizona solon spent sixty-seven of his ninety-four years in public office. Between 1900 and 1912, he learned the art of politics in a variety of local and county positions in territorial Arizona. After statehood, voters elected their native son to the U.S. House of Representatives, kept him there for seven terms, and in 1926 promoted him to the Senate, where he remained until his retirement in 1969. My father had met Hayden in the 1920s and regarded him as the ex officio leader of the Democratic Party in Arizona.

I recall that on the night of the election Hayden was still at Bethesda, recovering from the urinary tract infection that had kept him bedridden during the general election. Hayden tallied 199,217 votes against Mecham's 163,388, an extremely small margin for the veteran senator. Although Hayden won all but one county, Mecham had come close to pulling off an upset. The conservative Republican took Yavapai County, with its then two-to-one Democratic Party registration edge, by a margin of 5,745 to 4,911. Even more striking, he nearly carried Maricopa County, losing by only 6,092 votes out of 200,826 cast. My former political science professor, Neil Houghton, puzzled over the results, in particular the 73.69 percent turnout in a nonpresidential election. "I don't think I've seen a stranger election," he allowed. In fact, Mecham's surprising strength remained the subject of conjecture for days after the ballots had been counted. Houghton continued to speculate about what had transpired, and I carefully listened to his interpretation: "the sharp contrast of political philosophies of liberals and conservatives, for want of better labels, may have been partly responsible for Mecham's showing." An even more important factor may have been Hayden's advanced age. Professor Houghton added that "had Mecham received active support from the press or from ranking Republicans, he might have upset Hayden." Instead, I recall distinctly that Goldwater abandoned the party nominee, Mecham, in favor of Hayden in the general election.[1] Arizona voters—even Goldwater—many times looked at the person and not at the candidate's political affiliation.

Several important lessons could be drawn from this election, and they further illustrated some of the problems McFarland encountered in 1952 and 1958. It seemed that Hayden, the Democratic Party, and the politics of old Arizona—dependent on federal largess and well-placed congressional committee posts—had been put on final notice. Mecham's unique, inimitable brand of conservative politics—a mix of Goldwater conservatism, constitutional rectitude, and unadulterated candor—suggested that a new conservative agenda had taken root. Barry Goldwater, Paul Fannin, and John Rhodes—the first Republican congressman elected in the state's history—personified this new Arizona as they broke the grip of Democratic Party rule that had dominated Arizona politics since statehood. Mecham's surprisingly strong showing reiterated to me that fact and anticipated some dramatic changes that would shape Arizona's political culture as I entered the arena.

In a broader sense, this incremental transformation—the increasingly conservative posture of Arizona in particular and of the American West in general—contrasted markedly with the late-nineteenth- and early-twentieth-century mood reflected in radical politics, unionism, and socialism. As I thought about this contrast, I realized that when old Carl entered Congress in 1912, Arizona had embraced unorthodox political bromides, Populist insurgency, and radical political ideas such as giving women the vote and allowing voters to legislate directly. Hayden had supported these progressive reforms. According to political historian Paul Kleppner, Arizona reflected broader trends and changing patterns of electoral behavior in the American West. He characterized this transformation as the "radical West becomes conservative." Certainly, to my thinking, Arizona in the early 1960s had begun identifying with conservative Republicanism, entrepreneurial capitalism, and traditional values.[2] This warning-shot election, Hayden versus Mecham in 1962, captured vividly the radical-to-conservative drift that was taking shape in the region's electoral politics and political culture. As a Democrat, I realized that I could be bucking a historical trend, and when I began my political career in Arizona in earnest, I could not ignore the complex lessons to be learned from McFarland's two losses and from Hayden's breathless victory in 1962.

Almost immediately after passing the bar exam, I dove headlong into politics. In 1964, former state Democratic Party chairman Sam Goddard decided to run for governor a third time—he had most recently lost to Paul Fannin in 1962—and declared his candidacy. Goddard was a Tucson resident and close political confidante of my father, so his race excited me, and I volunteered for his campaign. In Tucson and throughout the state, I spoke for Goddard as he squared off against Goldwater-backed candidate Richard Kleindienst, who, as it turned out, defeated a defiant Evan Mecham in a vitriolic Republican primary campaign. While Goldwater chased the presidency in vain, his wounded former Republican Party chairman was not up to the parry and thrust of the political debate.

Goddard's distinct logo "Go Goddard," with a stylized roadrunner streaking against a dark blue background, taunted Kleindienst as he stumbled through the general election. Goddard carried the day by staying on message and benefiting from the Democrats' still substantial edge in voter registration. My family celebrated the victory, and shortly after Goddard took office, he asked me to join his staff and serve as legal counsel. At twenty-seven years old, I moved my family to Phoenix.[3]

Just prior to my move to Phoenix in 1965, I had been elected state Democratic Party vice-chairman. This position was a significant elevation from my previous service as vice-chairman of the Pima County Democratic Party. At the county level, I worked with the chairman, John Huerta, an affable Mexican American businessman who owned the popular La Fuente restaurant in Tucson. Friends with him for many years, I supported his candidacy for county chairman, and he reciprocated by including me in his inner circle. With Chairman Huerta, I helped select the eight Pima County delegates and four alternates to the 1964 Democratic National Convention. One delegate, former Arizona governor Dan Garvey, used his previous political post to secure a spot, and we selected the remainder of the delegation at a closed-door session at the Santa Rita Hotel in downtown Tucson.

I received a delegate appointment to the convention in Atlantic City, New Jersey. I learned a great deal and was exposed for the first time to the likes of President Lyndon Johnson, Senator Russell Long, and Senator John Sparkman (D–Alabama), among the most powerful figures in the U.S. Senate in 1964. We were, of course, Lyndon Johnson delegates because no real opposition emerged to his renomination. Although the convention was relatively serene, there was a notable exception. It concerned the seating of the Mississippi delegation, which allegedly had been discriminatory in its selection process. An alternative slate of delegates, dominated by African American citizens, was also present and demanded to be certified and seated as the delegates from Mississippi. I watched as a liberal lawyer from Tucson, Ed Morgan, took up their cause at the convention. Morgan maneuvered with purpose, cajoling the Credentials Committee to seat the alternative slate of delegates. He failed in this effort, but was able to gain some meaningful concessions in the Democratic Party platform. In the process, he achieved a degree of national recognition and added some progressive ideas to the political debate. I was excited about serving as a delegate and took little time to ponder what the convention might mean in terms of furthering my political career. As the convention came to an end, I refocused my energies on my new position in the Arizona governor's office.

This position was crucial because I broadened my political involvement significantly, building bridges for Governor Goddard with the Democratic-controlled Senate and the Democratic-Republican coalition in the House of Representatives. Leaders from both parties knew the DeConcini family, and many were good friends with my father. Goddard was considered a liberal Democrat from Tucson, a label that had to be muted and modified in order to accomplish legislative goals. I attempted to ameliorate differences with the more conservative Democratic old bulls in Phoenix as well as with Harold Giss from Yuma County, Bob Smith from Graham County, and Ben Arnold from Pinal County. Before the Supreme Court ruling of one man/one vote in 1961, each county had two state senators, similar to the principle governing election of U.S. senators. This setup gave rural senators great power, and they did not welcome the change rendered by the Supreme Court, which resulted in a dissipation of their political influence.

In addition to my valuable experience in the governor's office, I worked with Clayton Niles, Governor Goddard's executive assistant. Niles, Goddard's business partner in Tucson, was an outstanding individual who possessed an almost mystical aura. At first, I was wary, even fearful, of Niles, who had gained a reputation as a successful businessman but was deficient in political skill. I quickly learned that he possessed political attributes that matched his business acumen. He not only continued to run Goddard's Tucson-based business, but also oversaw daily operations in the governor's office with efficiency and decorum. Over the years, I grew close to Niles and his wife, Joanne, who maintained staunch loyalty to Goddard and later became supporters of and contributors to my campaigns for public office.

As I worked on legal issues for Governor Goddard, I met a young, rising political force in Arizona, Sandra Day O'Connor. At the time, she was deputy attorney general, serving in the administration of Attorney General Neil Smith, a Republican. Naturally, our office viewed the attorney general's opinions with a degree of suspicion. In fact, my primary duty for Goddard was to provide legal advice subsequent to that of the attorney general. O'Connor and I worked together on a number of extradition cases. I spent an inordinate amount of time checking statutes and citations before making a recommendation to the governor whether or not to sign an extradition request from another state. In fact, Sandra and her husband, John, who practiced law in Phoenix, socialized with Susie and me on occasion, and we forged a respectful and friendly bond during the Goddard years.

In this period, however, I squared off with the then deputy attorney general in a legal and political confrontation that left a profound impression on me. In fact, it had some future political and judicial implications. Governor Goddard and his top advisors wanted to make a political appointment to a state commission. Our office needed a legal justification to fill the vacancy. This commission slot, however, never occurred, and the existing commissioner refused to leave. I was charged with the task of substantiating the legality of the governor's executive authority to appoint his own commissioner subject to Arizona Senate confirmation. Clayton Niles and I worked vigorously to assure that the Senate would confirm Governor Goddard's appointment. With political considerations thus disposed, I completed the research to justify the executive authority to execute the change in commissioners.

My opinion, however, contradicted that of the attorney general. Sandra Day O'Connor wrote the conflicting opinion, and I recall making a visit to her office, located on the main floor of the state capitol. I wanted to argue my point. She politely yet firmly rejected my arguments, so I appealed to her superior, Attorney General Smith. I hoped to convince him that O'Connor did not understand fully the law that concerned executive appointments. I met with Smith, who also invited O'Connor to the meeting. I had hoped she would not be in attendance because I would have been more candid in my arguments as they pertained to the political advantage of our position in the matter. Her presence at this meeting, however, brought about a feeling of legal and intellectual challenge, and our discussion strayed little from the finer points of the law. In the final analysis, the Attorney General's Office—and Sandra Day O'Connor's argument—prevailed over ours. I had hoped that through eloquence and personal persuasion I could convince the attorney general to abandon his deputy's arguments and adopt my view.

In retrospect, though, I can see that her opinion was correct and that I was grasping for straws in this legal and administrative confrontation.

What struck me about this incident was O'Connor's professionalism and keen legal mind. She listened to my arguments carefully and respectfully, and then argued her opposing points methodically and logically. I watched her as she contradicted my suggestions at every turn. Her research was flawless, her eloquence memorable. I found it difficult to counter her opinion in the matter. I was disappointed that I had failed in gaining the political results desired, but this encounter was my first recognition that the deputy attorney general possessed the brilliance and vision that would one day catapult her to unprecedented political and legal leadership. Finally, despite the fact that she and Smith were Republicans, they were correct in their legal arguments, and the governor's office did not make the commission appointment.[4]

In late 1965, Governor Goddard promoted me to administrative assistant. I ran the daily operations and served as the governor's gatekeeper; I determined who gained access and who did not. Governor Goddard and Clayton Niles entrusted me, at age twenty-eight, with an enormous responsibility, and this position played a key role in my meeting influential Democrats throughout the state. As the governor's top assistant, I could review and present to him the résumés of potential advisors and candidates, then make recommendations.

At this time, I came in frequent contact with Rose Mofford. She had been part of Arizona history and government all my life. A longtime friend of my parents, she was an exceptional and gifted person in every way. Rose had watched me grow and develop as I attended grammar school and high school. In 1953, after working several years in the Arizona Treasurer's Office and Tax Commission and serving as business manager for *Arizona Highways* magazine, she became assistant secretary of state, a position she held for twenty-two years before running successfully in 1978 for her first full term as Arizona secretary of state. When I was working for Governor Goddard, Rose and her boss, Secretary of State Wesley Bolin, maintained offices directly across the hall from me. She was the most accessible government official I met in all my years in public office. She would always take time to talk to me and give me advice regarding the state legislature. I was always impressed by her keen intelligence and her breadth of knowledge. She knew not only the people who served in every position in government, but also the duties of the various offices. If Rose offered advice, I knew it was sound. She helped with the subtleties and nuances many others would have overlooked. I am grateful to Rose for her friendship and support from the time I first met her with my father when he was on the Arizona Supreme Court.

I enjoyed my work at the capitol immensely, and at this time I also recognized that I had developed a work ethic that matched the level of my father's dedication. In fact, after I left the governor's office in January 1967, I returned to law practice in Tucson, where I worked with my father and John McDonald. I would start work at 7:00 A.M. and often not return home until 9:00 P.M.—I was a workaholic, but this behavior had begun in earnest while I was in the governor's office. At the same time, my family, which now included three children, competed for my time, and I tried to make sure that I dedicated every available moment away from work to the family. In the mid-1960s, as I reflected on my career and my future, I kept arriving at the same conclusion that had percolated within me since the late 1950s: I wanted to run for elective office. The challenge lay in earning a living, raising a young family, and positioning myself to take advantage when the opportunity arose. My work ethic, so similar to my father's, would serve me well in this quest.

When Governor Goddard sought reelection in 1966, the DeConcini family in its entirety worked tirelessly for him. My brother Dino became chairman of the Democratic Party in Pima County. He was especially skilled at grassroots organizing and getting out the vote. Goddard should have won reelection, but Arizona House majority leader John Haugh, a Republican who also hailed from Tucson, proved to be a masterful adversary and caused dissension among Democrats, many of whom had joined the Republican-led coalition in the House. The 1966 gubernatorial campaign, pitting incumbent Goddard against establishment Republican and former radio personality Jack Williams, who defeated Haugh in the primary, was hotly contested and attracted a great deal of money.

I worked nights and weekends, dividing my time among my political job, the campaign, and state party activities. At that time, it was not illegal to keep your state position and work for a candidate. I represented Governor Goddard throughout the state, and on one occasion during this campaign U.S. secretary of the interior Stewart Udall made arrangements for a substantial contribution to the Goddard reelection effort. Organized labor in Washington, D.C., through Udall, delivered a large amount of cash in $100 bills, and all of it was reported in accordance with existing state law. I served as the conduit for these funds.

This money was never deposited in a checking account, nor was there a legal requirement to do so. This cash was used to "get out the vote." I designated where the funds were to be directed for neighborhood constituent vote recruitment. Although this sounded like buying votes with cash, it actually worked differently. It paid for neighborhood campaign headquarters, telephones, electric bills, and gas for cars that drove people to the polls on election day. The money also covered the cost of food for workers and volunteers and for other items that were generally paid for in cash. This process took place before election law reform, but many times I thought about my role as distributor of cash.

Stewart Udall had been a longtime friend of the family and always asked me about my father. Still, for reasons discussed around the DeConcini dinner table, I refused to explain to my father the details of this contribution until after the election because I knew he disapproved of this aspect of political campaigns. Although there was nothing illegal in these contributions and disbursements, he believed strongly that unaccounted cash in elections was detrimental to the political process.

Williams won the election, and I worked with his transition team to turn over the reins of power. During this time, I returned to Tucson and along with my father helped form the law firm DeConcini-McDonald. John McDonald, in fact, remains a senior member of this firm, which has offices in Phoenix, Tucson, and Washington, D.C. John is recognized as one of Arizona's prominent attorneys, and he remains a close friend. Today the firm has approximately thirty lawyers, but when we started there were only the three of us. John had a few clients, and I had none. My father fortunately brought us some business, and I spent long hours developing the firm. In 1969, we hired William Brammer as our first associate. Bill later became a state appellate judge and is recognized as a leading jurist in Arizona. Although now a full-fledged workaholic, I still kept foremost in my mind my long-term goal to run for elective office.

In 1969, a vacancy in the Pima County Attorney's Office occurred, and I made a concerted effort to gain the appointment for the balance of the term that ended in 1972. The Pima County Board of Supervisors, composed of two Democrats and one Republican, would make the appointment. My father supported my efforts and helped me make the appropriate overtures to the supervisors, whom we knew well. Soon, however, we learned that Rose Silver, deputy county attorney for the Civil Division, also sought the position. A dynamic, tenacious lawyer, she was one of the first women to graduate from the University of Arizona College of Law; she married a lawyer and later in her career became a well-known partner in the firm Silver, Silver, and Ettinger (her son-in-law). A pioneer in many ways, she also possessed one of the best legal minds in the state. Rightfully, she wanted to be considered for the position, especially if she did not have to run; she knew it would be difficult for a woman to run successfully for county attorney. She moved with determination. It was a sensitive situation, and my father and I considered the possibilities.

When Rose learned of my interest in the vacancy, she called my father to discuss the situation. They had known each other for years and were friends. In fact, when my father, who went to law school later in life, took a study course for the bar exam, Rose had tutored the course. As my father grew in social and political prominence in Arizona, Rose took great delight in telling the bar exam course story. Although I had never worked closely with her, I had worked with her two sons-in-law, Jack Ettinger and Gene Karp, who practiced with her. When Rose approached my father, she said that she thought she had the votes. I believed she had two of the three, so we met. Out of these discussions, we arrived at a compromise. If I did not seek the appointment, Rose agreed to support me in the next general election in 1972. Also, she generously offered to do all she could to advance my political career. She gained the appointment as Pima County attorney.

In making good on her promise, Rose appointed me special deputy county attorney to represent Tucson School District 1, the largest school district in Arizona. At that time, school districts in Arizona could not retain separate, individual counsel and were required to use the attorney appointed within the county where they were located. In rare cases, they could retain the state attorney general, unless there was a conflict of interest. Lawrence "Mo" Ollason, a lawyer with close contacts to Senator Hayden and his chief assistant Roy Elson, had a contractual arrangement for District 1, but Rose persuaded him to amend it and serve in another capacity. I was awarded the position at $10,000 per year, which was paid to the law firm DeConcini-McDonald. I took this job seriously, and I worked diligently with Bill Brammer and John McDonald to provide representation for District 1. I established good relationships with the school board and attended board meetings, which sometimes convened three times per month. Moreover, I attended executive sessions, which were held once a week, and consulted with administrators. A problem inherent in the arrangement was that the Pima County Attorney's Office did not have the resources to take on major litigation because of the numerous other duties required of the office. As it turned out, though my billing of $30 per hour to the district, with the $10,000 yearly retainer, was considered appropriate, it was not difficult to reach the limit of what was allotted to the position because of the tremendous amount of legal work involved.

The district administrators, aware of their dilemma, indicated they would pay less in attorney's fees on a monthly basis if they could hire their own counsel or contribute to the salary of a part-time deputy county attorney like me. As a result of the mounting legal work involved, I concluded that the law should be changed so that districts could hire their own counsel. I began lobbying for a change at the legislature in 1971. That year, with the help of a Republican family friend in the state Senate, Douglas Holsclaw Sr., legislation passed permitting school districts of a certain size to hire legal counsel from their own operating budgets. Tucson School District 1 fit the bill. This change not only benefited the various school districts statewide, but also helped law firms, including that of DeConcini and McDonald, to win lucrative contracts with the districts.

During this time, I made a foolish mistake in my fledgling political career. In the 1970 race for governor, I threw my support behind Lincoln-Mercury dealer and Democratic Party contributor Jack Ross. I knew Jack, as my father did, and he asked me to run his Pima County campaign. Before accepting the responsibility, I wanted to make sure that Raul Castro—former county attorney, Superior Court judge, and retiring ambassador to El Salvador—was not going to run for governor. My parents had known Castro for many years, and my mother had once taught him in the Tucson public-school system. If he decided to run, I would support him. When I contacted Castro, though, he informed me he was not going to run, so I joined Ross's team.

However, in May 1970, when Castro retired from the ambassadorship approximately one month before the filing date for the race, he became a candidate. I was perplexed by this about-face, but I had to fulfill my commitment to Ross, and I informed former ambassador Castro of that fact. He was gracious, and I ran the Ross campaign in Pima County. At the time, Castro was a popular politician who drew massive support from Hispanics and made inroads into powerful business communities and Republican strongholds. He won the nomination with relative ease, and I supported him to the best of my ability in the general election.

I worked with Alberto Moore and Jerry Sonnenblick in trying to win southern Arizona for Castro, and though they were somewhat miffed at my support for Ross during the primary, they overcame these initial misgivings, and we became political and personal friends in ensuing years. Castro came close, but lost to incumbent governor Jack Williams by less than 10,000 votes. I recall that Castro emerged from the campaign with a great deal of political appeal, and to his credit he never revealed a hint of animosity or resentment toward me over my support for Ross in the primary. In fact, he indicated that he planned to run again for governor in 1974.

Meanwhile, in late 1971 I commenced my campaign for the office of Pima County Attorney. My opponent in the primary, Lars Pedersen, served as chief criminal deputy for County Attorney Silver. The Republicans, under the direction of their young prominent county chairman, Richard Bilby, a lawyer in the prestigious law firm of Bilby, Thompson, Shoenhair, and Warnock,[5] turned the Democratic primary into the general election because they put forward no candidate for Pima County attorney in 1972.

I attempted to hire a campaign manager, Judy Berman, now Judy Abrams, who was a bright, young, active Democrat. She declined the offer but recommended nineteen-year-old Ron Ober, who, along with my family, opened a campaign office above my uncle Tony's beauty salon at East Broadway and Tucson Boulevard. "Tony's," of course, was named after my uncle Tony Gallo, who married my father's sister and had a prime location for his business. My family owned the building, and we placed a large campaign sign directly above the building and took advantage of the name recognition and prime location.[6]

Ron Ober impressed me from the beginning; energetic, innovative, and loyal, he worked hard, as did everyone else in the campaign. He attracted large numbers of young people to our effort, drawing on his years of contacts in the Jewish youth organization in Tucson. Although most of these volunteers were too young to vote, Ron mobilized them into a cadre known as "Dennis's Li'l Demons," who wore campaign T-shirts as they distributed campaign materials at rallies. My first campaign was enjoyable, but some noteworthy events also marked the election.

At the outset of the campaign, County Attorney Silver remained neutral, above the fray, while the office personnel outwardly supported Pedersen. Several county employees, however, supported my campaign, including David Dingledine.[7] As the campaign progressed, I gained more support, especially during the last sixty days of the campaign. Rose Silver declared publicly for me and brought with her a significant number of voters within the County Attorney's Office and in the community. With a month to go to the September 1972 primary, I grew increasingly confident of victory.

The campaign, nevertheless, was vigorous and active. Pedersen ran negative ads against me, alleging that the DeConcini family fortune was seeking to buy the elective office for me. His campaign ran television spots raising questions about the number of land parcels my family owned in Pima County and how that would raise issues of conflict of interest. Yet the media raised questions in response to these attacks. Unfortunately, Pedersen had been involved in a tragic automobile accident the previous year. His wife and child and a passenger in the other car were killed. His confident and aggressive demeanor seemed to belie the recent tragedy, and the press, on several occasions, addressed the issue. Several accounts pointedly suggested that he may have been culpable in the accident and had used the power of his office to deflect any serious investigation, adversely affecting his candidacy.[8]

Pedersen campaigned vigorously and with an unusual degree of self-assurance. He was, in fact, a seasoned prosecutor with dozens of convictions against felons. In contrast, I had participated in three jury trials in my brief legal career. My specialty at the time was transactional real-estate law and estate planning. I took criminal cases by appointment.

Criminal law brought me into the courtroom and was responsible for my limited experience in that realm. Pederson logically attempted to make my relative inexperience into a campaign issue. I knew, however, that the office did not require a trial lawyer's background because at the time thirty-four lawyers conducted the trial work. What was needed, I countered, was an administrator who could handle the mounting case load. We won a 60 percent to 40 percent victory in the primary, and with no opponent in the general election, I spent my time supporting other candidates throughout the state. This wise use of my time paid dividends for me in future statewide campaigns.

On January 6, 1973, I was sworn in as Pima County attorney. I immediately sought higher salaries and benefits for the deputy county attorneys and their assistants. My ability to deliver these economic benefits upon assuming office gained favor among long-time employees, many of whom questioned my lack of a prosecutorial background. I also appointed Rose Silver to head the Civil Division and at the same time launched an effort to organize a coordinated law enforcement team to investigate and prosecute drug cases in Pima County. The chief of police in Tucson, William Gilkinson, and his chief deputy, Clarence Dupnik, who worked directly with our office, initiated a new and mutually beneficial relationship that made inroads into the drug war at that time. Dupnik, in fact, later became sheriff of Pima County and coincidentally a friend and advisor to me.[9]

In addition to my role as Pima County attorney, I remained involved in electoral politics. In 1974, Raul Castro announced that he would run for governor and asked that I chair his statewide campaign. Neither state law nor county ordinance prohibited me from playing a major role in Castro's effort. I traveled the state extensively, renewed longtime friendships and acquaintances, raised money, and counseled the candidate. Castro was a solid campaigner and made appealing presentations to all groups. He won handily, and his victory generated political capital, goodwill, and contacts for me throughout the state. I helped Governor Castro organize his administration, and in that context I recommended that Dino, my older brother, serve as chief of staff.[10] At the time, Dino worked for the Williams Company in Oklahoma, and when called on to work with Governor Castro during his term of office, he readily agreed.[11]

During Castro's administration, narcotics activity along the border with Mexico demanded the attention of local, county, and state officials. Traffickers used airplanes, tunnels, trucks, cars, and pedestrians to funnel their illegal cargo into Arizona and other border states. In response, I organized the Border Counties Strike Force, which worked with several federal agencies. Thus, the Pima County Attorney's Office, the county Sheriff's Department, and the Tucson Police Department worked directly with the U.S. Customs Service (USCS); the Bureau of Alcohol, Tobacco, and Firearms (ATF); the Federal Bureau of Investigation (FBI); the Immigration and Naturalization Service (INS); and the Drug Enforcement Administration (DEA). I succeeded in setting up a single office of joint leadership, with my office providing the legal advice and services required for this effort. The press reported favorably on this intergovernmental cooperation, and Governor Castro, after receiving glowing reports on the success of the strike force, approached me to look into the possibilities of transforming it into a statewide program.

This drug enforcement initiative required much travel to Phoenix and placed me in contact with the state's most influential business and political leaders. The Phoenix 40, a self-appointed group that included community leaders such as Frank Snell and Richard Mallery of the immensely influential Snell and Wilmer Law Firm; Harry Rosenzweig, a businessman and close confidante of Senator Barry Goldwater; political insider Stephen Shadegg; and *Arizona Republic* editor in chief Pat Murphy, among many others. Mallery, an attorney who specialized in major business transactions and real-estate acquisitions, was also a friend of my brother Dino and was particularly helpful in this process. Tom Sheridan and Herman Chanen, prominent players in the Arizona business community, also demonstrated strong support. An amalgam of activists, law enforcement groups, and interested citizens augmented the strong support by the Phoenix 40 and led to the creation of a statewide narcotics task force. The Arizona state legislature responded and created the Arizona Drug Control District Strike Force.

The governor in 1975 appointed me director of the new agency, in addition to establishing a multi-million-dollar budget for it and a mandate to go after drug dealers. We opened offices in Phoenix and Tucson and received additional manpower from the Arizona Department of

Public Safety (DPS), thus strengthening our interdiction efforts.[12] Moreover, we initiated a sophisticated intelligence-gathering network composed of state and federal agents.

Among those agents I met in the mid-1970s, Joe Arpaio stands out as one of the most memorable. I met Joe shortly after going to Washington, D.C., when he became agent in charge of the DEA in Arizona. Nationally prominent and sometimes controversial, Arpaio is a real cop who doggedly pursues his goals. As the head of DEA, he worked with the strike force after I was elected to the Senate. He brought the DEA and the Arizona DPS under the umbrella of the strike force. We worked together as I took my antidrug efforts to the nation's capital. He appeared before the Senate Judiciary Committee and became a valuable resource to the committee and me. He retired from the DEA in 1983, was elected Maricopa County sheriff in 1992, and then was twice reelected by large majorities.[13] Though a Republican, he always supported me in my senate campaigns. Joe remains relentless in his pursuit of drug traffickers and continues to use every tool at his disposal to prosecute them. He continues to be a friend to me today.

The strike force proved an immediate success, with high-profile arrests, indictments, and convictions. Terry Grimble, a young attorney from Criminal Division of the Pima County Attorney's Office, directed the prosecutions unit. Unyielding in the pursuit of criminal indictments, he also demonstrated sound political skills and had a deft touch with the state legislature. After my election to the U.S. Senate in 1976, Grimble and later Steve Neely, a brilliant trial lawyer, succeeded me as director of the strike force. With jurisdiction in every county and the backing of the Arizona Attorney General's Office, the operation continued for several years until political winds shifted, support for the cooperative drug enforcement effort waned, and the Attorney General's Office assumed many of the strike force's operations. I take pride in having played a significant role in the effort to prevent the importation of drugs into Arizona and to prosecute those who trafficked in drugs.

A few other law enforcement initiatives marked my tenure as Pima County attorney. The Diversion Program and the Victim Witness Program garnered much good press and, I venture, were good public policies. The Diversion Program sought to divert nonviolent, first-time offenders—often users of small amounts of marijuana—from the criminal justice system if they pled guilty to the charge. They would receive community service and probation, but not face a criminal trial and potential incarceration. This program helped numerous nonviolent offenders reform their ways, and, ultimately, if they completed the probationary requirements, all records of their encounter with the justice system would be expunged. This program, supported by Tucson's deputy chief of police Clarence Dupnik, garnered press attention on a national scale, and the conservative *Arizona Republic*, the state's most prominent newspaper, championed the program.

The Victim Witness Program, which included the use of the skills of social workers and counselors for victims of crime, similarly attracted favorable attention from national media outlets. Fortunately for me, Debbie Jacquin, a longtime friend then married to the president of the Arizona State Senate, Bill Jacquin, maintained a deep interest in the program, and I asked her to direct it. A skilled administrator and savvy with the press, she brought the program to national prominence. My good relationship with the Pima County Board of Supervisors—who, to their credit, funded the initiative—helped start this model program for victims of crimes. In fact, the success of the Victim Witness Program helped me win awards from the National District Attorneys Association, which, of course, was a reflection on the foresight and vision of my fellow citizens in Pima County.

In a dizzying ten-year span, I had graduated from law school, grown increasingly active in Democratic Party politics, and won my first electoral victory. Walking the precincts, working at the county and state levels in various campaigns, learning from losses, and understanding victories were part of this decade-long education. My experience in Governor Goddard's office provided invaluable insight into the administrative dimension of the political and legislative process. My campaign work for Governor Castro in 1970 and 1974 introduced me to a host of potential supporters. Along the way, I met rising stars on the state and national stage. Moreover, I had practiced law in the public and private sectors, albeit from an administrative standpoint, I had served the public schools as a deputy county attorney, and, as Pima County attorney, I helped initiate some innovative law enforcement programs.

With my election as Pima County attorney in 1972, I thought I had achieved a lifelong goal. I could not have foreseen the changing political landscape four years down the road, a landscape that placed me in a politically opportune situation for a successful run for the U.S. Senate in 1976 (see chap. 1).

5 The Panama Canal Dilemma

On December 31, 1999, the United States ceded ownership of the Panama Canal and the Canal Zone to the nation of Panama, after nearly a century of occupation and control. I played a significant role in these developments, and my actions, controversial to many, shaped overall perceptions of my first term in the U.S. Senate. The Panama Canal Treaty—actually two treaties—carried with it an amendment that brought national and international attention to me, but at the same time the political fallout threatened to derail my political career in its earliest stages. In fact, opponents injected this issue into my reelection campaigns in 1982 and 1988, though they failed to convince voters that my role in transferring the Panama Canal and Canal Zone back to Panama required my removal from office.

Panama, in fact, did not exist when, in the mid-nineteenth century, Europeans began to explore the possibilities of creating a link between the Atlantic and Pacific oceans. The Panama Canal and the Canal Zone, stunning tributes to the engineering profession, are a unique part of the global community, and challenging questions regarding U.S. foreign policy, sovereignty, national security, and international commerce continue to swirl around the small and strategically significant isthmian waterway. But the so-called DeConcini Reservation altered the Panama Canal Treaty of 1977–78 and left an enduring American imprint in Panama.[1]

Little did I know that after four years of dealing with the local and regional problems associated with the duties of Pima County attorney—

drug interdiction, law enforcement, and legal administration—I would be thrust into one of the century's most emotional and problematic international issues. Many thought I was not prepared for such difficult and complex federal problems.

The Panama Canal has generated a significant amount of historical, political, and economic literature. Our nation's long-standing interest in a canal across the narrow, mountainous isthmus of land connecting North and South America was triggered in part by the Gold Rush of the late 1840s and early 1850s, when tens of thousands—a virtual wave—of Europeans and Americans traveled east to west via the isthmus to seek quick passage to the California gold fields. Most of those sojourners passed through Nicaragua, not Panama, for the latter was a pestilential place, and construction of the Panama Railway in the 1850s proved difficult and cost countless lives.[2] Yet the hopes of a Frenchman of questionable birth, Phillippe Bunau-Varilla, focused attention on a canal through Panama. As an engineering student in Paris in the 1880s, Bunau-Varilla had heard the great engineer Ferdinand de Lesseps, who conquered the Suez, describe his dream of another canal, one linking the Atlantic and Pacific. Unfortunately, jungles, mountains, and disease defeated de Lesseps, but this defeat only intensified Buneau-Varilla's desire to succeed in the effort.[3]

Meanwhile, during the American conflict with Spain in 1898, the USS *Oregon* had taken weeks to sail from Puget Sound around Cape Horn to come to the defense of the exposed and anxious eastern coast of the United States. The ship's slow progress underscored the advantages of a canal across the isthmus. With the war over and the United States an uneasy owner of a new Pacific empire, a canal seemed essential.

Two obstacles, however, blocked the way. The Clayton-Bulwer Treaty, an earlier agreement with Great Britain, denied the United States exclusive control over any isthmian canal. This problem was overcome by the second Hay-Pauncefote Treaty of November 1901.[4] Under its terms, the United States could build, control, and fortify a Central American waterway. Where to build a proposed canal, however, remained a problem. Concerned with costs, Congress could not or would not choose between construction in Nicaragua and Panama. The issue was decided, in dramatic fashion, for a Panama location when a hitherto dormant Nicaraguan volcano became active and convinced a majority of American congressmen that the region was too dangerous.

Another complication loomed, however, because Panama was a possession of Colombia. The Colombians initially proved receptive to the American proposal to build in Panama, but they changed their minds about the terms in the middle of negotiations—to the outrage of the assertive new U.S. president Theodore Roosevelt—and demanded more money. Residents of Panama grew alarmed, fearing the loss of the economic benefits the canal promised to bring to the region. Although Panamanians had revolted against Colombia in the past, they had never succeeded. Roosevelt encouraged some stealth military maneuvers and made some not so subtle diplomatic entreaties, causing the Panamanians to rise again. Fortunately for the revolutionaries, the USS *Nashville* had conveniently arrived at the port of Colon on the Caribbean coast. Inspired by the "implied" U.S. support, the rebels easily took the province and in a matter of hours the new Republic of Panama was born. President Roosevelt immediately forged an agreement with the new government. For an almost token sum, Panama afforded the United States the right to construct an interocean canal through a "zone" that would be controlled by U.S. authorities and fortified with U.S. arms.

On November 18, 1903, a treaty between the United States and the Republic of Panama was signed, making it possible for the United States to build and operate a canal connecting the Atlantic and Pacific oceans through the Isthmus of Panama. The treaty significantly granted the United States—in perpetuity—the use, occupation, and control of the Canal Zone, a zone approximately ten miles wide in which the United States would possess sovereign rights. These rights were "to the entire exclusion of the Republic of Panama of any such sovereign rights, power, and authority."[5] Soon the United States began to dig through the isthmus, one of the celebrated engineering feats of the early twentieth century, and by 1914 the canal was opened to world trade.

Another important aspect of the treaty was that the United States guaranteed the independence of Panama and agreed to pay the republic $10 million and an annuity of $250,000. In addition, for $40 million the United States purchased the rights and properties of the French, who had labored for years in an attempt to construct a canal. Finally, all private landholders within what would be the U.S. Canal Zone would be compensated for their property.

For the emerging state of Arizona and the rest of the trans-Mississippi West at the turn of the twentieth century, the opening of the Panama Canal was perhaps the most significant development in transportation to that time. In many ways, it signaled the end of the frontier West, a kind of coming of age. The canal, westerners hoped, would inaugurate a new era of economic self-sufficiency and would bring an end to the colonialism that had characterized the nineteenth-century economy. The canal could bring Arizona and the West into direct contact with the Far East, Latin America, the eastern United States, and Europe. As the completion of the transcontinental railroad systems had brought the West closer to the mainstream of American life in the nineteenth century, so the Panama Canal would bring the region in closer proximity to the rest of the world in the twentieth.

These hopes were best symbolized in the expositions with which California heralded the opening of the canal. San Diego's Panama Pacific Exposition in 1915 and San Francisco's equally spectacular Panama Pacific Exposition in 1916 boasted pavilions that represented the Pacific Coast, the mountain states, and the Southwest. These expressions of hope foreshadowed a new stage in the economic development of the region and tied Arizona and the West to the rest of the world.[6]

As a military, commercial, and cultural entrepot, the Panama Canal proved indispensable to U.S. global interests. As I earned my high school and college degrees, President Dwight Eisenhower initiated discussions to update the half-century-old treaty governing the canal. Many years earlier, on March 2, 1936, in a ceremony in Washington, D.C., President Franklin Roosevelt had signed the Treaty of Friendship and Cooperation, which not only increased the annuity to $436,000, but also, at the Panamanians' request, withdrew the guarantee-of-independence provision in the 1903 treaty. The Eisenhower administration elaborated further on the developing relationship and signed the Treaty of Mutual Understanding and Cooperation on January 25, 1955. Notably, Panama received more money and concessions: the annuity was increased to $1.93 million, and the Panama Canal Company and the Panama City Railroad Yards, valued at $22 million, were turned over to the republic. This historical process, which reflected the American virtues of comity and equity, would ultimately influence my controversial vote in the Senate more than twenty years later.

While our country modified the rental agreement for use of the canal, the canal's economic and strategic value increased dramatically, especially after World War II. In late 1962, the United States completed the construction of a high-level bridge over the canal's Pacific entrance, and in a symbolic gesture of unity the flags of both Panama and the United States flew jointly over areas of the Canal Zone under civilian authority. Presidents John F. Kennedy and Lyndon B. Johnson continued the dialogue. Later, presidents Richard Nixon and Gerald Ford held diplomatic discussions regarding U.S. status, use, and occupancy of the Panama Canal Zone. In 1972 and 1973, for example, following devaluation of the U.S. dollar, the annuity was adjusted proportionally to $2.1 million and $2.3 million respectively. President Ford never indicated to me that we should renounce our sovereignty, but he nevertheless authorized the State Department to enter into negotiations with the Panamanians over the issue of sovereignty. He and his handlers began positioning his administration to engage in renewed treaty negotiations, with an eye toward relinquishing sovereignty and operation of the canal to the Panamanians. Indeed, since the 1930s, various administrations, Republican and Democrat, had moved incrementally toward ceding more control of the Canal Zone and the Panama Canal to the Panamanians.

With the election of Jimmy Carter to the presidency, President Ford's plans were postponed, but not nullified. Carter, who took no firm position on the matter of sovereignty during the 1976 campaign, stepped into an increasingly volatile situation as he assumed office. The central question of physical and strategic control over the Panama Canal Zone remained an open one, while at the same time the issue of territorial sovereignty in Panama had to be addressed.

In July 1976, when I resigned my position as Pima County attorney and embarked on my first run for the U.S. Senate, I endeavored to articulate my positions with clarity and precision. I ran as a reformist outsider promising to balance the budget, eliminate the federal deficit, support campaign-finance reform, deregulate business, advocate a strong national defense, stop the spread of communism, and, among other things, keep the Panama Canal under U.S. control. When voters asked during the campaign if I would vote for a treaty that gave the Canal Zone and the canal back to Panama, I wrote on campaign stationery that I would not vote for such a treaty. Such a vote, I added, would debase the sovereign claims of the United States. Turning control of the Canal Zone over to the Panamanians, I was convinced, would be a huge mistake, primarily because the Panamanians possessed none of the equipment—military, security, and material—to protect international use of the canal.[7]

Moreover, U.S. strategic interests—including threats from the Soviet Union, Cuba, and other communist states—demanded that our nation control the canal at all times. Also, the long-term emotional attachment to the Panama Canal was palpable and undeniable: the Canal Zone was somehow an extension of the United States, an American outpost that served as a testament to the vigor and hopes of Theodore Roosevelt's successful, if controversial, foreign policy. These three major factors shaped my thinking as I formed my positions and indicated that I opposed the early proposals emanating from the Ford administration. A draft treaty had been circulated, but not executed, and as I took office in early 1977, there was discernible political heat surrounding a new Panama Canal treaty.

I realized almost immediately after taking the oath of office that the Panama Canal issue would trigger a political firestorm if President Carter and the Senate decided to enter into a treaty whereby the United States divested itself of ultimate control of the Canal Zone and the canal. Carter moved forward with dispatch, supporting such a treaty, which among other things, would turn over the Panama Canal Zone and the canal to the Panamanian government in 2000. (There were, in fact, two treaties: one that transferred the canal to the Panamanians in 2000, and one that affirmed U.S. operation and control of the canal from 1977 to 2000. These possible treaties, when confirmed, brought into sharp focus several political issues, including opportunities for Republicans to criticize the new president.) Most Senate Republicans opposed to the treaty excoriated President Carter for what they considered his naive approach and obvious lack of experience in foreign affairs. He possessed, they alleged, little of the necessary gravitas to craft and administer U.S. foreign policy. In addition, his support of the treaty, they claimed, reflected other deficiencies: he was soft on communism and ignorant of national-security issues, and, worse, his divestiture of the canal bordered on treason.

The Carter White House did not help matters. From the outset of his administration, his closest advisors committed a series of self-inflicted political gaffes that proved difficult to overcome on Capitol Hill and with the press. Similar to the shaky start of the Clinton administration, Carter surrounded himself with people unfamiliar with the ways of Washington. This inexperience, coupled with a kind of parochial and insular defensiveness, ill-served President Carter on the Panama Canal issue and other important affairs of state.[8] He nevertheless was a well-intentioned, dedicated public servant who wanted to do what was right, even if it was not politically popular. Had his staffers not continued to alienate allies at critical times, he may have accomplished more. Even family members, such as his brother Billy, embarrassed him, leading many to conclude that he was not really in total command.

These perceptions, real or imagined, provided political cannon fodder for those who opposed Carter's stance on the Panama Canal, so that Republican opposition crystallized during the debates over the treaty. Worse, inflation climbed to unprecedented levels, and interest rates grew almost beyond comprehension. Although these catastrophes were not entirely the president's fault, the public grew uneasy, and his liberal stance on the Panama Canal further compromised his political standing. When Senate hearings on the canal commenced, I was not sure that the treaty under discussion could garner the necessary two-thirds vote of the Senate to pass. I could not support the Panama Canal Treaty as submitted to the U.S. Senate. I would not vote for ratification. Speeches, pro and con, issued forth on the floor of the Senate, and for four months I remained firm in my position that it would be a mistake for the Senate to ratify such an agreement. As one of eighteen freshman senators, I was not in the forefront of the debate. The Panama Canal Treaty between the United States and Panama was agreed upon on August 10, 1977, and signed on September 7, 1977. The Panamanian electorate ratified the treaty on October 23, 1977, but ratification by the U.S. Senate remained problematic. I wanted to know more about the treaty and its implications, so I decided to take action.

In November 1977, I traveled to Panama, met General Omar Torrijos, the president of Panama, toured the canal, visited with American and Panamanian officials, and further analyzed the substance of the treaty. My wife, my mother, and my brother David accompanied me on this trip. Two staff members made the trip as well, and, in a troubling miscalculation, I invited John Kolbe, the political reporter for the *Phoenix Gazette,* to join the entourage.[9]

Along with a military escort, this almost unwieldy group took a commercial airline, via Los Angeles, to Panama. There I learned, among other things, that Kolbe was dedicated to working against me and my policies. Although his frosty demeanor on the trip was suggestive at the time, years of unremitting criticism in articles and editorials revealed his deep-seated opposition to my tenure in office.[10]

The tour proved critical to my overall comprehension and analysis of the Panama Canal Treaty. We spent four days in Panama City and the Canal Zone. We met with a wide array of people and organizations: the Catholic bishop, the American-Panamanian Chamber of Commerce, numerous businessmen, union employees at the canal, members of the Panamanian Parliament, and other government officials. We conferred also with U.S. military leaders at the canal and toured its length via helicopter. I was struck at this engineering marvel, today nearly one century old, and how the technology continued to be relevant and functional. The highlight of this visit, the meeting with General Torrijos, was memorable.

We flew to Torrijos's summer home, some ninety miles from Panama City, on the country's western coast. He conducted governmental business there, and a steady stream of advisors and officials came and went during our stay. Upon arrival, we had lunch at an enormous round table that seated not only our ten-member entourage, but also the several U.S. military and embassy people as well as the general and his staff. Torrijos was diplomatic, engaging, and even charming as he complimented me on having brought my mother to this meeting. In his eyes, I was a great political leader for this particular familial indulgence, and he spent no small amount of time extolling the virtues of successful political leaders and the significance of their mothers in their success. My mother enjoyed this immensely and later spoke glowingly of General Torrijos and his discussion of mothers' virtues.

As the discussion turned to the treaty, it became clear to me that the general assumed that the United States was giving up all sovereignty and rights to use any type of military force ever again in Panama without the direct request and approval of the Panamanian government. As I listened carefully to his reading of the treaty, I realized that the Carter administration, in presenting its pro-ratification arguments to the American people, interpreted the pending agreement in distinctly different terms. According to government officials, the United States would always have rights and would be able to use those rights to protect its national interest, and the Panamanians understood this perquisite. I asked the general whether under the treaty the United States would be able to deploy troops within the Canal Zone after the agreement became effective. I suggested that it would be inimical to our interests if the Soviet Union or some other communist power deployed troops in the Central American peninsula. Such a hypothetical provocation would threaten control of the canal. He scoffed at the very idea of such a scenario, and it became clear to me that he believed that the United States could not take such action under the treaty. This disparity of views troubled me greatly, and I decided to do something about it.

An interesting sidelight to this meeting was the presence of a colonel standing in the background. He was short and unattractive, with a pockmarked face. During our discussion, General Torrijos on more than one occasion turned to him to retrieve information. He was an intelligence officer, I was told. As it turned out, the figure was Manuel Noriega, future dictator of Panama and now a convicted drug dealer residing in a Miami jail. I remember this well because later, when President George H. W. Bush had problems with Noriega and was considering sending troops in to liberate the country, I reflected on our first coincidental meeting.[11]

After the very pleasant luncheon and three hours of diplomatic and social discussion, we parted ways with General Torrijos and returned to Panama City. The next day we returned to Washington via Arizona. At that time, I was convinced that I could not support the Panama Canal Treaty. Furthermore, I deplored the fact that the administration, knowingly or not, was misleading the Senate and perhaps the American public as to what rights the United States would maintain if the treaty were approved.

The inconsistent reading of the treaty was a problem that needed resolution. At first, I resisted taking a role in the debate, though I planned to make a speech in opposition to the treaty. I reaffirmed the notion that I would offer my reasons for rejection and vote against it. As I prepared my comments, my able, articulate, and politically astute legislative director, Dr. Romano Romani, helped refine my arguments.[12] Even Romano's skillful, cogent writing could not obscure the fact that the treaty, as crafted, was flawed. Though he was not intimately familiar with Arizona's political culture, his ability to work with my deputy chief of staff, Ron Ober, and administrative assistant, Gene Karp, helped make this foray into international affairs steady and strong. Together we crafted my public positions and focused on the specific reasons why I would vote against the treaty.[13]

As we worked and scrutinized drafts, the treaty was submitted for ratification. Majority Leader Robert Byrd, whom I had supported in his highly contested race for that coveted spot, approached me early in the process and asked that I take no public position. In sharp variance to established traditions and protocol, Senator Byrd came to my office, where our discussion was held, so I knew that this issue was of extreme importance to him. The majority leader customarily holds forth in his office suite, located beside the Senate floor, and all members, including committee chairmen, visit there. After asking me to take no position on the treaty, he informed me that he planned a trip to Panama with a number of other senators. He said that he knew I had been there and reiterated his request that I "keep my powder dry." In spite of his admonition, I told him that I had problems with the treaty as written and could not possibly vote for ratification. Our discussion ended with his acknowledging my reservations, but with the request to remain quiet until his return from Panama.

Byrd traveled to Panama with a group of mostly freshman Democrats. My good friend James Sasser was among those who went along, and he, among others, returned to Washington prepared to support the treaty with specific "Byrd amendments." These amendments included certain rights of passage and deployment of military vessels for national-security reasons. I was perplexed and did not agree with most of my fellow Democrats.[14]

As time grew closer for a vote and the various committees commenced hearings on the treaty, I became extremely important to the

Carter administration. Prior to the outset of senate hearings, no one from the White House had contacted me about the pending accord. I was considered an opponent and dismissed as a Democrat who would vote with the Republicans against the treaty. But as the hearings brought the treaty under increasing amounts of scrutiny and analysis, a subtle shift took place in the Senate. Some senators, whom the president considered strong supporters, began to express second thoughts, and others came out against the treaty. Soon, a dour-looking and deliberate deputy secretary of state, Warren Christopher, arrived at my office for a meeting to discuss the agreement. Was there any way, he asked, that I could support the treaty? I informed him that I could not vote for it as it was written. Visibly disappointed, Christopher left my office. In response to this rebuff, Secretary of State Cyrus Vance visited me and was as unconvincing in my office as he had been before various committees. I informed the White House and the State Department that I continued to oppose the treaty. Then, after speaking to Vice President Walter Mondale, to whom I reiterated my concerns and opposition, I was called to the White House for a meeting with President Carter. I explained to the president that I could not support the treaty unless certain changes were made. He impressed me with his knowledge of the intricacies and subtleties of the treaty and said that he would work with me if I were willing to work with him. I said that I would.

I returned to my office, where Romano and my staff worked on proposed amendments to the resolution of ratification. It should be noted that the Senate does not actually vote on a treaty; in other words, a treaty is not presented as a treaty before the Senate to vote yes or no. The process requires that a resolution be passed in the Foreign Relations Committee and then that this resolution be sent to the floor for approval. A resolution may be amended, and such an amendment, if it carries, modifies the treaty. In light of this constitutional rule, my staff, under the direction of Dr. Romani, drafted two reservations. The most important one, which came to be known as the DeConcini Reservation, provided that the United States at any time in the future and in perpetuity, could deploy its military forces within the sovereign country of Panama unilaterally at its sole discretion and without prior approval or requests. It was simply written, but complicated in its implications. Panamanian reaction to the resolution, best characterized as violent and negative, was the most obvious and immediate implication. In fact, I was burned in effigy in Panama. There were other implications as well. After assessing the negative Panamanian reaction to the DeConcini Reservation, President Carter called me to the White House again, where I reconvened discussions with Warren Christopher. I was adamant that I would not move from my position because I felt it was the right one. Further, I was not convinced that the administration would waver because of the strong Panamanian reaction. The Carter administration and I were at a political standoff.

The president sent his special assistant, Hamilton Jordan, to Panama to speak with General Torrijos. Though I was not informed of exactly what took place, I learned that the Panamanians adopted my amendment. To this day I am unsure whether they accepted my reservation.[15] But opposition to the Panama Canal Treaty became organized and politically potent. Throughout the country, a range of national-defense groups, religious organizations, conservative PACs, and individuals came out against the treaty. Arizona became a prime focus of media attention. My colleague Senator Goldwater, who had hinted prior to the 1976 election that he supported the treaty, announced against it, whereas fellow moderate Republican Howard Baker of Tennessee came out for it.

Baker's role was significant because a majority of the Republican caucus opposed the treaty. In fact, without Senator Baker, the minority leader, I am certain that the canal treaty would never have been passed in the Senate. He went against the wishes of his party. I spoke to him many times after the vote, and he stated simply, "It was the right thing to do."

The Republican Party spent large sums in Arizona building up anti-treaty sentiment and lobbying me to vote against the agreement. I realized that, in Arizona, I was in a no-win situation, especially if I were to change my previously stated position and vote for the treaty. This fact made me more determined than ever to stick to the wording of my reservation. President Carter, Senator Byrd, and Deputy Secretary Christopher tried in vain to persuade me to modify the language so that the United States could not unilaterally deploy troops in Panama. They argued that the Panamanian government should request the deployment of U.S. troops. Another White House meeting resulted in my standing firm against President Carter, even though he insisted, in vivid

The Damron Mercantile Store in Thatcher, built by my great grandfather, William Wallace Damron, as it looked in 1953.

My grandmother, Olla Damron Webster, along with my brother Dino *(right)* and me *(left)*, feeding chickens at the ranch in the early 1940s.

Dino and I helping our mother pick cotton at the ranch in the early 1940s.

My grandmother, Olla Damron Webster, in World War I riding attire at Hawk Canyon Ranch.

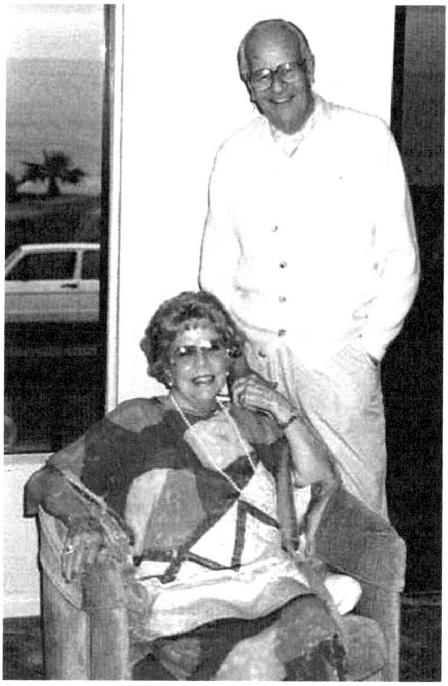

ABOVE: Evo and Ora DeConcini in 1981.
LEFT: Our stepfather, Dr. Morris Martin, and my mother in 2000.

LEFT TO RIGHT: Dennis, Dino, and David DeConcini in Tucson, 1947.

The cover of *Tucson Magazine* just prior to election day, 1976.

With General Omar Torrijos, Panamanian dictator, discussing the Panama Canal Treaty, 1977.

Shaking hands with newly elected president Jimmy Carter, 1977.

Testifying before the Senate Foreign Relations Committee, 1977.

A portrait of the Senate Appropriations Committee when I was a junior member, 1977.

ABOVE: Vice President Walter Mondale, who helped me in Arizona after the political fallout from my stance on the Panama Canal, 1978.

RIGHT: President Anwar Sadat of Egypt, whom I met during one of my first trips to the MiddleEast as a U.S. senator, signs a program for me, 1978.

BELOW: With Menachem Begin in Israel, 1979.

One of my many Republican judicial appointments, Judge Richard Bilby of Tucson, flanked by Senator Barry Goldwater and me, 1979.

Senator Goldwater and I flank Supreme Court justice nominee Sandra Day O'Connor during her confirmation hearings, 1981.

LEFT: With my good friend Senator Orrin Hatch at a hearing of the Senate Judiciary Committee, 1981.

BELOW: With my wife, Susie, at a White House reception hosted by President and Mrs. Reagan, 1981.

terms, that he could not accept my amendment because it would destroy the treaty and the good relationship that existed between the United States and Panama.

I remained courteous but resolute. I told the president that I understood his situation and would respect him, but I could not change the wording. I recall leaving the White House and speaking to the press with a sense of relief, realizing that, because of the administration's position, I would be able to vote against the treaty and thus alleviate my political conundrum in Arizona. Voting against the treaty would bring about far fewer political problems for me than voting for it. My Senate career, which had just begun, appeared to have avoided its first serious crisis.

Within twenty-four hours, however, my sense of well-being changed dramatically when Warren Christopher contacted me and told me he would take my reservation to President Carter. The president, he told me, planned to accept it. With this news, several undecided senators rallied behind the amendment, which meant that the necessary sixty-seven votes were secured if the DeConcini Reservation passed. Majority Leader Byrd, the redoubtable negotiator, seized the moment and moved with speed and determination.

He had the treaty on the floor of the Senate for debate, and he called on me to offer my reservation, but attempted to talk me into not having a roll call vote. I offered the reservation with Senator Paul G. Hatfield (D–Montana). Hatfield had been appointed to fill a vacancy and was up for reelection. His career was unfortunately brief because support for my reservation cost him dearly; he lost in his bid to be elected in the Montana Democratic primary. He thought my amendment might provide some political immunity, but at the same time he figured to gain favorable media attention. As it turned out, we were on the Senate floor for only thirty minutes, offered the reservation, and Senator Byrd accepted it, along with the other members. There was minimal debate. Senator Jesse Helms (R–North Carolina) complimented me on my effort, even though he voted against the treaty. My amendment passed overwhelmingly on a roll call vote. My second reservation passed as well. A victory on the floor of the Senate suddenly turned into the beginning of a political nightmare for me in Arizona: I was now committed to vote for the treaty.

To punctuate this anomalous situation, the treaty was voted on the next day, and I cast what turned out to be the deciding vote in favor of the Panama Canal Treaty. Official congressional ratification took place on April 18, 1978, and the treaty became effective on October 1, 1979. Indeed, the Panama Canal Treaty was ratified contingent upon my resolution that guaranteed the United States the right to use military force, with or without Panama's consent, to keep the canal open. I went home to Arizona and immediately faced numerous recall efforts.[16] Veterans' organizations were especially displeased, and I resolved to meet with them directly and face their criticism. I formed the Veterans' Advisory Committee and met with them to assist me in addressing the political fallout. No small number of Democrats expressed hostility toward me. The national and international attention that focused on my amendment seemed to be magnified upon my return to Arizona because the DeConcini Reservation was the key element in gaining passage of the Panama Canal Treaty. For weeks, it seemed, I was issuing statements on the nightly news or some other similar program. Although praised by some, I was condemned by many. The *Arizona Republic,* for example, though opposed to the treaty, nevertheless wrote complimentary editorials about my leadership role in this increasingly politicized atmosphere. The editors also commended me for getting something passed during my first year in Congress. Yet the state's largest and most influential newspaper was muted in its support and basically damned me with faint praise.

My Arizona constituents were not satisfied with a few kind words from the *Republic.* I undertook a grassroots, person-to-person campaign to explain the significance of the amendment and answer questions about why I had supported the treaty on the final vote. My 1976 campaign literature, disavowing the treaty, and other public utterances and press releases were used against me. I continued to explain the treaty and its importance. President Carter, unpopular in Arizona for reasons other than the treaty—especially because of his efforts to curtail federal funding for the CAP—was an incredible political detriment to me. I remember telling him one time that he had enormous political problems in Arizona. He frowned, looked at me, and said, "Do you believe that?" I responded: "Arizona, Mr. President, is very conservative. You did not carry the state against Gerald Ford, and indeed I think there is a large genuine feeling in Arizona that is very hostile to you.

Unfair as that may be, it is truly the majority in Arizona, in my opinion." I remember he grinned, expressing a feeling that he did not really appreciate my conveying this information to him. He evidently was used to hearing what he wanted to hear, or he did not fully appreciate the significance of the negative political reaction to him in his first few months in office. I viewed his leadership and administration with no small amount of frustration and concern, and in 1980 I crossed party lines and voted for Ronald Reagan for president.

For me, this first difficult political challenge imparted some profound lessons. Just one year in office and I found myself fighting for my political life in Arizona. I cast about for assistance and at first found few political friends. I learned that I could not change voters' minds with an explanation of facts, logically presented in the face of a media onslaught of information contrary to mine. Actor John Wayne, for example, a well-known Hollywood conservative, supported the treaty and my resolution and agreed to film commercials in support of me, but the media spots never ran owing to a lack of sufficient funding. I sought assistance from the national Democratic Party and the White House, but neither responded to my pleas in the days after passage of the treaty. Only Vice President Walter Mondale, himself a former U.S. senator from Minnesota, offered help and solace and displayed a keen awareness of the political problems I faced.

As it turned out, Mondale's sister was married to a Phoenix attorney, William Canby. I nominated him to be a judge on the Ninth Circuit Court. The vice president appreciated my efforts, though I am sure he could have found other ways to make this nomination. Mondale became quite friendly, offered advice, and tried to help deflect some of the vituperative opposition to my canal vote. He even visited Arizona at my request and had a modest influence in assuaging some of the criticism. I have always appreciated him for taking time to help a struggling freshman senator.

I took punishment from both sides, nationally and locally. I supported the Carter administration in the treaty vote, though I forced the administration to accept the DeConcini Reservation and other amendments. The White House was furious at my apparent insubordination. It had to answer to the Panamanians and mollify them. It was forced to realize that it had muddled its canal presentation to the public by making misleading representations, and my efforts at bringing forth a more accurate portrayal did not endear me to the new administration. I engendered little empathy and even less goodwill from the Democratic president, while at the same time I faced a political firestorm at home in Arizona. In fact, the consequences of getting caught in this crossfire stayed with me for the rest of my career in elected office.

In the 1982 election, the eventual Republican nominee, Pete Dunn, made the Panama Canal a key campaign issue even though numerous other issues needed serious discussion and debate. Early in my first term, I knew that I would seek reelection, and though I was at odds with the Carter administration on many issues, I remained on relatively good terms with the Democratic Party in Arizona. I knew in 1980, however, that with the election of popular conservative Republican president Ronald Reagan, with a Congress that had shifted dramatically to the right, and with the entrance of supply-side economic policies—Reaganomics—I faced a staunch electoral challenge in 1982.

Toward the end of my first term in the Senate, I called for a delay in the third stage of President Reagan's across-the-board tax cuts and during the campaign renewed my call for postponement of this measure. I was equally disappointed when the House of Representatives rejected the balanced-budget amendment, and I issued public statements to that effect. I stated that the Federal Reserve Board appeared insensitive to a floundering economy; urged a bipartisan effort to relieve unemployment by reducing interest rates; proclaimed my strong opposition to President Reagan's veto of a housing bill that would have reduced home mortgage rates by four or five points, thus creating nine hundred thousand new jobs and increasing sales by 650,000 units; and supported the extension of unemployment benefits by thirteen weeks and retraining for the long-term unemployed, particularly in Arizona counties hit hard by mine closures.[17]

Fortunately, I had a weak challenger in the primary. Caroline Killeen, a Tucsonan with little political experience, financed her campaign with money she had earned from recycling cans and traveled throughout the state on a bicycle until it was stolen in late July. She had only $800 to finance her effort, and she generated only a token opposition against me.[18] I had to stand on my voting record and public statements in the general-election campaign. Without a truly contested primary, however, my campaign fund of $1.72 million could be directed toward the general election.

The easy primary also allowed me to place my message before the voters in a systematic fashion. The six key challenges facing Arizonans, I contended, were unemployment, Social Security, the CAP, crime, a balanced budget, and environmental concerns. On these issues, I stayed on message throughout both the primary-election and general-election campaigns. Yet I knew to expect the unexpected, and the 1982 general-election campaign had its fair share of the unexpected.

Prolonged unemployment was a cancer, I maintained, and it ate away at the fabric of American society. It destroyed the spirit that made our country strong, and at every turn I argued that common sense required that we work together to make jobs available in the private sector to those who wanted to work. I supported our Social Security system and believed it was a solemn obligation that the federal government had made with its citizens. I refused to cut Social Security benefits or to amend the existing system.

The CAP was another centerpiece to my reelection campaign. Water was the fundamental resource without which Arizona could not prosper and grow. Through my position on the Appropriations Committee, I vowed to continue working to fund and complete the construction of CAP and bring Arizona's fair share of Colorado River into the state. Crime, I told audiences, was the most serious and immediate threat to our lives and property. Although we could not completely eliminate it, I said that we must try to control it and must never give up in our efforts to reestablish a society without fear. On the balanced budget issue, I held that it was the best remedy for the present and a safeguard for the future. I was proud to serve as the Democratic sponsor and floor manager of the constitutional amendment for a balanced budget. Concerning the environment, I maintained that there was no fundamental conflict between the responsibility to protect our environment and the legitimate use of the land for economic and recreational purposes. As a born and bred Arizonan, I was acutely aware of the abundant and magnificent resources our state possessed. Arizonans have a special responsibility not only to their children and grandchildren, I said throughout my reelection effort, but also to all present and future Americans to guard and protect this natural heritage.[19]

As in 1976, the Republicans had a contested primary, though unlike in the Conlan-Steiger campaign, the two candidates, Pete Dunn, a three-term state representative, and Dean Sellers, a Gilbert real-estate entrepreneur and rancher, virtually ignored each other and focused their attention on me. Predictably, both claimed that I had been too liberal during my term and that the U.S. Senate would be better served if I were replaced with a conservative Republican. Dunn's mantra was that "DeConcini talks like Ronald Reagan in Arizona and votes like Ted Kennedy in Washington." Sellers, too, used textbook political rhetoric, claiming I had been a thorn in President Reagan's side and too frequently had "flip-flopped."

In between attacks on me, the two Republicans also attempted to address what they called the "major issues." Dunn called for support of Reagan's economic plans, a strong military presence, lower taxes, and reductions in the food stamp program—standard Republican slogans. Sellers offered little more to the debate. He called for "strengthened national defense, [and] major changes in the income tax and Social Security systems," and he argued that "the federal Education and Energy departments must be dismantled."[20] Their assaults on me continued late into the primary, when Sellers, realizing he was behind in the polls by at least 14 percentage points, suddenly turned his attention toward Dunn. He claimed that Dunn had failed to vote on forty of two hundred bills passed in the state legislature. He reminded voters of Dunn's legal background, and, like Carolyn Warner in the 1976 Democratic primary, he suggested that there were too many lawyers in the Senate. On September 7, 1982, primary-election day, Dunn defeated Sellers for the Republican nomination for the U.S. Senate by a comfortable 18,000-vote margin. I faced Pete Dunn in my race for reelection, and on the day after the primaries we discussed having four separate debates in Phoenix, Tucson, Yuma, and Flagstaff. I had amassed a voting record, sponsored or cosponsored bills, established an image of political independence, and taken strong stances on controversial issues such as the Panama Canal. My record, in the context of the Reagan revolution, was clearly open for partisan scrutiny.

I centered the early portion of my reelection campaign on the failure of President Reagan's economic policies and "the urgent need for major changes." "The president's program didn't work," I told Frank Turco of the *Arizona Republic,* and "now it's time to take some corrective measures. We cannot follow blindly the same economic program." I provided information that the early stage of Reaganomics had not slowed inflation. It had not halted rising interest rates, and unemployment figures remained comparatively high. "We've got to do better than that," I said. Dunn came out of the primary as anticipated, attempting to identify with a president popular in Arizona. "I believe the people of Arizona want Ronald Reagan to succeed and they're going to send people to Washington who can help him succeed," he said.[21] Thus, our divergent positions on Reagan's economic program gave Arizona voters a clear choice.[22]

On September 15, just days into the general-election campaign, my staff took aggressive steps in response to information that an outside PAC based in Virginia, the National Conservative Political Action Committee (NCPAC), was working in concert with the Dunn campaign. As a result of this information, a member of my steering committee, Tony Mason, filed a complaint with the Federal Election Commission in Washington, D.C., against the Dunn for Senate Committee and the NCPAC. Critics had accused the NCPAC, which claimed credit for defeating at least four liberal senators in the 1980s elections, of relying on half-truths, distortions, misinformation, and lies. Its leader, John T. "Terry" Dolan, had been quoted in various interviews as saying, "We could elect Mickey Mouse to the House and Senate"; "I'm not after respectability. The only thing I care about is if we're effective"; "The Republican Party is a fraud. It's a social club where rich people go to pick their noses"; "I know I'm screwed up, but at least I admit it."[23] Arizona voters, I knew, did not want outsiders influencing the election, especially those who expressed themselves in such a cavalier and untoward fashion.

We charged that NCPAC lost its independence and came under federal campaign-spending limits when Dunn hired a researcher, Gary Giordano, as NCPAC's researcher in Arizona. Giordano, an unsuccessful Republican candidate in the September 7 primary in Legislative District 24, at first denied he worked for NCPAC. But Tony Mason, from our campaign, produced documents showing that Giordano, who dabbled in a variety of right-wing causes, was deeply involved with the NCPAC and Dunn and that the group reported spending $26,417.89 against me through the end of July. Of that total, $17,850 was spent on a poll.

Furthermore, because Dunn paid Giordano $500 in March for information he had researched, and because Giordano had been recognized as the point man in Arizona in NCPAC's July newsletter, Mason concluded correctly that money spent by the NCPAC on the Arizona race amounted to in-kind contributions to Dunn. In that case, the group would be limited to spending $5,000 in the primary and $5,000 in the general elections, which was roughly $10,400 less than they reported spending. Mason reminded Dunn that the penalty for a conviction of violating campaign-spending laws was one year in prison. He added that Dunn was "cowardly and dishonest" for bringing the NCPAC in to do his dirty work. After some chest thumping and equivocation, Dunn relented: "I am planning to ask NCPAC to stay out of Arizona. We can beat DeConcini without them."[24]

Besides taking on the NCPAC and Dunn in the legal arena, Ron Ober moved quickly to shoot and air some remarkably effective television spots that framed the issue in vivid terms. In machine-gun fashion, an off-camera voice recited some of the budget cuts the NCPAC favored: less money for water projects such as the CAP, less money for programs such as Social Security, and no money at all for the Veteran's Administration hospital system. Then Dunn's campaign headquarters phone numbers appeared on screen as the voice urged people to "Call Pete Dunn, and tell him we don't need NCPAC here. Tell him that's not the way we do things here in Arizona."[25] Dunn's office was flooded with calls. By September 25, NCPAC announced that it would not become involved in the DeConcini-Dunn race, and I ordered my commercials tying Dunn to NCPAC pulled from the air. We could turn our attention, I hoped, to issues such as the economy, unemployment, inflation, crime, and water.[26]

My staff and I agreed that we should frame the campaign debate on our terms. In Tucson, shortly after the NCPAC emerged as a campaign issue, I addressed the Democrats of Greater Tucson and pointed out some of my opponent's inconsistent actions. Dunn portrayed himself as an enemy of organized labor but had sought and won labor's endorsement when he ran for the state legislature in 1976. He extolled the importance of solar energy but had opposed solar tax credits in 1979. He labeled himself a fiscal conservative but had voted for 96.4 percent of all state House spending bills between 1977 and 1980. The inconsistencies in his record enabled me to call on him "to start running a campaign based on what he has done and what he intends to do." "Up to now," I asserted, "it has been a campaign of half-truths and lies." Tough rhetoric in a suddenly confrontational race, but we realized we had to engage Dunn directly and aggressively.[27]

Our newspaper, radio, and television spots were especially effective. I attribute this success to Ron Ober, Michael Hawkins, Gene Karp, and others, who helped fashion the delivery of my message in these various forms. One memorable newspaper ad, with a photograph of me wearing a bola tie and wide grin, asked, "Why is this man smiling?" Beneath the photo and copy was a list of hundreds of "Republicans for DeConcini," many of whom were among the state's most prominent citizens. Jack Pfister, a prominent Republican member of the Phoenix 40 and former director of the Salt River Project, was one of the Republicans listed in the ad, and he commented that it "was one of the most effective political ads" he had seen.[28] This aspect of the 1982 campaign was memorable for its high level of achievement.

The 1982 campaign, as in my other campaigns, featured fringe issues related to my Italian surname and the possible existence of the Mafia, or organized crime, in Tucson. On September 24, the *Sacramento Bee,* a leading California newspaper, published a story based on the manuscript of Joseph Bonanno's autobiography. According to the *Bee,* the work criticized my family, in particular my father, Evo, for distancing himself from the convicted Mafia leader. My father addressed the revelation directly, informing the media that "[a]t one time we were friends, but he had a lot of publicity, you know." Bonanno, drawn into the controversy, said, "Evo and I had a clean relationship. I want to clear Evo's name forever on this score. Evo DeConcini never did anything crooked." I was convinced that the release of Bonanno's statement was an attempt to embarrass me in an election year.[29]

As Pima County attorney, I had orchestrated an investigation that enabled undercover officers to seize Bonanno's garbage, recovering notes and other materials that led to a felony conviction in 1980. Bonanno, who was seventy-seven at the time of the 1982 story, was found guilty by a federal jury in San Jose, California, of conspiracy to obstruct a grand jury that was seeking evidence about Santa Clara Valley businesses operated by his sons. I added that I thought the story about Bonanno's relationship with my father was another example of vindictiveness on the part of Bonanno because I had begun the investigation that led to his felony conviction and ultimate sentence. "I realize what the attempt is," I said, "I've had a lot of criminals that I have convicted not like me." Bonanno, of course, denied that he was trying to embarrass me during an election year by bringing up his old relationship with my father, but nonetheless this was one of several attempts to link my family to organized crime.[30]

Throughout the campaign, Dunn persisted in assailing my vote on the Panama Canal. He favored keeping the Panama Canal under U.S. control and spoke to numerous veterans groups throughout Arizona in his attempt to gain political traction. At the same time, he called for making cuts in veterans' benefits and Social Security and for lowering funding for the CAP.[31] I opposed these positions. Dunn's claims that I had sold out American interests with the DeConcini Reservation were contradicted by tape recordings of General Torrijos condemning me and my plan after the treaties had been signed.[32]

Dunn nevertheless tried to make political capital on the Panama Canal, claiming that Torrijos had turned my efforts to his advantage. But I had the tape. At joint campaign appearances, Dunn would make this claim, and I would bring out the tape recorder, push the "on" button, and play Torrijos's vitriolic denunciation of me. The audiences invariably listened and began to view Dunn as someone who was not credible. This byplay soon became a kind of a warm-up routine that preceded our debates: he would say, "Let's get this out of the way" and then make his statement, and then I would play the tape.

One final incident of the 1982 campaign was memorable. As my campaign staff knew, the only way a challenger could gain any political credence was to have a forum with the incumbent and cause him or her to blunder. On October 13, 1982, Dunn and I appeared together on KAET, Channel 8, the Public Broadcasting System station located at Neeb Hall on the campus of Arizona State University in Tempe. The one and one-half hour live debate was to be telecast statewide. The month of October, I knew, was filled not only with political campaigns but also with sports activities, including the World Series. As the moderator introduced us, I informed the live audience that I appreciated their tuning in to the debate, and then I told them the score of the World Series game, which was in the third inning at the time our debate started. Naturally, television viewers turned their channels from the debate to the game, thus allowing Dunn little chance of winning over large numbers of voters. I watched him smile wryly, knowing that I had played a successful political gambit.

An *Arizona Republic/Phoenix Gazette* poll conducted one week before the election held good news for my campaign. Both papers endorsed my reelection and announced that I held a thirty-one-point lead over Dunn —55 percent to 24 percent, with 19 percent undecided—though he stated that he had conducted a poll that showed the race was much closer. A separate poll conducted by the Public Opinion Research Center mirrored the results of the *Republic/Gazette* survey; I led Dunn 57 percent to 23 percent. Dunn scoffed at the results and said, "I take heart in a number of things. . . . I saw a poll in the primary that I was trailing my opponent 3 to 1 in Pima County," but "I won Pima County 2 to 1." Like most politicians, he uttered the familiar refrain, "We're going to have the election anyway; we're not going to let the pollsters decide this election."[33]

In the end, I won reelection handily, defeating Dunn 411,970 to 291,749 and losing only one county, Yavapai, by 154 votes out of 25,618 cast.[34] I won Pima County by a margin of 67 percent of the vote to Dunn's 30 percent. Because the results showed a trend of two to one in my favor, I issued some statements interpreting the significance of my reelection. I avoided using terms such as *overwhelming, unanimous,* or *mandate,* but I thought that a message had been sent to the Reagan administration that "the American people wanted a cooperative effort to work out the problems of the economy." My record in Congress demonstrated a "moderate to conservative" bent, and, as the punditry wrote the day after the election, "DeConcini's ratings by national organizations of both the left and right tend toward the middle."[35] I agreed with this assessment. After some time to evaluate the broader issues involved, Arizona voters appeared to have agreed not only with my Panama Canal vote, but also with my stance on other important issues, which might best be described as moderate to conservative.

Those pressures and outcomes notwithstanding, I felt I had done what was right. I realized once again that my father's axiom was correct: do the right thing, and you can always look at yourself in the mirror and will not have to apologize to anyone. That moral philosophy helped me persevere through a significant amount of political fallout, and I rededicated myself to hard work and hoped that through these efforts I could overcome the political problems engendered by my vote for the Panama Canal Treaty.

Put another way, I created an immense problem for myself when I took a position prior to an issue's coming before the Senate for final determination. When I reversed my stance because of changing circumstances, I endured public criticism and political attacks. Press coverage and media spin doctors persuaded the public, in remarkably effective fashion, that I appeared to be a sellout, a disingenuous public official who switched his vote for political gain. Yet I lost from both sides of the issue. The Panama Canal Treaty vote exemplified in vivid terms a profound dilemma that challenges elected officials. I voted with reason and heart; I voted as I believed in spite of my initial perceptions. I found myself in this difficult situation, one in which many members of Congress find themselves. It is a dilemma that will always vex public officials. It is a dilemma also for those who grow astute at avoiding the types of tough choices illustrated in my role in the Panama Canal Treaty ratification process. Many hedge their bets, do not take positions immediately, or straddle issues. Reporter John Kolbe, my inveterate detractor, took me to task for playing both sides against the middle and, quite frankly, was surprised at my actions as reflected in the DeConcini Reservation. As the 1982 campaign proved, the Panama Canal vote persisted as a key campaign issue. It framed to a significant degree the nature and direction of my reelection campaign. Though other issues were put before the voters—Reagan's economic policies, unemployment, water, and crime—the Panama Canal remained a large part of the political dialogue surrounding my tenure in the Senate.

6 A Day in the Life
Senate Culture, 1977–1995

In 1913, the Seventeenth Amendment to the Constitution, calling for the direct election of senators, became the law of the land. Prior to this amendment, state legislatures appointed one of their members to the upper house of Congress. In this age of reform, progressives in both major parties succeeded in creating a more responsive and accessible electoral system. Indeed, the direct election of senators and women's suffrage seven years later reflected this progressive spirit and will forever provide testament to the presidencies of Theodore Roosevelt, William Howard Taft, and Woodrow Wilson.

Before World War II, representatives and senators served approximately six months of the year in Washington, D.C. Their allowances provided for only one round-trip ticket per year from their state to the capital. By the 1960s, Congress began nine- and ten-month sessions, thus eliminating the tradition of members of Congress maintaining a separate profession. By the time I arrived in the Senate in 1977, Senate culture and work habits had been modified dramatically, yet some traditions remained unchanged.[1]

I served eighteen years as a member of the U.S. Senate from the state of Arizona, and no day was exactly like the next. I learned immediately that my fellow elected officials fell into three distinct categories. Many senators—whom I considered good friends—viewed their elected status with such reverence that they chose to minimize their public appearances in an effort to maximize their effect. They tended to delegate work and negotiations to trusted staffers. Others, who were a bit more down to earth, participated in daily office activities, took a direct role in their committee work, and helped staff plan their schedules. This hands-on group tended to be everywhere: attending committee and subcommittee hearings, entering statements into the record to demonstrate to their constituents that they were effective, and much more. A third type of senator focused on one particular issue, developed an area of expertise, attended innumerable hearings, held weekly press conferences, called study sessions, and sought constituent exposure. In effect, the Senate maintained a history and culture that enabled senators to execute their duties in a variety of styles that produced, of course, varying degrees of success.

A typical day as a senator began with a morning meeting or breakfast anywhere from 7:00 to 8:30 A.M. I tried to minimize breakfast meetings, so I scheduled no more than two of these types of meetings per working week. I was usually up late at night, either working or attending a social function, and I preferred to arrive in the office around 8:30–9:00 A.M. If we had breakfast meetings, we were usually addressing constituent issues or delivering a short speech. The day, however, always began with a dose of urban reality: driving into the city from the suburbs. The drive from McLean, Virginia, where my family and I lived, took from thirty to fifty minutes, though I lived only fourteen miles from the Capitol. By 1980, I acquired a car phone, a unique item at that time. I used this car phone—though primitive compared to today's models, with its limited range and poor reception—a great deal. In general, when I arrived in the office, I attempted to see staff members for prescheduled appointments, review mail, and finish up leftover duties. Then I would take phone calls, return messages, and prepare those phone calls I would make at night. It was better to return calls later in the day because of the two- or three-hour time difference between Washington, D.C., and Arizona.

Committee meetings usually started at 10:00 A.M. Sometimes lasting into the afternoon, committee hearings occupied Tuesdays, Wednesdays, and Thursdays. Senate votes occurred on these days, and sometimes, as I was conducting business, I would be called to the floor to vote. If I were not chairing a committee, I would take my mail with me, read it, outline memos, and keep listening to testimony—a kind of sensory and intellectual juggling act. Had I not done this work while attending committee hearings, I could never have completed tasks. If there were a topic of special importance to my constituents or the country under discussion at the hearings, my staff always alerted me, and I prepared to engage in the discussions.

When I had particular interest in a piece of legislation, I would be on the floor managing the bill. This task took me away from committee or constituent meetings and broke the continuity of the day. Again, my staff alerted me to dealings on the Senate floor and advised me on commitments and voting choices. When voting on an issue, I considered several variables. What was the significance of my vote for my constituents? What was the significance of my vote for the White House? Did I have commitments to honor there? And, of course, what was the significance to the nation? Therefore, when a vote commenced, I had fifteen minutes to cast my vote.[2] I would talk with a staff member who was observing the proceedings and assessing the information. Amendments to bills were often complicated, and astute staffers needed to brief me on all of the subtleties and nuances in a very short time—sometimes two minutes—then I would cast my vote. This process was not always difficult. Procedural votes to support the administration's position on an issue, for example, were easy. At other times, the vote could be difficult; I would have to reconcile the pros and cons, analyze my convictions, and interpret my history on an issue. For example, if I had to vote on an education issue that benefited one state but set a bad precedent for the nation, I found myself conflicted. Senators find themselves in this dilemma almost daily, whether the issues center on highways, health, tax policy, appropriations, financial and regulatory affairs, or education. My staff helped me immensely in dealing with this aspect of voting.

As I approached a vote, I always had confidence in my staff. They would explain the circumstances of an issue, answer my questions, and recommend how I should vote. For the most part, I sided with my staff, though on occasion a Senate member persuaded me to vote the opposite way. My staff naturally expressed their displeasure when this took place, but I would immediately ask them to draft a memo defending my vote. Drafting a convincing argument that contradicted their original suggestion was truly the test of an outstanding staff. I recall so many times when legislative staff such as Romano Romani or Mary Hawkins, who had advised me to vote another way, generated convincing memos to explain my votes to the press and my Arizona constituents.

Controversial issues, such as the death penalty, proved to be little problem for me because my views were well known. Both the staff and the press knew that I supported the death penalty. Problems emerged on highly volatile issues. On a controversial amendment to the Medicare authorization bill that gave seniors greater rights yet took away the economic incentive for hospitals, how would I vote? Even today, seniors on fixed incomes are pitted against the health-care establishment. My staff studied such issues, and my constituents—seniors and health-care providers—knew I faced a serious choice. I would speak with doctors, seniors, businesspeople, and labor and health-care professionals. These challenges are actually a dynamic part of the political process and form the heart of being a legislator. The fact that I made decisions at the final moment on issues of this nature provided me with a sense of purpose and faith in the electoral process. I always tried to use good judgment.

The abortion issue was always a struggle in the Senate. Most members were decidedly either pro-life or pro-choice. Providing federal funding for abortions or permitting early-term abortions generated clearly defined positions. Yet legislation designed to permit aborted fetuses for use in research for the development of medicines to address disease created a whole new warehouse of politically charged debates. I heard testimony that these fetuses could be used for research, and, indeed, it was clear that medical applications for Parkinson's, Lou Gherig's, and Alzheimer's were real. I opposed abortion, and now I was presented with an amendment that complicated the abortion issue even further by focusing on the use of fetuses from abortions that had already occurred. Along with other pro-life members, such as Strom Thurmond (R–South Carolina) and Mark Hatfield (R–Oregon), I supported the amendment. The right-to-life organizations descended on me, though they did not use this issue to oppose my reelection. I became convinced that if abortions took place, there was no reason not to use aborted fetuses for scientific purposes. Of course, the hard-core right-to-life people saw my vote as a kind of moral and political waffling, but I am convinced my position was right. I was concerned about voter backlash, as were other pro-life senators who voted with me, but voting on controversial and emotional issues was part of the job description.

At 12:30, we would break for lunch, and, more often than not, we spent this time with constituents in the Senate dining room. The Senate, in fact, has three dining rooms. One public dining room on the first floor has an inexpensive menu, average food, and less than desirable furnishings. Down the hall is the formal senators' dining room, with enough space to seat two hundred people. I recall Senator Spark Matsunaga (D–Hawaii) each day reserving a table of twelve for his constituents—a ritual that all Hawaiian visitors to Washington, D.C., could expect. When I was there, he would call me over to meet them. These courtesies reflected Matsunaga's penchant for personal contact and constituent service. He was also one of the few senators I knew who read all his mail.

The senators' dining room, in fact, is formal. Linen-covered tables, elegantly appointed crystal and silverware, and the famous Senate Bean Soup are the distinguishing characteristics of this venue. Across the hall from the senators' dining room is the senators' private dining room. Only members and former members are allowed in this small, divided room, with an open door to aid food delivery. Republicans sit in the first of two long tables, and Democrats in the second. One can choose from the menu or the buffet, and waiters assist if necessary. Here, the seniority system is not important, and I sat with whom I wanted. In my time in the Senate, there always were a few who boasted or tried to impose their seniority, but for the most part the atmosphere was casual. Warren Magnuson, for example, was chairman of the Appropriations Committee, and when he sat at the table, everyone grew quiet to see what "Maggy" had to say. If he wanted to discuss something, then everyone else talked about the same subject. After that, everyone could return to their discussion. If Maggy appeared quiet, then others could lead the discussion.

I remember well John Culver (D–Iowa), who could facilitate a discussion on any subject. Lloyd Bentsen (D–Texas) seemed always in a sober mood. When he chose to speak, all listened with great anticipation but were usually disappointed. He seemed to have a high opinion of himself, though he was always cordial to me.

Two of the best conversationalists were Louisiana's Democratic senators, Bennett Johnston and Russell Long. Both were smart, competent legislators and told great tales of Louisiana political culture. Watching and listening to Johnston at lunch or on the floor of the Senate was a joy. He listened and considered carefully other points of view. Long told stories of his legendary father, Huey P. Long, the governor and senator who in 1935 was assassinated. He recounted one well-known anecdote about an early gubernatorial campaign in which his father promised a small community that he would build a bridge across a river to link the town with a nearby highway. He promised the state senator that if the senator would vote for him and endorse him as well as support his budget, he would see that the bridge project was accomplished. After his election, Governor Long did not come through on his promise. The state senator, asking how he would explain this to his own constituents, received the reply, "Tell them I lied." While evoking laughter, the story was uncannily accurate concerning Huey Long's political tactics.

The Senate dining room provided an environment for political deal making and legislative discussion. One majority leader, George Mitchell (D–Maine), atc thcrc often and would discuss legislation. Mitchell knew exactly what he was doing; he would float various legislative scenarios and listen to members' responses, then ask them to drop by his office to discuss the issues. Once there, you were in his net. He would invite other members with differing opinions, and a compromise would ultimately be reached. Mitchell was fascinating, bright, yet unassuming, and he put everyone at ease. His staff was excellent, and he was always prepared. President Clinton's 1993 tax budget act brought out the best in Mitchell. Throughout the process, he indicated to the Democratic side that he did not have the votes, and it would be a tragedy if this proposal did not pass. He asked us what items should be excised or included, and he would revisit these issues. He would work out details in the Senate dining room, and he was astute at putting together this legislation. I admired his methods and his resolve.

After lunch, usually between 1:30 and 2:00 P.M., senators would leave the dining-room area to take on afternoon duties: committee hearings, constituent meetings, and related matters. Many senators returned to their offices for naps. If a member's Senate seniority dipped below seventy, he or she was assigned an office in the main Capitol building, which served as a private suite. Some offices were spacious and included bathrooms, wet bars, and stirring views of Washington, D.C. Others were less inspiring. My first office was next to Senator Donald Riegle Jr. (D–Michigan) in the basement with no windows. The furniture consisted of a desk, couch, and chair, and I often saw rats crawling around outside. I spent minimal time in this office. The advantages of having an office at the Capitol were many; if you worked late, you could stay in the office, have a drink, or take a rest. As I gained seniority, I inherited former Idaho senator James A. McClure's (D–Idaho) hideaway, which was on the third floor of the Capitol. Although it was windowless, it nevertheless boasted a beautiful chandelier, eighteenth-century office furniture, and ornate appointments. It also had a wet bar, television, sofa, and fireplace. I used it on rare occasions—for meetings with staff and constituents or for later meetings.

Dinner was often at a local restaurant or the Senate dining room if we were in session. Two to three nights a week, the Senate would meet past 6:00 P.M. Once in a while, my wife would join me, though often I ate with other senators. When I first came to the Senate, I was able to go to the Secretary of the Senate's office and have a cocktail. Stan Kimmit served in that position, and he had a continuous bar, with a bartender, in his office.[3] Many nights, from 5:00 to 9:00, we would sit in the bar drinking and talking. Older members, such as James Eastland, Henry "Scoop" Jackson (D–Washington), or Herman Talmadge, would hold forth, telling stories and advising the younger members. Over time, this Senate haven became less available as new people filled the Secretary of the Senate post.

Although I never served in the House of Representatives, I observed and formed friendships with numerous members. The much larger House—435 members compared to 100 senators—operated in far different fashion from the upper chamber. Freshman House members, for example, faced great difficulty gaining recognition or influence upon taking office. Moreover, new members might get appointed to one or two committees and usually no more than one subcommittee of each full committee. It was extremely rare for freshman and even sophomore representatives to receive multiple assignments.

I noticed a positive consequence to this apparent limitation: because House members could focus their attention on only one or two subject areas, they were often prepared to address issues, whereas senators struggled to gain knowledge on the more numerous bills facing them. House members served on only two subcommittees of the Appropriations Committee, so the opportunities for conflict were minimized. In the Senate, if a member served on the Appropriations Committee, he or she might also serve on five subcommittees and an additional major committee, such as Appropriations or Judiciary (known as an A committee). That A committee might include up to seven or eight subcommittees, with a senator being required to serve on three or four. A senator might also serve on one other A committee or several B committees, as well as on additional subcommittees. It was thus not unusual for a member of the Senate to serve on two A committees, such as Appropriations and Judiciary, and five subcommittees, perhaps chairing one of them. My chief of staff, Gene Karp, informed me that I served on more committees and subcommittees than any other member of the Senate.[4]

On a number of occasions, I attended conference committee hearings, consisting of both House and Senate members, and noticed that the House member possessed more information and greater command of the details than the corresponding senator on the same committee. In Defense Appropriations Subcommittee conferences, Representative John Murtha (D–Pennsylvania) would demonstrate much deeper knowledge of a particular system than fellow subcommittee members Senator Daniel Inouye (D–Hawaii) or Senator Theodore (Ted) Stevens (R–Alaska).[5] Other House members developed expertise on one or more weapons issues before the Defense Appropriations Subcommittee. It was not at all uncommon for their knowledge to be superior to mine. Representative Norman Dicks (D–Washington) exemplified the House defense expert. In fact, he spent most of his time on defense issues. He was a great colleague and a friend, and he knew more about defense policy and issues than most of the senators on the subcommittee.[6]

Not enough time exists in the day to devote appropriate attention to each committee or subcommittee assignment. For example, as a committee chair, I would choose the subject matter and develop it, but I did not want to exclude other issues. I tried to stay involved, and I relied heavily on my staff. Indeed, these positions as staffers for members of Congress are highly desirable, and competition for them is fierce. Although the highest-paid staff members may make more than $100,000 per year, most staffers take home modest incomes. I found senate staffers competent and hard working, and they often took on the personality of the senator for whom they worked: tough, mean, jovial, or genial. The ideal staff participates in many aspects of the senator's various political positions and in fact often negotiates for the senator as if he or she were present. This situation, of course, requires an intimate and trusting relationship between senator and staff member. I observed many senators who did not have close, daily contact with their staff, and I concluded that it rendered them less effective in the execution of their duties.

Some other aspects of daily activities in Congress drew my attention. During my tenure from 1977 to 1995, I observed that House members behaved less congenially than Senate members. The House, of course, with 435 members, offers less opportunity to form friendships and acquaintances than does the Senate, where I worked with 99 other members. In fact, at a personal level I enjoyed getting to know my fellow senators. Through the friendship-building process in Congress, I concluded that the types of individuals I met reflected the public at large. There were brilliant and outstanding individuals who at the same time possessed little or no practical social skills. Nevertheless, somehow, constituents elected these individuals. Others arrived in the Senate with average intellectual qualities, but were "good guys" from fraternity days.

The Senate is truly a representative democracy. All types of people served. The same diversity marks the chamber today, and a broad range of men and women from all walks of life will serve in the future. Some senators lacked in intellectual capacity or, at least, were not as intelligent as portrayed in their public images and press releases. Although they might impress me as being very nice persons, they oftentimes did not possess the ability to analyze issues before speaking. When, for example, *Regardie's,* a popular Washington publication, voted William Lloyd Scott (R–Virginia) the dumbest member of the Senate, he held a press conference to announce that he was not the dumbest senator. Not totally ignorant, such members were out of their depth and somewhat ineffective in the chamber.

My impressions sometimes led me astray, however. Although one former member, Larry Pressler (R–South Dakota), was a friend, I thought he perhaps lacked the necessary gravitas to focus on issues. He claimed a distinguished education and a Phi Beta Kappa award, but I never sensed that he paid careful attention to discussions of significance. He did, however, have a press office that effectively publicized his positions and made the most of his legislative career. Many years later I discovered that he compensated for a learning disability by not responding immediately to questions, which is a fundamental requirement in the political arena. Pressler's example, one in which image and capacity were dissimilar, illustrates the significant role played by public perception.

Jeremiah Denton (R–Alabama), a retired admiral from the U.S. Navy and a former prisoner of war in Vietnam, could not place issues in a broader context; he would be so determined and focused on minutiae that I wondered if he really understood what he was doing. I grew to know Senator Denton well; we served on the Judiciary Committee together, and it happened that we shared the same views on abortion as well as on other issues that came before the committee. We held numerous hearings and press conferences together, and Denton, so emphatic and demanding, would make incomprehensible statements that made it seem as if he had no clue about the issue under review.[7] Other members had short tempers and intense opinions, and they often registered strong objections to positions contrary to their own, although the press allowed significant leeway in this regard.

Many senators had formidable intellects and thus held great interest for me. The late Senator Daniel Patrick Moynihan (D–New York), for example, was a very bright former cabinet member and ambassador, and I consider him one of the more fascinating members with whom I served. His floor presentations gained him a reputation for elitism because he emanated a sense that his position was the only viable one. That time-honored debate tactic sometimes does not persuade others, and I witnessed him lose some votes because of his haughty demeanor. Senator Moynihan also possessed a large ego, like many of us, and although he embraced causes, he had difficulty following through. I recall many evenings when he had placed objections before some amendments or legislation, but then could not be found to debate them. His staff, aware that he was off somewhere relaxing with a drink or two, would stall until early the next morning, when he would be available and in good form. More than once, in efforts to get bills passed, I had to circumvent Moynihan's staff to convince the leadership that if Senator Moynihan could not come to the floor, then the Senate should proceed with pending legislation. This became a pattern. Parliamentary maneuvering notwithstanding, Senator Moynihan, whatever form he was in, would always be a tremendous advocate and formidable ally. In spite of the previous night's activities, he was as intellectually able as usual, and the few times I debated him I recall thinking that I did not understand what he said. I asked a few colleagues on the floor, and they said that they did not understand him either. In effect, his intellectual capacity was difficult to overcome in debate, and though I may have won some arguments, I know I lost many to the New York senator. He was compelling, charismatic, and unique—an intellectual in the Senate and a man I admired greatly for many years.

Senator Bill Bradley (D–New Jersey), Rhodes Scholar, college basketball star at Princeton and with the New York Knicks, was probably one of the least effective senators who served in the upper chamber. An engaging and friendly celebrity, he always joked with me. He even spoke at some of my early fund-raisers in my 1988 campaign, and I have been forever grateful for his efforts. But Bradley rarely extended himself beyond his own self-interests. If there were any politically negative implications for him on an issue, he disappeared. He often wavered. I remember the 1986 tax reform legislation in which Bradley was touted as the major reformer on the Senate Finance Committee. He participated in the drafting of the tax bill, but the measure was in my opinion a disaster, and his machinations raised many questions. He made promises to a number of constituents about supporting the indexing of their capital gains tax. I put forward my own bill, as did other members, which also called for indexing capital gains, and I spoke with Senator Bradley about it. He promised to support the capital indexing amendment. As the legislation moved through the Senate, Bradley was on the floor debating different parts of the bill. When the time came to speak on behalf of the capital indexing amendment, however, he remained silent. What I considered to be Senator Bradley's unreliability nevertheless did not detract from the carefully cultivated public image he created for himself.

Senator Warren Rudman (R–New Hampshire) deserves attention,

for he too typified the disparity between image and reality in the Senate. A former state attorney general and Korean War veteran, he possessed a keen intelligence and strong political opinions. His book *Combat: Twelve Years in the U.S. Senate* reveals that he was never the same after the passage of the Gramm-Rudman-Hollings budget act. In this budget, Rudman advocated placing budget restraints on Congress. The legislation set targets that could not be overruled without a majority vote. In fact, I voted for the first Gramm-Rudman-Hollings Act but changed my opinion after analyzing its implications because I saw that it was a political fraud perpetrated to create an impression that Congress was bringing about a balanced budget. In time, one of the original sponsors, Fritz Hollings, likewise changed his position because of the continuous modifications, alterations, and maneuverings surrounding the bill. In my view, Rudman orchestrated these actions for political purposes, especially to benefit the Reagan and Bush administrations. Indeed, Republican efforts to balance the budget were a valuable part of the political process, but the advancement of a specific political agenda utilizing the budget became a running joke among many members, Republican and Democrat alike. Rudman, however, defended his actions, and though he claims in his book that the legislation was historically significant, I dispute that notion.[8]

Rudman carried himself as a statesman above the fray, removed from the small details of constituent service, able to carry forward the responsibilities of the republic. He was also a very partisan individual, though he tried to portray himself as nonpartisan. My experience with Rudman and his work on the Senate Select Committee on Ethics, specifically with regard to the issue surrounding Charles Keating and the savings-and-loan scandal, was extremely disappointing. He took up the ranking cochairmanship of this committee, which was to consider senators on a nonpartisan basis. In this case, however, he approached me—twice—to lobby on behalf of his issues and was decidedly partisan in dealing with the various senators under investigation in the hearings (see chapter 8 for a full discussion of both the hearings and Rudman's behavior while serving on the Ethics Committee).

Another fascinating and intelligent figure was Senator Alan Simpson (R–Wyoming). He seemed down to earth and far from an elitist. Simpson had served in various statewide offices in Wyoming, and when he arrived in the Senate, he immediately distinguished himself with a great sense of humor, self-deprecating personality, and big smile. At nearly seven feet tall, he impressed everyone who saw him. We served on the Veterans and Judiciary Committees together, and over time I grew to know him quite well. Simpson was quick—quicker than most; he used humor to reach legislative compromise. On many issues, we found ourselves in opposition, and I know from experience that he was a formidable legislative opponent. On veterans' affairs issues, we tangled more than once, and in most cases I prevailed because I was an advocate for the veterans. Although he was well liked on both sides of the aisle, he lost his bid for reelection as deputy majority leader. Still, people like Senator Simpson, though in the political opposition, made the Senate a better place.

At the end of the day, several members retired to their offices, many of which had well-stocked bars. I knew the senators who maintained these libation outposts and on occasion would join them. Sometimes I would go to my own hideaway to have a beer or glass of wine. While I waited to vote, I would make phone calls, converse with my staff, and look forward to getting home for the evening. The Senate becomes much more congenial in the evening hours as idle time leads to a more relaxed posture and socializing. The cloakroom was the main gathering place as we waited to vote. After my first term, I developed a kind of internal radar that enabled me to anticipate whether or not there would be a vote. For some reason, I knew I could leave, though the cloakroom assemblage never stopped chiding me for my actions. One night I walked in around 10:30 P.M. and said to the staff, "I'm leaving because there won't be any more votes." One of the clerks asked how I knew this, and I responded, "Trust me, I know," although I was actually basing my assumption on that newly developed internal radar. I left, and about halfway home I was buzzed to return for a vote. Frustrated, I decided to pass and not return for the vote. The next day the cloakroom staff had a big laugh at my expense. Still, I usually returned to vote even on less-important legislation because it was my duty to vote on as many bills as possible.

Thus, on a night when the Senate was in session, I would arrive home between 10:00 P.M. and 1:00 A.M. My home life was limited, and I found myself going to bed and waking up just to restart the process. If the

Senate let out early, and I was not traveling to Arizona, I made time for family. At least two weekends per month found me in Arizona. I would leave late Thursday or early Friday and proceed to a full schedule of speeches, constituent meetings, and briefings. I would return to Washington either late Monday afternoon or early Tuesday morning. The three-hour time difference wore on me, but this was part of the job. I found that I could not sleep in my office, like some Arizona House members, from Tuesday through Thursday and fly to Arizona on Friday. A day or week in my life in the Senate was never the same, though the framework for conducting business was tradition bound. The people, places, and activities are forever etched in my memory, and I am grateful for them.

During my three terms in the Senate, I successfully sponsored or cosponsored more than four hundred bills, resolutions, continuing resolutions, and joint resolutions. The legislative process works through an admixture of centuries-old parliamentary rules, traditions, committee duties, and personal and political relationships. Efficient and outstanding staff work was essential to the passage of any successful legislation, and, as noted elsewhere, I was fortunate to have assembled what was arguably the best staff on Capitol Hill. Out of hundreds of legislative battles I fought, one of the most rewarding was the introduction and passage of the Anti-Drug, Assault Weapons Limitation Act of 1989.[9] This significant lawmaking effort illustrated how staff and senator worked together to bring about a positive result.

During the 1980s and especially toward the end of the decade, the number of cases where assault weapons were misused was increasing. On the morning of January 17, 1989, a troubled drifter named Patrick "Eddie" Purdy opened fire with an AK-47 and two handguns on a schoolyard full of children at Cleveland Elementary School in Stockton, California. In a few minutes, Purdy had fired 105 rounds, not including the self-inflicted single bullet that ended his life. Thirty-three students and one teacher had been shot, and five children lay dead—four girls and one boy who ranged in age from six to nine years old.[10] As a direct result of this tragedy, I decided to investigate and review automatic weapons.

Prior to this event, I was a strong Second Amendment supporter who claimed that people, not weapons, were responsible for crimes. I had the support of the National Rifle Association (NRA). My reputation as a "tough-on-crime" conservative Democrat, committed to the war on drugs and a supporter of police groups and prosecutors, combined with my voting record in that regard made me an NRA "100 percenter"—one of a small group of legislators who always voted against legislation opposed by that organization. In one instance where I defended gun owners' rights, I was named the NRA "Person of the Month" for July 1988. In my reelection campaign that year, the NRA mailed out a member letter endorsing me as one of its "best friends in the Senate."[11] In effect, despite my Democratic Party affiliation, the gun lobby supported me.

But the firearm used in the Stockton massacre, an inexpensive Chinese version of the Soviet AK-47, drew considerable media attention, and I wanted to know more about this weapon and others like it. The AK-47 was familiar to Vietnam veterans and millions of Americans who saw them on the evening news. In 1987 and 1988, the Chinese dumped into the U.S. market nearly eighty thousand AK-47s that sold for between $300 and $400 apiece; they were a bargain. Even First Lady Barbara Bush was surprised to learn that they were legal in the United States. She thought they had been banned, but following the Stockton massacre, she said, "They should be."[12]

In this changing context, on February 8, 1989, three weeks after Purdy's tragic actions, Senator Howard Metzenbaum (D–Ohio) introduced S 386, the Assault Weapon Control Act of 1989. Responding to a reporter's question, Metzenbaum announced his motivation for the federal legislation, which put him at stark variance with my usual position. "No," he said, "we're not looking at how to control criminals . . . we're talking about banning AK-47s and semi-automatic guns."[13] Indeed, the great national debate over federal legislation dealing with automatic weapons had reached a milestone.

In addition to Metzenhaum's legislative proposal, the newly installed George H. W. Bush administration took action that further placed gun control at the forefront of public debate. On March 14, 1989, after several cities and states had passed laws banning various automatic weapons, including the California Assembly, which voted to outlaw forty models of automatic weapons, William Bennett, on his first day as "drug czar," issued a one-page statement that was in essence a reversal of Republican policy: "Treasury Secretary Nicholas Brady and I have discussed assault weapons and he has decided to suspend, effective immediately, the importation of several types of assault-type weapons."[14] Bennett mentioned specifically the AK-47, Uzi carbine, Austrian Steyr Aug, and two semiautomatic weapons manufactured by Fabrique Nationale of Belgium. Three weeks later, on April 5, 1989, President Bush, who had taken a few tepid steps toward the gun-control supporters, expanded on Bennett's pronouncement and on the suspension on the importation of assault weapons.

Even my recently retired Senate colleague Barry Goldwater distanced himself from the NRA and its unyielding adherence to the Second Amendment. He had served as an NRA spokesman, appeared in commercials for the group, and in many ways personified the right to bear arms. He too now claimed that he and the NRA were in disagreement. "I've never used an automatic weapon or semiautomatic weapon for hunting," Goldwater announced. "There's no need to. They have no place in anybody's arsenal. If any SOB can't hit a deer with one shot, then he ought to quit shooting."[15] Goldwater's vivid language mirrored my views.

The NRA left nothing unchallenged. Wayne La Pierre, the NRA executive director, and his chief lobbyist, James Jay Baker, cranked up their formidable public-relations apparatus, began making calls to congressional offices, including mine, and sent a clear message to all federal elected officials: that the Bush administration, through its reaction to what the NRA called "short-term political hysteria," had reneged on its campaign pledge to protect the rights of gun owners.[16]

At this time, I received intense lobbying from both camps. Several police organizations, supportive of gun control in general and of the Metzenbaum bill in particular, approached me with the intent of seeking my endorsement of the legislation. At first, I rebuffed these overtures because I thought Senator Metzenbaum's bill was too draconian and could not generate enough support to become law. I agreed with the motivation and intent of the Ohio senator's legislative proposal, but after seriously reviewing the bill I had deep reservations about its broad provisions. For example, I was strongly opposed to giving complete discretion to the Treasury secretary to add weapons to the list already prohibited and to implementing a registration system in the sale of lawfully owned assault weapons. Moreover, as a member of the Senate

Judiciary Subcommittee on the Constitution, where gun-control legislation originated, I felt compelled to get actively involved during these early stages of the debate rather than merely stating my opposition to pending gun-control legislation.

I consulted with my majority counsel to the Judiciary Committee, Dennis Burke, who rightfully informed me that I should not turn my back on the police organizations, who, like the NRA, had supported me. So I met with the NRA's Wayne La Pierre and James Baker to explain the emerging situation.[17] I suggested that there was room for compromise, but they were resolute: no compromises, especially with legislation introduced by a liberal like Metzenbaum. Their inflexible stance, coupled with the pressing need to take action, prompted me to offer a middle way through this political quagmire.

On April 11, 1989, I stood at my desk on the floor of the Senate and introduced S 747. "Mr. President," I began, "I rise today to introduce the Anti-Drug Assault Weapons Limitation Act of 1989. This bill addresses the increasing problems associated with the use of assault weapons by illegal drug dealers, while protecting the rights of citizens who legally own assault weapons and continue to abide by the law. The story is familiar to us all," I continued, "Every night on television, the front page, or the radio, we learn of someone killed with an assault weapon. More often than not the carnage is committed by an individual engaged in the illegal drug trade. Whether it is the Medellin Cartel or the Crips or the Bloods youth gangs, drug dealers have found a weapon of choice that gives them an advantage over all adversaries, including the police." I knew also that I would be attacked from both sides. "Mr. President," I added, "I am certain that arguments will be made that this legislation does not go far enough. I am equally certain that others will contend that the bill goes too far. I view those two arguments as supporting the position that this legislation takes—that there must be a reasonable middle position which will protect the public from physical harm while ensuring protection of constitutional rights under the law."[18]

In effect, my bill banned future sales of several types of semiautomatic assault weapons, both domestic and imported, but allowed present owners to keep their firearms. S 747 called for the prohibition of nine specific firearms, none of which were typically used for hunting: (1) the Norinco, Mitchell, and Poly Technologies Avtomat Kalashnikovs; (2)

Action Arms Israeli Military Technologies Uzi and Galil; (3) Beretta AR-70 (SC-70); (4) Fabrique Nationale FN/FAL, FN/LAR, and FNC; (5) Steyr Aug; (6) INTRATEC, TEC-9; (7) Street Sweeper; (8) Colt AR-15 and CAR-15; and (9) MAC 10 and MAC 11.

Dennis Burke helped navigate this legislation through seemingly innumerable obstacles. He has recalled that NRA officers and members "went through the roof" because to them I had defected to the other side. They immediately began a direct mail campaign against me. They also instituted a mass phone campaign to derail the proposed legislation. One humorous memo from Senator John McCain (R) suggested the degree of commitment the NRA had in trying to scuttle my bill. "I thought there was something wrong," the McCain memo stated, "when I kept finding staffers cowering under their desks and wandering around the halls screaming, 'I JUST CAN'T TAKE IT ANYMORE!!' I think it was the ten thousand phone calls a day from the NRA that finally did everybody in. I mean, how many times can you hear the argument that it's every red-blooded American's right to carry an AK-47 to defend himself against those really vicious attack deer wearing Kevlar vests?"[19]

In fact, the NRA mailed more than fifty thousand letters in Arizona decrying my apostasy. Recall petitions were being passed around Arizona gun shops, and the state's two leading newspapers, the *Arizona Republic* and the *Arizona Daily Star*, published the predictable letters to the editor calling for my ouster from the Senate.[20] Dennis Burke reported that the lies and exaggerations stretched credulity and were almost humorous, but we had to acknowledge that the NRA was sending this material to the voters of Arizona. Although this mailing no doubt caused me political damage, I knew that the NRA was hurting itself with this extreme reaction. My bill would prevent even harsher legislation.[21]

Meanwhile, President Bush, despite assurances to the NRA that his administration would not ban domestically produced weapons, took definitive steps in that direction. For example, in June 1989 Treasury Secretary Nicholas Brady issued a letter listing seventeen domestic assault rifles that would be banned if they were made overseas. Shortly thereafter, ATF director Stephen Higgins issued the results of a three-month study of assault weapons. Not only would the temporary ban on twenty-nine imported semiautomatic weapons become permanent, but he also expanded the list to forty-three models. I supported the Bush administration's actions, but, like me, President Bush took criticism from both sides. The NRA wanted to expel him from the organization. Among those who wanted a more comprehensive assault weapons ban, Representative Pete Stark (D–California) feared that although Bush deserved praise for having the "guts to stand up to the NRA," the prohibition extended only to foreign guns. Congressman Stark correctly predicted that the ban of these foreign models would be a bonus to domestic companies because they could raise their prices while demand skyrocketed.[22]

On July 20, 1989, the fourteen-member Judiciary Committee voted on my bill in its first legislative test. The committee was divided equally among Democrats and Republicans, and, after some informed and lively debate, it seemed destined to a tie vote, thus killing it before it reached the Senate floor. I tried to break the logjam and at the last minute inserted a "sunset" provision that had the overall effect of having the ban expire in three years. Moreover, my last-minute provision included the caveat that the Justice Department would determine the impact the law had on gun-related crime. So if the ban had a positive impact, I would reintroduce it. If not, the law would lapse.

As the voting progressed, it appeared to break along partisan lines; Democrats for my bill, Republicans against it. When the count reached seven to six in favor, there was some confusion because Arlen Specter (R–Pennsylvania), who was also sitting in on the impeachment hearings of a federal judge, was not available to cast a vote. This situation was not unusual because many committee hearings take place simultaneously, and when Congress is in session, lawmakers walk in and out of committee rooms at all times. Although the Republicans on the committee remained calm, my counsel, Dennis Burke, informed me that in this particular instance Specter could be a wild card.[23]

A former district attorney from Pennsylvania's largest city, Philadelphia, Specter was a moderate. Despite his prickly demeanor and well-known abrasive personality, I maintained good relations with him. I knew also that Pennsylvania had the second-highest rate of NRA membership per capita in the country, and he tended to vote with this important constituency. However, as Dennis and I waited and watched while the deadline for voting approached, we noticed that the Republicans on the committee grew increasingly nervous. Several aides were sent to find Specter. Judiciary Committee chairman Joseph Biden (D–Delaware) counted off the final seconds. As he prepared to announce that the bill passed seven to six, Specter entered the room and stunned all of us with his actions. He looked at Biden and said, "I'm sorry, Mr. Chairman, I can't vote on this bill. My staff has not briefed me adequately." Then he turned and walked out.[24] With that weird ending to the hearings, the Judiciary Committee moved my bill to the Senate floor.

It turned out that Senator Specter also had the support of several national police organizations, such as the Fraternal Order of Police, the National Association of Police Organizations, and the International Association of Chiefs of Police, and they backed this bill. In effect, Specter, whose background was not dissimilar to mine, had arrived at the same conclusions I had and supported this form of antigun legislation. I did not have to use a political chit for Specter's tacit support; his motivations, at least, mirrored mine.

During the summer of 1989, I detected a shift in the political winds; I received letters of support, and I sensed that the NRA had overplayed its hand. In September 1989, Sarah Brady, wife of President Reagan's press secretary James Brady, who was tragically wounded in John Hinckley's attempt to assassinate the president, was then chair of the lobby group Handguns Control Incorporated and wrote a strong letter of support for S 747: "Your courageous Senator Dennis DeConcini has defied the National Rifle Association and authored legislation to halt . . . the sale of deadly assault weapons. The NRA is putting enormous pressure on Senator DeConcini to back down by orchestrating a mail campaign against him from Arizona residents." She continued, "Senator DeConcini needs to hear that citizens like you support what he is doing."[25]

The lobbying continued through the end of the year and into 1990. In late May, as the bill headed for a Senate vote, Dennis Burke reported to me that twenty-five members were sure to vote for the bill, but that twenty-nine were immovably opposed. He also determined that fifteen senators were leaning toward voting for my bill, twelve tilting against, and nineteen undecided. It was a dynamic, fluid situation.

On May 22, 1990, I decided to send a long letter by courier to President Bush asking him for support of S 747. Besides seeking his endorsement, I provided facts and figures that detailed how the drug war was being fought in the streets of America. "Mr. President," I wrote, "today's drug dealer is armed to kill. Unfortunately they do not hesitate to use these weapons against our police officers. . . . The weapon of choice for the drug dealer is the assault weapon." Beneath my signature at the end of the letter were eight additional signatures from the most prominent law enforcement leaders in the nation. The letter ended, "Help us make our streets safe again, and end the carnage of our police officers." Daryl Gates, then chief of the Los Angeles Police Department and an advisor to President Bush on crime issues, was included in the list of eight.[26]

I also had Bob Maynes, my press secretary, issue a press release—much shorter than the lengthy plea to the president—that stated the same message. At that moment, there were three separate assault weapons bills in the Senate: Senator Strom Thurmond's alternative bill not mentioning the weapons by name, Senator Metzenbaum's extreme measure, and mine. Because my bill had been passed out of committee the prior year, it was included in the Comprehensive Crime Control Act, S 1970, spearheaded by Senator Joseph Biden, which was being debated at the same time as the three competing antigun bills.

A few days before the vote, Biden, the Senate Judiciary Committee chairman, who supported my plan, approached me and said he had some bad news. He claimed I did not have the votes and that inclusion of my bill would bring down the entire package. He said the Democratic leadership had decided that they were going to remove my assault weapons ban from the bill, and I would have to offer it as an amendment from the floor. I told Senator Biden that this approach was unacceptable.

The legislation was important to me. It had earned a place in the larger gun- and crime-control package because of the committee vote. I asked to meet with Senate majority leader George Mitchell, Biden, and Metzenbaum. We met late at night in Mitchell's office, and I convinced them that my bill should remain where it was because my good friend Orrin Hatch, one of the NRA's staunchest supporters and leader of the opposition to my bill, would have to garner the votes to remove my bill from the larger package. At this meeting, we also agreed that Senator Metzenbaum's bill would be voted on first.

On May 22, 1990, Senator Metzenbaum passionately spoke in behalf of his bill, though he focused his comments on the NRA, calling it a "paper tiger." His bill was soundly defeated, eighty-two to seventeen.

The Senate then turned its attention to Senator Hatch's motion to strike what he called the "DeConcini ban" from the crime bill, S 1970. I recall how Dennis Burke and I prepared for defeat, believing we had done everything we could to win. After two hours and fifteen minutes of debate, the Senate chose to recess at around 10:45 that night and would reconvene at 9:30 A.M. the next day, May 23.

That morning Dennis Burke and other staff members placed a number of postersize photographs of the assault weapons to be banned on easels at the back of the Senate chamber. The impact was that these guns looked nothing like hunting rifles. Senators began gathering in groups, gazing at the photos and shaking their heads. I stood before the photo of the Streetsweeper and asked a senator standing beside me, "Would you go hunting with this?" I talked with Senator Tom Daschle (D–South Dakota), who was leaning toward voting against my bill. I assured him that his local police groups would campaign with him and that a vote in support of the ban would have no political ill effects.

An extraordinary thing took place on the Senate floor that day. Floor debate was aimed more for the record rather than to convince colleagues to vote one way or the other. Most votes were decided long before being cast. In this case, however, senators were making their decisions on the Senate floor. As they lingered around the photos and talked, Dennis Burke, thinking quickly, contacted several law enforcement leaders and had them call the senators, saying they would provide political cover from any NRA attack.

Lloyd Bentsen, against gun control for a long time, was watching C-SPAN as the cameras focused on the posters at the back of the chamber. He came down to the Senate and told me, "I think you're right." Then, as the voting started, Sam Nunn (D-Georgia), Robert Packwood (R–Oregon), John Warner (R–Virginia), Al Gore (D–Tennessee), and James Sasser—all who were undecided or leaning toward voting against the bill—voted for it. Senator Alfonse D'Amato (R–New York), coming to the floor, noted that the vote was close and from the corner of his eye saw me approach. "Al," I said, "could you give me a possible vote on this issue?" He turned to me and said, "Sure, D!" He often referred to me as "Big D," and his vote, which doubtlessly caused him problems among his conservative base, proved crucial. I grew cautiously optimistic, and Dennis could scarcely believe what was happening. When the clerk reported the final tally, fifty-one to forty-nine, to uphold the assault weapons ban, we could barely contain ourselves. Though the pro-gun delegation forced another vote a few hours later, the bill stood.

I returned to my office, and the staff was cheering. This was not only a legislative victory, but also a deeply personal one. I had withstood the NRA-backed wrath of gun owners, pickets, an unsuccessful but vicious recall effort, harassing phone calls, and death threats. After thanking my staff, I asked that they return to their desks, get on the phones, and thank those senators who supported me in this effort. I was very concerned for Senator David Boren (D–Oklahoma) and Senator Jay Rockefeller (D–West Virginia) because they were especially vulnerable to political fallout from their pro-gun constituents. As Dennis Burke described the reactions of the various administrative aides he contacted in this fight, "One moment their boss was going to the floor to vote no on the bill, then a half-hour later he comes back voting yes. A lot of staffs were just blown away. I was on the phone the next two weeks helping them deal with the fallout from the vote."[27]

I went to work as well. I drafted a letter of gratitude and sent it to every senator who voted with me. James Baker, the director of NRA federal affairs, mailed an interpretation of the vote to his membership, singling out what the NRA considered to be significant defectors: "Several historically pro-gun Senators deserted firearm owners when the votes were cast. These included Senators Lloyd Bentsen (D–Texas), Jim Sasser (D–Tennessee), John Warner, Quentin Burdick (D–North Dakota), Kent Conrad (D–North Dakota), Robert Byrd (D–West Virginia), Jay Rockefeller (D–West Virginia), Sam Nunn (D–Georgia), and Tom Daschle (D–South Dakota)."[28] The inherent threat to these senators notwithstanding, I was pleased to issue a press release about the passage of S 1970 on July 11, 1990, indicating, "Today the Senate gave final passage to the Omnibus Crime Bill of 1990, which includes Sen. Dennis DeConcini's (D–Arizona) legislation that prohibits the importation of five foreign assault weapons and the manufacturing of four assault weapons most often used in violent drug-related crimes and [that] also increases the penalties for usage of these assault weapons."[29]

Though unique in many respects, the teamwork required in gaining successful passage of the anti–assault weapon legislation typified my office's approach to the legislative process. From beginning to end, the bill required negotiation and compromise, though we never wavered from our central position. As I said when I introduced s 747 on April 11, 1989, "Some legislators have proposed intrusive procedures and extensive background checks for all owners of semiautomatic weapons. Others have suggested confiscating these weapons from law abiding owners. Admittedly, the assault weapons problem is serious; our response, however, must be sober."[30] Indeed, I suggest our approach *was* sober, thoughtful, and deliberate and reflected the essence of my service in the U.S. Senate.

7 Judicial Politics

My work on the Senate Judiciary Committee began with a combined sense of anticipation, excitement, and responsibility. As a junior member during my first term, I observed that the committee was composed of the most formidable personalities in the Senate. In 1977, the Democrats were the majority in the Senate and controlled the committee, which was chaired by James Eastland, a conservative Democrat.[1] The minority Republicans were mostly conservatives, though Senator Charles "Mac" Mathias of Maryland, a moderate, was the ranking member. Next in line was Strom Thurmond of South Carolina, who later forced Mathias aside and became chairman of the committee when the Republicans gained control of the Senate in 1980.[2] But in 1977, the Democrats on the committee, save Chairman Eastland, were liberals. Ted Kennedy of Massachusetts, Joseph Biden of Delaware, Howard Metzenbaum of Ohio, James Abourezk of South Dakota, John Culver of Iowa, Patrick Leahy of Vermont, and Senator Birch Bayh of Indiana formed the liberal core of the Democratic majority.

Then there was me. I considered myself a middle-of-the-road Democrat, with an independent streak. Indeed, in time, I would part ways with some of my Democratic colleagues on some critical and historic votes.[3] Robert Dole (R–Kansas) was also on the committee and wielded significant influence. He was emerging as a Republican leader at this time, and he viewed my background in law enforcement and my moderate politics as potential for common ground on the committee. Senator Dole and I quickly developed a good working relationship on the Judiciary Committee, and this rapport extended to our personal relationship as well. I could tell that his ability to work well with members of both parties bode well for him in the future.

Chairman Eastland conducted business in inimitable fashion, smoking cigars and wheeling and dealing with both parties in order to control the appointment of judges through the Senate selection process. President Jimmy Carter, however, intervened in this time-honored process in unprecedented fashion; he established a series of judicial commissions to select federally appointed judges. This decision naturally caused grumbling because it had always been the prerogative of sitting senators of the same party as the president to nominate for federal positions those judges who were serving in the courts of their respective states. I worked with Chairman Eastland in resisting this ill-conceived program. After much negotiation, a compromise was struck. The commissions would limit their recommendations to appellate court judges only, and, in turn, the names of these nominees would be submitted to the senator who was from the state where the federal position was open and of the same party as the president, and that senator would select one or two names from the list. Concerning district court judges, senators retained control of the process. The senior senator in the same party as the president, in coordination with the other senator from that state, would maintain control over the nomination process.

Another fascinating part of the judicial nomination process centered on the "Blue Slip." When a nomination was sent up from the White House, presumably approved by the senior senator from the president's party and the state in question, it was sent to the other senator from that state regardless of his or her party affiliation. Whether signed or not by the junior senator, the Blue Slip was honored. In my case, for example, if I wanted to nominate a judge, I first had to submit the name to the White House, gain approval, and then send a formal nomination to the Senate, which of course, was then referred to the Judiciary Committee. The Judiciary Committee would then send a Blue Slip to Senator Goldwater, the senior senator from Arizona, and then wait for him to send the slip back to the Judiciary Committee. If the Blue Slip was not sent, I, as the senator who suggested the name, would have the right to press for consideration without the Blue Slip. I witnessed Chairman Eastland reluctantly move forward on nominees with no Blue Slip when there was pressure from members to hold hearings, even though the lack of a Blue Slip represented a lack of consensus about a nominee for a federal judicial position within a state.

Chairman Eastland had a number of judicial nominations sent up by the Carter administration. In addition, U.S. marshals, U.S. attorneys, members of the Justice Department, and commissions and boards that required Senate confirmation were under the jurisdiction of the Judiciary Committee. Eastland, well into his seventies at the time, could not chair all these sessions, so he delegated noncontroversial hearings to junior members. As the most junior Democrat, I conducted hundreds of hearings during my first two years in the Senate. From bankruptcy to the nomination of appellate court judges, I chaired hearings and learned much about the judicial nomination process. It provided me with an opportunity to meet judges, read their files, ask questions, and gain insight into the tremendous amount of influence a member could have in shaping federal judicial policy. I asked the majority of the questions at the hearings under my direction, though on occasion a senator or two who knew the nominee might ask questions on certain issues. I always asked each nominee a certain set of questions. The most important question to me then and now was: "Will you maintain a temperament of respect to those that appear before you, whether they are defendants, plaintiffs, witnesses, or lawyers, after you are sworn into office?" Naturally, every nominee swore he or she would.

Another issue of extreme importance to me centered on whether or not judges believed in a disciplinary process—within or outside the judiciary—that could in fact remove federal judges.[4] This issue, of course, was contentious, and many judges asserted that Congress should stay out of the process, whereas others argued that there should be a process to hear complaints against judges. Ultimately, I introduced legislation that took ten years to pass, but resulted in establishing the federal judiciary to recommend setting up a disciplinary commission composed of judges who, in the various appellate courts, would listen to complaints, review them, and make recommendations to the full court for a decision. Then there would be a formal vote.[5]

Although a significant number of judges opposed disciplinary oversight, I always worked closely with the judiciary for pay increases, benefit increases, buildings, and amenities to carry out duties. Moreover, I served on the Appropriations Committee and eventually became chairman of the committee that appropriated money for federal buildings, so I was keenly aware of the judiciary's needs.

In addition to the aforementioned questions I asked of nominees, I probed into prior Supreme Court decisions and the candidate's views on them. I was concerned whether or not the nominee believed in what is known as stare decisis, which concerns following previous decisions by a higher court. Of course, nominees always said they did believe in it, but often, as the record in numerous cases indicates, they did not.[6] My early experience in conducting these hearings was invaluable, and I appreciated Chairman Eastland's indulgence in allowing a freshman senator to learn by doing.

During Carter's administration, I was the Arizona senator from the same party as the president, so my first nominee for a position as a U.S. district judge was for a vacancy in Tucson, and, as often happened during my three terms in the Senate, I found myself at cross-purposes with my political party. That district had two federal judges, and one, a thirty-year veteran of the federal bench, decided to retire. This situation gave me the opportunity to select and recommend the person whom President Carter would nominate. Richard "Dick" Bilby, then a prominent lawyer and active Republican in Tucson, Arizona, was my first nominee. Dick and I had been casual friends for years; we had law offices in the same building. Dick's father, also a prominent Republican, was one of the powerhouse lawyers in Tucson. My father, of course, knew the elder Bilby, and they had a respectful working relationship. Dick was a friendly, affable, and smart lawyer. We would discuss politics as we rode up the elevator in the old Valley Bank building in downtown Tucson, joke at our differences, and see each other at political functions. He became Pima County Republican Party chairman in 1970—a difficult job in the predominantly Democratic county. Nevertheless, with an optimistic outlook, he would promote the candidacies of Republican office seekers.

As noted in chapter 3, when, in 1972, I decided to run for county attorney, Dick demonstrated pragmatic goodwill toward me and made sure that I faced no Republican opposition in the general election. Though I would probably have defeated any Republican that year, it would have cost a great deal of money to run a general-election campaign. Also, I got off to a great start in January 1973, which could not have happened if there had been a contested general election. Dick never told me that he discouraged anyone from running, but it was obvious that he had cleared the path for me.[7] Later in our careers, Dick and I would discuss that election, and in his own inimitable way he would smile wryly and say that the best man had won and that "I'm proud of you, Dennis." So it was with great pleasure that I nominated Dick Bilby for a U.S. district judgeship. I believed strongly in his legal abilities and cared not that he was a Republican. I felt indebted to him for his subtle assistance early in my electoral career, but that was not the prime reason for my support. He was indeed the deserving candidate to be a district judge, and he wanted the position.

Dick had had a previous judicial nomination experience, during the presidency of Richard Nixon. He had been nominated to serve on the Ninth Circuit Court of Appeals, but the Democrats had controlled the Senate, and my friend and former colleague, Senator Kennedy, derailed the nomination. Another dear friend of mine, John P. Frank, also opposed Dick for the Ninth Circuit. In short, he was rejected and not confirmed. Dick later told me that this rejection was a blessing in disguise because he really did not want to be on the appellate court, but preferred to serve on the district court as a trial judge. When I sent his name to the Democratic White House, there were questions about his Republican credentials, but I expressed my complete confidence to Attorney General Griffin Bell and to President Carter that Richard Bilby was my nominee and that I truly wanted to forward his name to the Senate. They put his name forward, and he became a U.S. district judge with the unanimous consent and approval of the committee and the Senate.

I conducted the hearing as if it were for the most noncontroversial nominee. And it was with great joy and pride that I witnessed Dick sworn into office. In political life, when you help someone, you often do not expect to receive expressions of gratitude except at the moment of service or the appointment. For years afterward, Dick would write to me, first on an annual basis, and then about every three or four years, to thank me for nominating him and recommending him to President Carter. He repeatedly said it was the best job he ever had, and he was extremely grateful for my support. It always gave me great satisfaction to receive these messages because Dick always maintained his even temperament and humility in his approach to other people.

Justice Bilby served with great distinction and not only modernized the district court in Arizona, but also spread his innovations throughout the court system at the district level. I am convinced that this was one of the best appointments I made, though Tom Chandler—a close family friend, a prominent lawyer in Arizona, and a strong supporter—objected to Dick's nomination. A staunch Democrat and partisan activist, he called and took me to task for putting in a Republican as U.S. district judge for Tucson. Tom knew Dick, liked him, and had even practiced with him on many cases, but he thought it was almost an act of political treason to place a Republican in that seat when the country had a Democratic Senate and president. I explained to Tom my reasoning, emphasizing Dick's professional background and everything else, and I recall Tom's rejoinder, "I understand that, I know him better than you do, Dennis, and I have great respect for him. He would be a great judge, but you should have put in a Democrat." Tom and I revisited this conversation over the years, and he concurs that Dick Bilby was one of the outstanding jurists of our time.

Over time, as I served on the Judiciary Committee, I had the opportunity to recommend others to various positions. One was Earl Carroll, who practiced law in Phoenix. An outstanding lawyer and a Democrat, he had clerked for my father when he was on the Arizona Supreme Court. I also nominated Val Cordova, the first Hispanic to be nominated to a district court. At the time, I was consulting with local attorneys, my father, and others regarding these nominations. I evaluated the feedback and with the help of staff developed a list of nominees. One of the nominees to the Ninth Circuit Court of Appeals was Thomas Tang, who, like Carroll, had clerked for my father when he was on the Supreme Court. Tang had been elected to the Maricopa County Superior Court and had served there with distinction. He was not reelected, however, because he had placed a juvenile defendant on probation when the press and the public preferred more severe sanctions. The newspapers, especially the *Arizona Republic*, criticized Judge Tang unmercifully. I nominated him because I knew him to be an excellent lawyer and therefore felt he would be an outstanding judge. The challenge, of course, was getting him through both the Carter nominating process and the attorney general–appointed commission for assigning appellate court judges. One of the commissioners was my good friend John P. Frank, whom I had offered a nomination to the Ninth Circuit, which he declined.[8]

In effect, John P. Frank had emerged as the gatekeeper for appellate court judges in Arizona. Although he himself declined the position, he had a list of candidates he wanted nominated. Among them was Mary M. Schroeder, then a state judge in Arizona and one of Frank's former partners.[9] I knew Schroeder through Frank's glowing recommendations and had no particular problem with her nomination, but I wanted Thomas Tang appointed as well. Fortunately, during the Carter administration, Arizona was entitled to three appellate court nominees, so I struck a deal with Frank. I would move the nomination of Mary Schroeder to the Ninth Circuit if his commission would recommend Thomas Tang for the Ninth Circuit, and that is how these two judges were appointed. Judge Tang was one of those people whom I admired because of my father's relationship with him. Moreover, he had been William "Bill" Mahoney's partner for years. Tang and Mahoney had a good firm with an outstanding legal and public-service record. Mahoney, who had served as Maricopa County attorney in the early 1950s, was also a longtime friend of the DeConcini family. He later was appointed ambassador to Ghana by President John F. Kennedy and was considered one of the outstanding public servants on the Democratic side in Arizona.[10]

After Judge Tang was sworn in, he and his wife could not thank me enough because it gave him the kind of credibility he deserved after his defeat in the election to the Maricopa County Superior Court. Judge Schroeder, after her swearing into office, took to the Ninth Circuit like a duck to water. She was smart, good with people, and strong on women's issues, and she did her homework with consummate skill.[11] Ultimately, she became chief judge of the Ninth Circuit Court of Appeals.

John P. Frank, who played such a significant role in this process, was someone steeped in the law, profoundly keen of mind, and liberal in his approach to political issues. He mentored numerous legal and political careers, including those of Mary Schroeder and the present governor of Arizona, Janet Napolitano. He took great pride not only in helping people who worked with him on legal issues, but also in helping them move up the political ladder. We were longtime friends, and though I was not as liberal as he on most political issues, he nevertheless supported and counseled me. He usually had an agenda, was smooth and clever, and rarely burned a bridge. He passed away in 2002 and is missed by many, including this admirer.

I also nominated William "Bill" Canby, brother-in-law to Vice President Walter Mondale. Jack Brown, a Democratic party activist and Canby's law partner, urged me to consider Canby, who had an outstanding record and fine reputation in Phoenix and throughout Arizona. In fact, I knew Canby because he was a counsel of record on the U.S. Supreme Court case that enabled lawyers to advertise their services publicly. Prior to Canby's Supreme Court case argument, bar associations, courts, and various state agencies prohibited lawyers from advertising. Canby persuaded the Supreme Court to find that this prohibition was an infringement on the constitutional right of free expression and speech. I was, in fact, opposed to lawyers' advertising, but, that difference in opinion notwithstanding, I supported Bill Canby for appointment as a Ninth Circuit judge.

Vice President Mondale, to his credit, took a subtle approach in his support for Canby, though I am sure he could have made short work in securing confirmation. He showed wisdom and patience concerning Canby's nomination. He came to see me in my office, which had a strong impact on me. He told me that he would really appreciate it if I would suggest Bill Canby's name to the White House for the Ninth Circuit. As I thought about it, I realized that I had no choice because, had I objected to Canby's nomination, Vice President Mondale would have been able to use his influence to overcome my objection if he wanted. But I was impressed with his understated yet firm support for his brother-in-law, and my nomination of Canby cemented a long-lasting good relationship with Mondale both during his term of office and after he retired from the vice presidency. I suggested to the attorney general's commission that Bill Canby's name be placed on the list for review. John P. Frank approved immediately, and the Senate unanimously confirmed Canby's nomination to the Ninth Circuit.

Although most nominations went smoothly, others were derailed or undermined, as happened with John Collins, a dear friend and a superior court judge in Pima County. He had married into an Italian American family, the Cracchiolos. One of the sons, Andrea, was my classmate and friend, and eventually became a prominent orthopedic surgeon.

The two other Cracchiolo sons, Daniel and Joseph, had clerked for my father. Through my early legal career, I saw John Collins work long, hard hours. He also had a soft spot for pro-bono cases; he was a compassionate person in this regard. He ran for Pima County Superior Court judge, was elected, and served there for twelve years. He was an excellent judge, had his heart in the right place, possessed a good sense of the law, and never grew too full of himself.

The presiding judge ultimately placed him as the juvenile court judge. John took this job seriously and with unusual focus. He changed the legal perspective on juvenile justice in Pima County. He instituted counseling and special programs for problem students; he involved family members in the process and recruited skilled counselors. In short, he established new, innovative, and award-winning approaches to juvenile justice. I worked closely with him while I served as Pima County attorney. He supported my programs to divert young first-time offenders from the criminal justice system into alternative programs. He supported the Victim Witness Program, and I supported his efforts in the juvenile court.[12]

Shortly after my election to the Senate, another vacancy occurred for the position of district judge in Tucson. I nominated John Collins, but unfortunately for John, some of his fellow judges, who by then had secured positions on the federal bench, opposed his nomination. I spoke with President Carter and Attorney General Griffin Bell, but could not pry loose John's nomination. His innovative practices and sometimes controversial rulings, opposed by more conservative and traditional judges, played a major role in bottling up the nomination.[13] He continued to aid those unfortunates in society, and I regret that he was not named to the district court.

A second profound disappointment was my effort to nominate and confirm Nicholas Udall to the district court in Phoenix. A Democrat and part of the politically prominent Udall family, Nick had been mayor of Phoenix, Maricopa County attorney, and Maricopa County Superior Court judge. He was an outstanding judge and lawyer, but at the time I nominated him, he was approaching sixty-five years of age. He volunteered to waive retirement benefits, and I put forward his name to President Carter. I wanted to put him on the bench because he was an outstanding person and a dear friend of the DeConcinis. Unfortunately, the Carter White House viewed the Udall nomination with trepidation and refused to move forward with the process. I approached Attorney General Bell and urged the White House to approve this nomination. The White House gave it some consideration, but after two years I was forced to withdraw his name and place Val Cordova's name in Udall's place. Cordova, as pointed out, was the first Hispanic to serve in this position. It seems that the politics of age and experience worked against Nick Udall, who would have contributed greatly to the federal judicial system in Phoenix.

Meanwhile, as I was pushing the nomination of John Collins, his brother-in-law, Dan Cracchiolo, came to see me in Washington. I had known Dan all my life, admired him, witnessed his outstanding legal abilities, and appreciated his friendship to my family and me. He wanted to be nominated to the district judge position as well. I told him that I would nominate him at the appropriate time, but that I could not do it while I was fighting for John Collins. Dan evidently saw sooner than I that John was not going to be confirmed, but my sense of loyalty, which has on occasion caused me problems, made me see John's nomination through to the end. Nevertheless, I intended to nominate Dan later, if the opportunity presented itself. Dan would have made an excellent judge, but unfortunately for him, for me, but perhaps not for everybody, Ronald Reagan defeated Jimmy Carter in 1980, and the political landscape concerning the appointment of judges changed. To this day I regret not nominating Dan at an earlier time.

After Reagan's election, it was Senator Goldwater's turn to send nominations to the White House, which would then send them (or not) to the Senate for confirmation. A couple of Barry's good friends who were also his close legal advisors helped select some outstanding Republican judges, including William Browning, a Tucson lawyer I had known for years. In fact, I had considered nominating Browning, but I had already successfully recommended one Tucson Republican, and I did not think I could pull off a second. As the Reagan administration insinuated itself into the federal judicial culture, I worked in concert with Senator Goldwater and his nominations. Barry wanted them, I supported them, and I got to know them. The senators with whom I worked and the one who succeeded me in the office—Barry Goldwater, John McCain, and Jon Kyl (R)—have supported some outstanding lawyers and judges to serve on the federal bench. Ideologically, the nominees have been balanced and have avoided the extremes of the political spectrum.

The names Sandra Day O'Connor and William Rehnquist hold great significance to me as an Arizonan and member of the Senate Judiciary Committee. When I was elected to the Senate, Justice Rehnquist, who had been nominated and confirmed during the presidency of Richard Nixon, was a sitting Supreme Court judge. With the retirement of Chief Justice Warren Burger, President Reagan sought to promote Rehnquist to chief justice. In short order, Reagan nominated Antonin Scalia to the Supreme Court to take the newly opened seat. I recall vividly that the Democrats on the Judiciary Committee and several others in the Senate commenced a diligent effort to keep Rehnquist from becoming chief justice of the Supreme Court. From my perspective, Rehnquist was an outstanding lawyer—intellectually gifted and well respected in Arizona. Both he and Sandra Day O'Connor, classmates at Stanford Law School, graduated at the top of their class and, of course, were active in the Republican Party. Rehnquist had served in the Justice Department under Attorney General Richard Kleindienst, and it was there that he came to the attention of the Nixon administration.[14]

The Democratic Party in Arizona strongly opposed Rehnquist's nomination for chief justice. My good friend Charlie Pine, state chairman of the Democratic Party, opposed him, testified against him, and encouraged others from the liberal wing of the party to fight the appointment. As it turned out, I supported Rehnquist, fought hard against my own party in Arizona, and differed sharply with many of my fellow Democratic senators.

From my perspective, two main issues galvanized the opposition to Rehnquist's promotion to chief justice. The first and most obvious to me at the time concerned his extremely conservative legal philosophy. The second centered on his past political activities in Arizona. His conservative interpretation of the Constitution was well documented in his written opinions when he served as an associate justice. Liberal opponents intended to expose him as out of touch with "American values." Some senators may have pushed their liberal agenda too far in efforts to block the appointment, yet I understood that they wanted members of the Supreme Court to be open to other views than a "strict interpretation" of the Constitution. In the areas of reproductive rights and individual freedoms, many found Rehnquist's views a potential threat.

Another objection involved the fact that when Rehnquist was a young lawyer in Phoenix, he had volunteered to do legal challenges at polling places on election day for the Republican Party. Significantly, he was not there soliciting votes for candidates, but instead was there to question whether voters met the legal standards to cast ballots under Arizona law. Rehnquist was obviously concerned with issues of citizenship, age, and domicile. Those questioned were often Hispanic, registered to vote in south Phoenix precincts, and could not speak English. These challenges slowed the voting process and discouraged others in line from voting. Whether because of the time spent waiting or the questions about one's minority status, the result was that there appeared to be the presence of racial and cultural prejudice.

The Democrats, however, practiced the same kind of election-day politics. We challenged voters and monitored Republican challenges. I recall monitoring the more affluent Republican areas and attempting, as a representative of the Democrats, to challenge votes. This exercise in futility—questioning upper-middle-class Anglo voters—only slowed down the voting process. The voters I attempted to challenge spoke English and were not intimidated. Nevertheless, this was the Democratic response to Republican voting challenges in minority precincts. More than once I went to polls in northern Phoenix and in northern and eastern Tucson—affluent Anglo areas in Arizona's two largest urban areas. I also went to polls with high Democratic registration in order to discourage Republican challenges.[15] So Rehnquist's activities in this regard were not unique and certainly were within the law. Nevertheless, he remained a Democratic target in this process.

When President Reagan nominated him for chief justice, Rehnquist came to see me at my office. I told him I would support him, though I allowed that I would have a difficult time with my support because of his past voter challenges in Arizona. He downplayed these past activities and wisely moved on to other issues. I read a number of his opinions and, indeed, I found them very conservative. I agreed with some, and others I did not, though I found his legal writing clear and precise.

When Senator Kennedy opened the hearings, it was clear from the outset that he would lead the opposition. Though I disagreed with him on this issue, I always maintained great respect for his legislative and debating ability. In Rehnquist's case, Kennedy made constitutional arguments put forward under the Equal Protection Clause of the Fourteenth Amendment.[16] In addition, reproductive rights, prisoners' rights, individual freedoms, and issues of probable cause entered the discussion. Others joined Senator Kennedy, such as James Abourezk from South Dakota and Howard Metzenbaum from Ohio, who believed that Rehnquist would lead the Supreme Court even farther to the right than had his predecessors. I defended Rehnquist by asking him questions that revealed his knowledge of the law and by demonstrating to my fellow committee members that both Republicans and Democrats in Arizona participated in polling-day challenges. Rehnquist stood his ground, and on very sensitive issues he refused to answer questions specifically. He had already created a record as an associate justice on the Supreme Court, though. He had left a trail of opinions, and on those he was questioned. As the hearings developed, several Republican members of the committee joined me; Senators Hatch, Dole, Specter, and Thurmond, in particular, defended Rehnquist and his record. The hearings grew testy as the Republicans accused the Democrats of opposing Rehnquist's nomination only because they abhorred President Reagan and his policies. The Democrats cried foul, and the hearings moved forward with increasing acrimony.

Once again I found myself in an awkward political position within the Arizona Democratic Party. I was supporting a conservative Republican whom Democratic Party insiders viewed as anathema to their ideals. I recall spending an inordinate amount of time mending fences at various district meetings and explaining why I supported my fellow Arizonan for promotion to chief justice of the United States. As part of my explanation, I would tell Democrats that I too had worked as a polling-place challenger and that Rehnquist had the right to challenge, even though his actions had been directed at discouraging voting in a minority-dominated precinct. Though I disagreed with this tactic of targeting a minority-dominated precinct, I defended his right to challenge in a lawful fashion.

Finally, after several weeks, the Judiciary Committee voted to report Rehnquist's nomination to the full Senate. As I said, I parted ways with my fellow Democrats and joined the Republicans to report a favorable recommendation. On the floor, I spoke again in favor of Justice Rehnquist. My view about Rehnquist's nomination and that of others remained consistent throughout my service on the Judiciary Committee. I presumed that the president of the United States would nominate a qualified candidate, meaning that the candidate had a reputation for integrity, distinguished legal experience, and sound temperament. On that basis, I supported the nominee. I never decided based on a single issue or according to litmus tests. For example, I voted for nominees who were pro-life, pro-choice, pro-gun, pro–gun control, pro–prayer in schools, or anti–prayer in schools. If they met my standards, I would vote for them even though I disagreed with them on one or more issues.

Sometimes the system was flawed. Louisiana's senator Russell Long, chairman of the powerful Finance Committee, submitted nominations just as other Democratic senators could during the Carter administration. Several district judge nominations came forth for New Orleans, and in one case Senator Long nominated Richard Collins, a practicing lawyer from that city. Senator Bennett Johnston—one of my neighbors in McLean, Virginia, and the junior Democrat senator from Louisiana—acquiesced, and, as it turned out, I was designated to chair some of the hearings on Collins.[17]

Collins had a thriving criminal law practice that focused on middle- and low-income plaintiffs and defendants. He was African American and very active in New Orleans Democratic Party politics. As the hearings commenced, Senator Eastland provided me with access to the FBI report on Collins. The FBI would customarily conduct an investigation on a nominee and send the report to the committee chairman. The chairman would then share this report with the ranking member, and, on occasion, the ranking member might share it with other senators.

Much to my consternation, Collins had a record of violating judicial ethics, bribing jurors, and paying voters to turn out at the polls. He had successfully avoided conviction of these charges, however, though the nature of these alleged transgressions raised serious questions about him. As a result of these red flags, I recessed the hearings, discussed the Collins nomination with Chairman Eastland, and met with the FBI investigators.[18]

After analyzing and synthesizing the information, I commenced preparation of a written argument that I would make before the Judiciary Committee: we should turn down this particular nominee. Chairman Eastland, however, expressed displeasure at my recommendation and said that he would take up the issue in executive session, which meant that the press and most staffers would be excluded from the meeting. In this session, I laid out the case against Collins and noted that even though the American Bar Association had recommended him for appointment, it had done so with the lowest recommendation. We voted unanimously to turn him down. We went back to the full committee, which similarly voted down the nomination. I was pleased that the nominee would not be reported to the floor for consideration.

When Senator Long learned of the outcome, however, he was very upset. He contacted Chairman Eastland, who told him, "We need to talk to Senator DeConcini about this." We met, and as I reviewed the Collins file with the two powerful southern senators, they listened carefully and quietly. Then Senator Long explained to me why he had nominated Collins. The explanation disturbed me, but I learned a great deal about the process and how it worked. According to my senior colleague, there were several Anglo nominees with sterling records and impeccable reputations. The Carter White House, however, told Senator Long that he must submit the names of some African Americans. Senator Long searched to find African Americans he could recommend for district judge in New Orleans, and in the course of this effort he came across two individuals, one of whom was Richard Collins. The other potential nominee, as it turned out, had more ethical and legal questions about him than Collins. So Collins was the lesser of two evils. I expressed my astonishment, raised some mild objections about selecting the best-qualified person regardless of race, color, or creed, but Long had an agenda. He wanted to address the Judiciary Committee and make a case for Collins. Long's good friend Senator Eastland agreed to this unusual request, and the case was made before the full committee. Collins was not the best or most competent lawyer available in New Orleans by any means, he acknowledged, but there was great need to move forward on this particular nomination. Much to my distress, the committee reversed itself—there were enough Republicans to support Eastland and the majority of the Democrats—and one week later in another full hearing of the committee Collins was brought up and reported out favorably. I voted against him. He was affirmed in a unanimous consent vote. After ten years on the bench, he was ultimately indicted for corruption and was forced to resign.

Meanwhile, another Supreme Court nomination followed on the heels of the Rehnquist hearings: Court of Appeals justice Antonin Scalia, an outstanding scholar and extreme conservative, had been nominated to the Supreme Court. His U.S. Court of Appeals nomination, put forward during Gerald Ford's presidency, was approved unanimously, and he brought to his Supreme Court hearings a sterling reputation and affable personality. Scalia's nomination benefited from following so closely behind Rehnquist's. The critical scrutiny that surrounded Rehnquist's legal opinions, law review articles, and past political activities never clouded Scalia's hearings. When I met Scalia for the first time, he impressed me immensely with his great sense of humor, keen intellect, and common touch that enabled him to communicate with all types of people. I could not help but like him, though his opinions almost always took on a narrow interpretation of the Constitution. His good nature and solid credentials enabled him to sail through the process with unanimous consent in the Judiciary Committee and on the floor of the Senate.

The next Supreme Court nomination of great significance concerned another Arizonan, Sandra Day O'Connor. As noted earlier, I had known her from my years in state government. She had been elected to the Arizona State Senate, had served for eight years, and had become majority leader when Republicans took control of the upper House. Her husband, John, graduated from Stanford Law School at the same time, and they both practiced law in Phoenix.[19] Her career blossomed in the state Senate, and, later, Governor Bruce Babbitt, a Democrat, nominated her to the Arizona State Court of Appeals. The Republican-controlled state Senate easily confirmed her, and Babbitt received much good press with this inspired appointment. When Justice Byron White announced his retirement from the Supreme Court during President Reagan's first term, speculation ran rampant about whom the president would nominate to replace the aging White.

I issued a statement to the Arizona press and wrote a letter to President Reagan, urging him to nominate Sandra Day O'Connor for the Supreme Court. The Arizona press gave many column inches to my suggestion, though it attracted little attention elsewhere. I visited

Senator Goldwater in his office and informed him that I had written a letter to the president and had told him that I thought O'Connor would be an excellent choice. Goldwater chortled a very happy response, laced with a few light profanities, and said he would call President Reagan to second my idea. With Goldwater's intervention at this time, I learned that the White House had decided to interview Sandra O'Connor. This interview, I understand, left an outstanding impression on the Reagan White House. Still, when I spoke with her after this meeting, she allowed that she did not think she would be nominated because there would then be two justices from Arizona on the Supreme Court.

President Reagan put forward her name for consideration and approval. I supported this nomination and helped her by taking her to see every Democrat and most of the Republicans on the Judiciary Committee. Ironically, those most skeptical about O'Connor were Republicans. Some of the most conservative committee members—Thurmond, Denton, and Charles "Chuck" Grassley (R–Iowa)—had questions about whether or not she was pro-life on the abortion issue.[20] As I took her to visit Senate Democrats, I could see they were impressed and that she was not a prisoner of any particular conservative ideology. My wife and I sponsored a large tea at our home for all of the Senate wives, at which O'Connor left a great impression and demonstrated that she was engaging, competent, and able to assume the position on the Supreme Court.

I organized witnesses on her behalf, including the Arizona House minority leader Art Hamilton, an African American and a Democrat who was pro-life, and Republican State Senator Diane McCarthy. Longtime Republican political leader Tony West, who had served in both the Arizona House and Senate and as state treasurer, testified. As the hearings progressed, the question remained whether O'Connor was conservative enough. Again, I spoke with Senators Thurmond, Grassley, and Denton and assured them she would not disappoint the conservatives on the Judiciary Committee or in the Senate as a whole. Thurmond, not entirely convinced, took me aside yet another time and asked, "Is she for real, is she really conservative, is she really pro-life, and will she do the right thing from our perspective?" "Yes," I replied. The president hosted another dinner, and Nancy Thurmond, Senator Thurmond's wife, hosted a tea so that O'Connor could be further scrutinized. In the end, the Democrats wholeheartedly supported her confirmation, and the Republicans came around as well. I found a great deal of satisfaction in helping shepherd her nomination and confirmation to the Supreme Court.

Justice O'Connor has been an exemplary leader for women, for lawyers, and for those who aspire to the bench. Her opinions reflect an ability to synthesize differing points of view into a coherent whole. And though I am pro-life, Justice O'Connor's masterful and subtle work in the case challenging *Roe v. Wade* demonstrated that she could put together a coalition of five members who did not reverse the decision, but who found a middle ground that did not prove divisive and problematic for the country.

The Rehnquist and O'Connor nominations were historically significant and made me proud to hail from Arizona. The most difficult and most publicized nominations were those of Robert Bork and Clarence Thomas. Bork had been serving on the U.S. Court of Appeals, and President Reagan, early in his first term, nominated him to the Supreme Court. Bork was an outstanding scholar who had served as a professor of law and later as solicitor general during the Nixon administration. A patriotic veteran, he had gained a reputation as a spokesman for the conservative right.

Upon his nomination, I asked myself if I had looked at his record during his previous hearings—in his confirmation for the U.S. Court of Appeals—before our committee. I had not.[21] I commenced analyzing his record, and as I progressed through his files, Senator Kennedy and other Democrats raised questions about his writings on abortion, individual rights, privacy, and a host of other issues. The Judiciary Committee and the FBI investigated his record. Opponents were soon running advertisements in newspapers, some of which were outrageous and bordering on libel. One charge, I recall, claimed that Judge Bork favored "sterilizing workers." In fact, he had ruled that companies had the right to use certain chemicals and found that the workers in the particular case in question had not been harmed. It was not a decision that in any way suggested that he favored the sterilization of workers. I grew concerned about the fairness of the process. I had not decided how I would vote on Judge Bork—though, as I indicated earlier, I was inclined to support the president by assuming that he had nominated a qualified candidate. Other charges surfaced. On several occasions, for example, the Supreme Court had unanimously reversed Judge Bork's decisions in lower courts, so it was claimed that he was out of touch with mainstream legal thinking on any number of issues and certainly not in line with the Constitution. There was, indeed, a concerted effort to undermine his nomination.

These unfair efforts notwithstanding, Judge Bork helped himself little during the process. He didn't seem to understand that he needed to portray himself with a degree of humility. He also appeared to resent that the Judiciary Committee had to ask questions about his qualifications and his professional career. Some nominees debated or argued with the committee, but Bork crossed the line of propriety and waged rancorous debates concerning the Constitution even if the subject had nothing to do with his prior writings or opinions. I recall vividly long arcane discussions about the Fourteenth Amendment, the Due Process Clause, and the Fifth Amendment and its application. At this juncture, Bork's nomination became problematic. His attitude was unyielding; he made no apologies: he was right, the Judiciary Committee was wrong. This intellectual elitism alienated the Democrats especially, and the Republicans grew defensive. At the same time, the cheap shots in the press continued and, not surprisingly, found their way into the hearings. Nevertheless, I withheld judgment and went back to the files. I revisited his decisions and speeches. As I contemplated them, the Republicans on the committee were defending Bork's every action, and the Democrats were challenging every statement, every issue. Bork's nomination became a partisan deadlock, and politics rather than legal issues ruled the day.

An underlying theme to these hearings was *Roe v. Wade,* and observers correctly assumed that Bork would lead the Supreme Court in overturning this decision. It was clear, however, that no matter what, President Reagan would nominate pro-life judges. Rehnquist, Scalia, and O'Connor reflected this pro-life agenda, though Justice O'Connor helped steer the Court into a moderate position on this issue. Bork's strict, unalterable interpretation of the Constitution influenced me to vote against his confirmation, however. I would not vote against him because he was Republican—I had just voted yes for three previous Republican judges—or because I disagreed with some of his opinions. The Republicans and Democrats dug in their heels. At the final order, when the vote came before the Judiciary Committee, I cast a vote against Judge Bork. I had read closely his decisions on the Fourteenth Amendment, and he had not defended himself well when asked whether or not the Due Process Clause applied to minorities other than African Americans and women. In addition, my vote reflected a concern for his arrogance and his placing himself so far to the right of the political spectrum; I could not, in good conscience, vote for adding this person to the Supreme Court. My vote was not an easy one, and I struggled with it because I thought Judge Bork had been demeaned through the process. He was not confirmed because some Republicans—including John Warner of Virginia, who told me he agreed with my reasoning in the matter—joined Democrats in turning down this nomination.

President Reagan then nominated district judge David Ginsberg, who ran into problems early in the process. Among other things, Ginsberg admitted to smoking marijuana in college, so that, given the recent history of the nomination process, he could not be confirmed. The president then nominated Anthony Kennedy, who served on the Ninth Circuit Court of Appeals. I had met Judge Kennedy a number of times at judicial conferences and came away impressed with his temperament and with the manner in which he handled cases. I read all his cases, and when the hearings began, I could tell that the Democrats were relieved that Judge Kennedy was moderate and that his interpretation of the Constitution was more flexible than Bork's. Quiet, well-spoken, and respectful, he generated positive feelings among the Judiciary Committee and no controversies. The Senate in the end confirmed him in a unanimous vote.

After Judge Kennedy's confirmation, I heard the Republicans complain that they had never subjected a Democratic president to this kind of political pressure for a Supreme Court appointment. This claim, of course, was nonsense because President Carter and later President Clinton experienced extreme difficulties with Republicans on the Judiciary Committee, who exacted their pound of flesh for the Bork fiasco.

During the George H. W. Bush administration, David Souter was easily approved to the Supreme Court. His sponsor from New Hampshire, Warren Rudman, introduced him to each member of the Judiciary Committee. Rudman's use of his position on the Senate Ethics Committee caused him no qualms when he told me that it was one of the most important accomplishments in his career to see his friend David Souter confirmed by the Senate. I voted for Souter, but I would have voted against him in an instant if he were not qualified. (My vote almost became an issue because Ethics Committee cochairman Rudman put pressure on me to vote for Souter while I was before that committee facing charges of ethics violations on the Charles Keating situation. See chapter 8 for a fuller discussion of this incident.)

In 1991, President Bush nominated Judge Clarence Thomas to replace Justice Thurgood Marshall. Thomas, with help from President Bush, stumbled out of the gate. The president, vacationing in Kennebunkport, Maine, presented Thomas at a press conference. Bush announced that with Thurgood Marshall's retirement, he sought the best judge in the system and found Thomas. This statement raised many eyebrows because Thomas was not the most outstanding, brilliant, or knowledgeable judge sitting at that time. In effect, Bush threw down the gauntlet to liberals and Democrats.

I did not know Judge Thomas at the time of his nomination; I may have met him when he was nominated to serve as head of the Equal Employment Opportunity Commission (EEOC) or when he was nominated and had a hearing on his appellate court appointment. The White House and a very well-respected senator, John Danforth (R–Missouri), elected to the Senate in 1976, took great interest in this nomination. Danforth had served as Missouri attorney general, and Thomas had been his deputy attorney general. Thomas had also worked in Danforth's Senate office. He quickly gained an appointment as assistant secretary of education and then moved on to the chairmanship of the EEOC. Coincidently, he and Anita Hill, both graduates of Yale Law School, met at the EEOC.

He was controversial at the commission. He initiated change in an awkward and aggressive manner, and at the same time the Republican administration expressed little interest in advancing minority employment in a significant way. The EEOC served as a conscience, or inquisitor, into whether or not employers were being fair in their selection of individuals for hiring and promotion. Though not perfect, the EEOC was better than having to file action in court when a complaint arose.[22]

Judge Thomas had risen from the lower middle class and had worked hard all his life. He believed in "pulling your boots up by yourself." I have often wondered why he has not been more sympathetic in his decisions about minorities, given the difficult economic situation in his early years.[23] His rationale, I suspect, is that the system provides a fair shot if you work hard. As the nomination process progressed, Senator Danforth took Judge Thomas to each member of the Judiciary Committee. I met with him twice. I told Senator Danforth that I would be very careful in scrutinizing Thomas, reviewing his record, and remaining open-minded.

As I thought about this nomination, I concluded that it was unfair to compare any African American nominee with Thurgood Marshall. Justice Marshall was a pioneer; he had been on the cutting edge of public opinion and racial issues. He had been the legal director of the National Association for the Advancement of Colored People (NAACP), an appellate court judge, and a solicitor general of the United States. He was lead counsel on numerous cases before the Supreme Court prior to his selection as justice to the Court. And *Brown v. the Board of Education,* his testament to racial and cultural justice in America, altered significantly the direction of U.S. history. So any nominee was bound to comc up short in the comparison.

The perception that the Bush administration was trying to create an "African American seat" on the Supreme Court marred the process. Administration opponents, racial rights activists, and liberals viewed this nomination as token gesture—an attempt to turn back the clock on racial progress with a right-wing nominee such as Thomas. From my perspective, no matter what race or what gender, the person nominated must be qualified for the position. As Thomas came before the Judiciary Committee and the microscope grew more focused on various charges, Senator Danforth, his sponsor and mentor, responded promptly and effectively. Judge Thomas answered the growing number of charges and complaints as well.

The political left charged that Thomas was another strict interpreter of the Constitution and that he was just like Judge Bork, only not as intelligent. He stated that he found merit in "natural law," which to liberal intellectuals served as a way to overturn or subvert the Constitution. Unlike Judge Bork, who debated and argued endlessly, Thomas refused to answer many questions. He even evaded some of my questions. Democrats grew mistrustful and skeptical. Interestingly, Thurgood Marshall, during his own hearings, had refused to answer some questions concerning racial issues. He had been advised to avoid direct answers to these questions because his answers might jeopardize his confirmation, and in that case Senator Ted Kennedy had defended him against charges that he was evading answers to direct questions.

Committee members asked Thomas questions about *Roe v. Wade*, and, like Rehnquist and O'Connor before him, he issued an evasive answer. I was disappointed and wished he had been more specific, but his evasiveness on this issue would not cause me to vote against him. To his credit, Judge Thomas's deportment before the committee was exemplary compared to Judge Bork's behavior. Nonconfrontational and humble, he was well aware of the subtleties and nuances concerning testifying before committees. Thomas was there not to make enemies, but to answer questions put before him—some he answered, and others he did not.

Thomas possessed other abilities. He understood the circumstances of race and politics and was adept at working within this political framework. When Senator Kennedy raised questions that Thomas was not loyal to his race, he responded with intelligence and force. It was a masterful performance in this regard. He made reference to heroes in his family—Martin Luther King Jr. and John F. Kennedy—and added that a picture of John F. Kennedy hung prominently in the family home. Senator Kennedy smiled, realizing the nominee had trumped him on this occasion.

The hearings grew lengthy, with more than fifty witnesses for and against the nomination. The Democrats controlled the Judiciary Committee at this time, so most witnesses opposed Thomas. In September 1991, when the committee voted, all the Democrats except me voted against Thomas, which created a tie as all the Republicans voted in his favor. The committee had a standing rule that a tie vote would be referred to the floor with "no recommendation from the committee." At this time, it appeared that my vote would help push Thomas over the top on the floor of the Senate. Some disgruntled Democrats threatened an unprecedented filibuster, but it never occurred. A final vote was scheduled for October.

Then the political environment changed dramatically when a newspaper published a leak from a senator on the Judiciary Committee. I knew the senator who leaked the information, a well-respected individual I had known and served with for years, and I was very disappointed in his action. The leaked information concerned Anita Hill, who had worked for Clarence Thomas and had complained about sexual harassment when she worked for Thomas at the Labor Department and the EEOC as far back as 1981–82. Senator Biden, chairman of the Judiciary Committee at this time, conferred with ranking minority member Strom Thurmond, and Thurmond in turn informed the rest of the committee. One of my staff members told me that there had been a reference to this claim in the FBI file, but that it had been refuted. The charges were more than nearly a decade old, and Ms. Hill had not wanted to testify at the Senate hearings on Thomas's nomination; she had in fact refused to testify. When Senator Biden spoke with her, she said she would testify anonymously. Biden refused, saying he would not consider information relevant if the person did not sign his or her name to it. In effect, Ms. Hill wanted the committee to consider this accusation, but with no identified person behind it. Biden rightfully refused her offer.

Unfortunately, the media printed the accusation, and we were forced to address Ms. Hill's statements. Soon thereafter Ms. Hill reversed her attitude concerning testifying before the committee. She began holding press conferences with various groups, in particular women's groups, describing her accusations in detail and urging the Senate not to confirm Judge Thomas. The press seized on the issue, suggesting that the Senate Judiciary Committee had covered up the accusations and that some of the Democrats on the committee did not help to dispel this notion of a cover-up because they now believed the door was open to reverse the decision to send the nomination to the full Senate.

The Democratic caucus met, and Biden explained the entire case. I recall Senator Allen Dixon (D–Illinois) urging the Judiciary Committee to revisit the issue. I agreed, and the caucus directed the Judiciary Committee to hold hearings on the sexual harassment allegations. Vigorous debate ensued concerning whether this approach was fair, but the committee would hold the hearings anyway. The Republicans met and decided that Senator Specter from Pennsylvania, a former prosecutor and U.S. attorney with a brilliant legal mind, would lead the questioning.

The Judiciary Committee reconvened before a packed house. Senator

Biden gaveled the hearing to order, and Judge Thomas testified first. He denied any and all charges, expressed exasperation, and appeared dumbfounded about how something like this could happen to him. A seat on the Supreme Court, he said, was not worth going through stress like this, and he said confirm me or do not confirm me, but the process has to end.

This statement rang a strong bell with me, as it did with others. Biden then said he would not refer to the FBI report when he questioned Ms. Hill, which was her request. The Republicans objected, and Senators Specter and Hatch announced that they would refer to the FBI report. The committee recessed, and Chairman Biden worked out an arrangement whereby Ms. Hill would answer questions, even on information in the FBI report, but Judge Thomas would have the right to respond no matter how late the hearings went into the evening. Senator Danforth wisely worked to make sure the press would write not only on Ms. Hill's statements, but also about any rejoinder from Judge Thomas.

This hearing became one of the most widely viewed television events in history. Our offices were inundated with calls. Each Democrat on the committee was allowed to ask as many questions as he wanted. Ms. Hill testified to a number of instances of sexual harassment relating to her relationship with Judge Thomas. Senator Specter methodically elicited testimony and raised questions. In my view, he never insulted her or diminished her status as a lawyer and a witness. He approached this situation as I would if I were questioning a "hostile witness," but not wanting to upset the jury. In a skillful way, he placed her veracity and credibility before the committee and the public. I noted that the press was split as to the fairness of the hearings, and many reporters, with whom I chatted during breaks, wondered if Thomas could survive the process.

We heard witnesses from both sides. Some attempted to verify Ms. Hill's statements that Judge Thomas made unwanted sexual advances and used sexual descriptions in their conversations. Ms. Hill, according to these witnesses, would report these alleged transgressions to her roommates and friends. Witnesses in support of Thomas, women in particular, claimed they had never seen such actions or heard such statements. Ms. Hill's central position was that she had to keep her job because she could not find another one. This position troubled me because an intelligent African American lawyer—Republican or Democrat—is a much sought after person in Washington. A person with her background and set of skills, I reasoned, should not have great difficulty finding employment. In my opinion, for some reason she was attached to working with Clarence Thomas. She said she had no choice, but I did not believe her.[24]

As the record demonstrated, Hill eventually left the EEOC and took a job at Oral Roberts University in Tulsa, Oklahoma. While there, she asked Thomas to serve as a guest lecturer to her class, and he agreed. She picked him up at the airport, took him to the school where he spoke, drove him to his hotel, then took him back to the airport the next morning. There were also reports that she had stated recently that it was a good thing that Clarence Thomas had been nominated for the Supreme Court.

In my view, she compromised her credibility. I questioned the validity of her accusations, concluding that she had used Thomas to advance her career and now was "blowing the whistle" on him. If I had believed or wanted to believe Ms. Hill, I would have had to conclude that the people who had worked with Thomas and her in the same place and proximity—the EEOC, Oral Roberts University, the American Bar Association, and other professional places of work—would have come forward and said that Judge Thomas was lying and that Ms. Hill was telling the truth. I arrived at the conclusion that Ms. Hill had little if any evidence to substantiate her claims.

Nevertheless, I felt strongly that Ms. Hill had been sexually harassed at some time and that the harassment had left an indelible impression. This was doubtlessly true with many women—and, for that matter, men as well—who have been harassed. These degrading types of actions can be burned indelibly into one's psyche. During the hearings, I commented how my mother told my brother Dino and me that she had been harassed in Los Angeles when she was a young, single workingwoman. Her supervisor had approached her with a sexual invitation, which she declined, and the following day she was issued a pink slip. She told us numbers of times that this incident had left an everlasting impression on her. I also stated that my daughters, Denise and Christine, and my son, Patrick, now lived in a world where they could pursue their careers in an environment that would not degrade them and that sexual misconduct would not enter their professional lives. Having issued that statement, however, I could not arrive at the conclusion that the evidence was there to substantiate Ms. Hill's charges against Judge Thomas. Further, I felt that we were being asked in the Judiciary Committee to be a jury, not a judge and jury. We were to determine whether or not there was evidence or probable cause to conclude that these actions took place. The committee system is not, in fact, a jury system. It listens, asks questions, and makes judgments as to qualifications and whether or not a person possesses the temperament and capability to carry out the job in question and to use good judgment in that most important process. In the end, the Senate confirmed Clarence Thomas by a vote of fifty-two to forty-eight.

8 Keating Five

Charles Keating and his business ventures have generated many books and much commentary about the savings and loan travails that rocked the country in the late 1980s and early 1990s.[1] The "Keating Five" became the favorite media tag line to describe the five sitting U.S. Senators who became associated with Keating and his activities. Alan Cranston (D–California), John Glenn (D–Ohio), Don Riegle, John McCain, and I—four Democrats and one Republican—became ensnarled in a series of complicated and controversial political events that formed the most trying period in my Senate career. The nine months of investigations and twenty-three days of hearings before the Senate Ethics Committee were especially difficult for my family and me. During the hearings, Robert Bennett, the special counsel hired by the Senate Ethics Committee, focused his questions on my ethics as related to fund-raising, which embarrassed me and forced me into a position of defending my actions. My efforts to address Charles Keating's situation and to intervene with regulators on his behalf clearly had a profound impact on my career in the Senate in the late 1980s and early 1990s.

Tied closely to the Keating situation were my personal finances. Over my father's objections, I published my financial statements immediately upon election to the Senate and issued my income tax reports every year. I recall my father stating, "Why do you want to disclose all that information when it really isn't relevant and doesn't make any difference?" I countered that I considered achievements in public service were not directly related to personal income or financial holdings.

Of course, my father was right. In reality, financial disclosure made little difference, and, in fact, my partnership in the family real-estate business and my successes in Arizona real estate in the period from 1970 into the 1990s—my time in the Senate—proved problematic for me. Reporters looking for stories concluded that I had somehow used public office to aid in the growth of these assets. Thus, the booming real-estate market in Arizona during my tenure in office and the consequent success of the family business, coupled with the Keating problems, contributed to a very difficult period in my Senate tenure and produced some serious personal challenges.

I first met Charles Keating in the early 1980s, when he formed a national organization that opposed pornography.[2] He targeted not only child pornography, but also men's magazines such as *Hustler, Playboy,* and *Penthouse.* Keating came from a wealthy, politically connected family in Ohio that owned real estate, newspapers, and other businesses.[3] His antipornography organization invited me to speak at a conference in Phoenix, Arizona, and I accepted the request. I made the speech, which was well received, and the press gave my appearance a great deal of coverage. Bishop Thomas O'Brien attended, as did Keating's lobbyist, James Grogan.

Shortly thereafter I introduced and cosponsored legislation that sought to enable government entities to restrict locations of pornographic businesses. The U.S. Supreme Court, however, has a long history of hearing pornography cases, with the result that local standards and "obscenity" are inchoate concepts, and adult pornography, for the most part, has not been subject to judicial or legislative sanctions. Child pornography, in contrast, has produced another set of circumstances, and prosecutions against the exploitation of minors have met with greater judicial and legislative success.

A few months after my Phoenix antipornography speech, in 1982, I accepted an invitation to attend a dinner party at Keating's palatial home off Lincoln Drive in north Phoenix. It sat on seven or eight acres, included a lavish pool and stunning vistas, and provided an impressive setting for the elaborate outdoor barbeque. I learned that Keating had organized American Continental Corporation in 1978 and was a leading home builder. My wife, Earl Katz, who was my chief fund-raiser, and I arrived to see more than one hundred people mingling with drinks in hand and enjoying Keating's opulent hospitality. A hostess escorted us to the ramada, where, at a large round table, Keating and his party, which included then Arizona congressman John McCain, engaged in lively conversation. Keating rose abruptly, greeted my party warmly, and introduced us around to several people. We ate and left for another function in south Phoenix. I came away impressed with him and his associates but had no other contact with him for more than a year.

Then Mother Theresa came to Washington, D.C., and appeared at the National Right to Life reception at the Capitol Hyatt Hotel, about two blocks from the Senate Office Building. As a pro-life senator, I was invited and ventured over to meet Mother Theresa in the late afternoon. The hosts escorted me to the front of the line, and several of my pro-life Senate colleagues joined me, including my good friend Orrin Hatch. I was introduced to Mother Theresa, told her I was from Arizona, and her first remark to me was, "How is my dear friend Charles Keating?"

I fumbled for an appropriate response, something like, "Oh, he's fine; I have seen him on occasion, and I understand that he is a big supporter of your efforts." I then praised Keating for his generosity, his Christian pronouncements, his efforts to save the unborn, and his crusade to diminish the distribution of pornography. I told her I followed her efforts, admired her indefatigable energy, and hoped to visit her orphanage in Calcutta. (In fact, she invited me, and I visited the orphanage a year later.) After thirty minutes, I left the reception and continued on with the daily activities that occupied my time in the Senate.

A few months later Keating's lobbyist, Grogan, asked for an appointment to see me. By that time, Keating had invested heavily in Arizona, and in 1984 his American Continental Corporation purchased a California-based thrift, Lincoln Savings and Loan. He also became involved in shopping centers, real estate, and other enterprises. Keating quickly became one of Arizona's premiere home builders, and his company, Continental Homes, outpaced others in the state. Grogan entered my office and right away focused his discussion on home-building interest rates and the role of the National Home Builders' Association. I had strong positions that encouraged the federal government in general and the Department of Treasury in particular to allow home builders to issue bonds at low interest rates so that new home buyers would qualify.

Though some mortgage and banking interests opposed this policy, it became law. Grogan wanted to discuss some of the specifics, and when he asked if he could pursue these talks at a later time, I said, "Of course."[4]

Shortly thereafter I attended a huge reception and dinner sponsored by the Arizona Home Builders' Association at the Camelback Inn in Phoenix.[5] There I had another introduction to Continental Homes. I sat at the head table, was introduced and received a nice round of applause, and noticed many dignitaries scattered throughout the crowd. The evening progressed with the distribution of awards for various areas of home building; Continental Homes won a significant percentage of these awards. I came away impressed and noted later that this company had become the sixth-largest employer in Arizona, reflecting an enormous commitment of fiscal and human resources to the state. Many relied on this company for jobs, housing, and economic development.

After that evening, Keating invited me for lunch. Earl Katz and I went to his office on Camelback Road in Phoenix. We walked through the office, met many people, and were struck by the fact that we saw no minorities in the building. There were no people of color; all were Anglo-American. This observation did not disturb me immensely, though I thought to myself, "What is this? This is kind of a peculiar thing." If one arrived in the executive offices of a major bank, copper company, or manufacturing concern in Arizona, there was almost always a minority presence in the facility, even though it might be below the national average. In the case of Keating's executive offices, a minority presence did not exist. I pondered this situation later and realized it was probably because of Keating's views on minorities.

The Reagan administration's policies on savings and loans during the 1980s provide an appropriate starting point for placing this early meeting with Keating in context. President Reagan promised to get government off the backs of Americans; he endeavored to deregulate the private sector. On August 15, 1982, less than two years into his presidency, he invited a small gathering of supporters to witness the signing of one of his administration's major pieces of deregulation legislation. The audience—a mixture of savings and loan executives, public officials, and journalists—were informed that they were taking a major step in the deregulation of American financial institutions. The Garn–St. Germain

Act of 1982 cut loose the restrictive federal regulations on savings and loans. Indeed, for more than half a century, Americans had relied on savings and loans to finance their homes, but anachronistic regulations, a legacy of the Great Depression, prevented these institutions from competing effectively in the financial marketplace of the 1980s. The Garn–St. Germain bill, Reagan promised, addressed this pressing need. As he put it in his closing remarks that day, the bill was "the most important legislation for financial institutions in 50 years," and it meant more housing, more jobs, and growth for the economy. "All in all," he added ironically, "I think we've hit the jackpot."[6]

In effect, savings and loan associations—also called thrifts—were significantly deregulated in the early 1980s. Among other things, this deregulation allowed them, after much legislative struggle, to invest in commercial as well as residential real estate. Over the course of the 1980s, however, many of these thrifts made commercial real-estate loans involving substantial risk. As the Federal Home Loan Bank Board (FHLBB), which regulated the thrift industry, uncovered these problems in the mid-1980s, it tried to impose stricter regulations to prevent a worsening of the position of savings and loans. Some of this re-regulation required congressional action and new legislation. The federal government ran into significant problems in attempting to fix an industry that could not control itself in the changing environment of deregulation. By 1987, it had become an industry on the edge.

As President Reagan pursued his policy of deregulation, Congress, in contrast—and especially the House and Senate Banking Committees—wrestled with this volatile financial situation. I supported Reagan's policy of deregulation and competition within the banking industry. It was clear later, though, that Keating's reckless actions eventually created problems beyond the give and take of legislative compromise, and he became a symbol for the excesses of deregulation.

Much later, in 1989, when the House Banking Committee heard testimony on the collapse of Lincoln Savings and Loan, Keating suggested that the problem centered on overzealous regulators, whom he said were out to undermine his business. Others countered that the FHLBB was anything but activist in its auditing practices. FHLBB administrators claimed that they were approached by a number of influential senators to discontinue investigations of Keating and Lincoln. I was one of these senators. During the course of hearings and press coverage, it was revealed that five senators—McCain, Cranston, Glenn, Riegle, and I—had received substantial campaign contributions from Keating, totaling more than $1.4 million.

The aftermath of these revelations included investigations and press accounts accusing the five senators of acting improperly and raising questions whether Keating had been able to buy influence through his campaign contributions. At times, Keating was outrageous, and the press dubbed him "the man who bought Washington." The *Arizona Republic* later reported that "at a nationally televised congressional hearing, Representative Jim Leach (R–Iowa) called Keating 'a financiopath of obscene proportions.' "[7] And Keating, in possession of an outsized ego, helped the feeding frenzy with untoward utterances. Asked during the height of the controversy if he thought his money "influenced recipients to act in his behalf," he shot back, "I certainly hope so."[8]

The investigations into Keating and his activities included the state of California, the U.S. Department of Justice, and the Senate Ethics Committee. Whereas the California and Justice Department investigations concentrated on Keating's actions, the Senate Ethics Committee investigation, as noted earlier, concentrated on the actions of the five senators—now known as the Keating Five—implicated in intervening with federal regulators on Keating's behalf.

Keating, as he let it be known, was a great swimmer, an Olympian, and his son-in-law, eye surgeon Gary Hall, was a gold medalist. His grandson, Gary Hall Jr., has continued this tradition. Keating loved the Olympics and traveled to them wherever they were and whenever they took place. Athletic, outwardly successful, tireless, he lived a splendid material life, with boats, planes, travel, and the very best accommodations.

The purpose of one of our earliest meetings in Phoenix in the spring of 1987 was to ask me to intercede with federal regulators concerning the rules (re)imposed on savings and loans associations and the various investments these institutions could make. Keating told me that in 1984 he had purchased California-based Lincoln Savings and that in the past he had been in the banking business in Ohio. Further, he indicated that he, or at least his family, had run successful banking enterprises. However, he said that his savings and loan, like many others in the country at the time, was not doing well, and he asked for help. I listened, took notes, and assured him that I would look into the matter.

I spoke with the Savings and Loan Association in Arizona and learned that savings and loans had problems competing with banks. This group had earlier requested my support for legislation, introduced in the House of Representatives, that gave savings and loans the right to invest in real estate in percentages greater than allowed under existing regulations. The proposed changes, in theory, would have leveled the competition with banks.

Prior to the Reagan administration, savings and loans faced strict regulations—some beneficial to them, others not. For example, they were required to pay a quarter percent more than banks on savings deposits. Banks objected to this advantage, called Regulation Q. They sought to eliminate this advantage and succeeded in getting the legislation introduced and passed. I voted against it because I supported the notion that savings and loans encouraged Americans to save more money because of the slightly larger percentages in interest. This modification, combined with the inability to invest in real estate, some close observers argued, placed savings and loans at a further disadvantage. In response to the increasingly troublesome fiscal environment, savings and loans sought to gain lost ground and tried once again to modify the rules that governed the FHLBB and the Federal Home Loan Mortgage Corporation.

Edwin J. Gray, a political friend of President Reagan from his days as governor of California, had been named head of the FHLBB. Gray represented American First Savings Bank of San Diego, where he was the head of public relations. He previously had served then-governor Ronald Reagan as press secretary. When Reagan ascended to the presidency, Gray took a job with the administration as assistant to the president and director of White House policy and development. But Gray's wife, Monique, could not bear the Washington weather—humid, hot, sultry—and returned home to salubrious San Diego. Gray left the administration and returned to his post at American First.

In the thrift industry, powerful trade groups, such as the U.S. League of Savings Institutions, worked diligently to make Reagan's new policy work and at the same time to sell it to the public. In November 1982, at this organization's annual convention held in New Orleans, Ed Gray made the rounds and was pulled aside by U.S. League chairman Ed Shane. The chair of the FHLBB—the agency that regulated the nation's federally chartered savings and loans—was open because Richard Platt, the current chairman, had announced his retirement and plans to return to Utah. The U.S. League, Shane said, traditionally played a major role in selecting the FHLBB chairman. The convention attendees, almost on cue, approached Gray and announced their support for his candidacy. On May 1, 1983, Gray was sworn in as the seventeenth chairman of the FHLBB, a three-member board that consisted of the chairman and two directors. By law, one director had to be a Republican and the other a Democrat.[9]

Gray was far from qualified for the position and was controversial from the day he assumed the job.[10] He promised his wife he would stay for two years, and he thought he would make many speeches about how well the industry was doing under the new Garn–St. Germain rules.[11] From the outset, a negative perception of his personality dominated conversation on the Hill and was reinforced in various newspaper articles and other publications.[12] I had no personal dealings with Gray, but he wanted to maintain a strict interpretation of the various rules regulating savings and loans.[13] Some suggested that his background in the industry clouded or narrowed his perspective on regulating savings and loans institutions.

Then the mid-1980s real-estate slump placed pressures on both banks and savings and loan associations. New housing starts suffered as well, though in Arizona there were signs of hope in this sector of the economy. The financial industry suffered, and Keating and others continued their pressure for further deregulation. I spoke with him in Phoenix, and he came to Washington several times to see me, issuing long dissertations about the problems he faced. Other Arizona savings and loans executives echoed Keating's complaints. Keating asked four other senators—McCain, Glenn, Riegle, and Cranston, whom he had known and to whom he had donated campaign funds—to join me in talking with the FHLBB about these restrictive regulations. I said that I would, but that I would need some supporting information.

For this research, Keating employed Allen Greenspan, longtime chairman of the Federal Reserve Board, who was at the time a well-known economist working in the private sector in New York City. Greenspan produced an impressive one-hundred-page analysis of the issue. He argued forcefully and effectively that the real-estate investment restriction was unfair and that savings and loans should also be able to invest in market securities to raise capital for expansion and investment purposes. As it turned out, Congress eventually sanctioned this modification, and Lincoln Savings and Loan as well as some Arizona-based associations supported these changes. Meanwhile, unbeknownst to me, Keating stood ready to issue securities on an expanded basis, which some rules modifications would enable him to do.

After he commenced issuing these risky securities, he continued to complain about regulators executing expanded audits, something he called "harassment." In addition, the availability of capital for home building remained problematic, and many institutions had resorted to creative forms of fund-raising for construction. As noted earlier, in this financial milieu Keating had purchased Lincoln Savings and Loan in Los Angeles so that he could access much-needed capital for Continental Homes. This move, it turned out, proved to be an enormous error. Keating used insured funds, and as a guarantee he floated bonds (junk bonds) on behalf of Lincoln Savings and Loan. In turn, these funds were used to purchase real estate and to finance construction of hotels and subdivisions. Junk bonds have been part of the financial landscape for many years. They are high-yield bonds, offered at 10 to 12 percent interest, which must be paid off, including the principal payment, in ten years. The company guarantees these bonds, but often they are issued in excess of the net value of the sponsoring enterprise. This was the case for Lincoln Savings and Loan, as well as for many other similar institutions in the late 1980s: Keating was in the process of issuing bonds in excess of his companies' net values—a procedure that the five senators and others in Congress were unaware of at the time.

Later I was criticized for failing to detect what amounted to a constituent's elaborate Ponzi scheme. Keating was indeed one of my constituents and in fact was the leading home builder in Arizona. This fact prompted me to respond to his requests to intervene with federal regulators, armed with Greenspan's analysis and other recommendations. I had no qualms asking federal regulators why the Lincoln audit had lasted more than two years, when normally such an audit lasted twelve months. That fact notwithstanding, Keating had taken all possible steps to avoid answering some specific questions.

Keating had donated millions of dollars to political candidates across the country. Though he favored Republicans, many Democrats, like me, received political contributions. As federal auditors crawled around Lincoln in 1987, Keating informed me that he was not content to take the harassment lying down. He had spread much money around, and he wanted access to the institution where laws were made. Almost every Arizona member of the House and Senate had received some form of political donation from him. He gave money to Representatives Jon Kyl, Morris Udall (D), Ed Pastor, and Eldon Rudd (R). For my 1982 and 1988 campaigns, he had raised $85,000. And for Senator McCain, as it turned out, Keating and his associates raised approximately $112,000 in funds.[14] As I approached my reelection campaign in 1988, I was aware that it would take $3 to $4 million dollars to make a successful campaign in Arizona. At that time, federal rules limited maximum contributions to a candidate to $1,000 per person, with $25,000 total contributions given by any individual to various federal campaigns. Thus, it was no easy task to raise the necessary funds to win reelection in 1988.

At a meeting at my office on March 24, 1987, Keating, in a long, rambling statement, asked if I could intervene with federal regulators to end the audit of Lincoln Savings and Loan. He hoped not to have to explain any longer a pending audit with federal regulators on his financial disclosure forms. The government was destroying Lincoln Savings and Loan, he told me, and that in turn would destroy Arizona. I considered his seemingly unending complaints about FHLBB regulators, though I knew they were exaggerated, and, with the audit entering its third year, I concluded that there had been abuse, so I agreed to help a constituent. In the meeting, Keating indicated that the other four senators would join me in this effort, and I spoke with each of them. They believed that Ed Gray and his regulators had abused their regulatory authority, so they were enthusiastic about raising the issue. After this meeting, I called the first of two meetings in my office, the first with Ed Gray and some of the other senators. Cranston, who attended this meeting, and Riegle, who did not, were important players because they were on the Senate Banking Committee, which oversaw Gray and his regulators at the FHLBB.

I asked Gray to come to my office, though later he testified before the Senate Ethics Committee that I told him to come. That was nonsense. I said, "Ed, can you come by my office?"[15] I may have suggested that I go to his office, which was something I often did with various agency heads because the offer helped in solving bureaucratic problems. In the early evening of April 2, 1987, Gray arrived at my office, and he had no assistant with him, though that was not a prerequisite for this meeting. He was polite, yet defensive in demeanor. Senators McCain, Glenn, and Cranston also attended this meeting.[16] We discussed Lincoln, presented our case, and expressed our hope that this audit would come to a conclusion. We wondered why the examiners from the Eleventh District FHLBB in San Francisco were being so arbitrary about Charles Keating. We also disagreed about the application of the direct investment rule, which limited the degree of risk thrifts took. Gray explained that he had confidence in his San Francisco staff and the people working the case. He suggested that the people who were actually conducting the audit come to Washington to talk to us. Jim Cirona, president of the Eleventh District FHLBB, was the person directly responsible for overseeing Lincoln, and Gray suggested that I call that office to set up a meeting. The assembled senators did *not* request or suggest the proposed meeting with the auditors. We also asked Gray if he thought the Lincoln audit was impartial and typical because we knew that this investigation, compared to other cases, was taking an inordinately long period of time. Chairman Gray once again referred the question to the Eleventh District FHLBB, so we thanked him for his time, and he departed.

My office called and set up a meeting with Cirona and his assistants. The meeting, which took place in my office on April 9, 1987, included all five senators. At this point in time, none of us knew that Keating had contributed to our campaigns, although we later determined that he had, but none of us concluded that contributions were forthcoming because of these meetings. Cirona; his second in command, Michael Patriarcha; and the supervisor in charge of the examination, Richard Sanchez, arrived in Washington. There they picked up William "Bill" Black from the Federal Savings and Loan Insurance Corporation (FSLIC). Black was preparing to transfer to San Francisco to serve as general counsel at the San Francisco FHLBB.[17]

They came armed with excuses. McCain, Riegle, and I were vociferous and assertive. Glenn and Cranston also expressed their views. The regulators explained their position, and the meeting ended with the regulators' promise to look at the abnormal period of time being taken to conduct the audit. Unbeknownst to us, of course, the two regulators, prompted by Ed Gray, took copious notes, so that later, as it turned out, they had some quotes from the meeting. In fact, Bill Black's notes were later published in a book about the savings and loan industry.[18] I got to the point immediately: "We wanted to meet with you because we have determined that potential actions of yours could injure a constituent." The exchanges were specific and sharp, and the regulators avoided answering questions about the nature of the audit and what prompted it. Cirona claimed Lincoln was a "ticking time bomb," and Patriarcha's comments that "I've never seen any bank or S&L that's anything like this . . . [their practices] violate the law and regulations, and common sense" were far from diplomatic. Then Patriarcha announced, "We're sending a criminal referral to the Department of Justice. Not maybe, we're sending one."[19] This comment indicated that efforts toward compromise had ended and that the Keating saga had entered a much more problematic phase.

I am unsure whether or not the meeting was taped, but in a few weeks Ed Gray wrote a letter to the five senators expressing his dismay at our intervention on behalf of Keating and Lincoln Savings and Loan. He leaked the letter to the press. McCain responded first and took issue with Gray in the most forceful terms, saying there was absolutely no truth to Gray's assertions that there was improper conduct by the senators in meeting with his subordinates. The rest of us responded in similar fashion.

The press naturally loved the story and jumped on it with alacrity. Common Cause, an ally of mine in the past, immediately filed a complaint with the Senate Ethics Committee against all five senators. The committee, feeling a tremendous amount of public pressure, initiated a preliminary investigation, so the nightmare of the Keating Five began in earnest. The press became omnipresent, and the only story that ran on the nightly news at that time focused on investigative reporters digging out how much money Charles Keating had contributed to the various senators' campaigns. It turned out that Senator McCain had failed to disclose a number of trips on an airplane owned by Keating and a few visits to the Keating vacation home in the Bahamas. As indicated earlier, I received campaign contributions approaching $85,000 over several years, and even Representative Jon Kyl had garnered $25,000 in Keating-related campaign contributions.[20]

I was confronted with the issue of hiring legal counsel, though my instinct was otherwise: if I were to appear before my peers, it would be far more difficult for them to discern the truth if it were filtered through a legal counsel. I acquiesced to the suggestion, though, and interviewed several lawyers with experience in white-collar crime and ethics violations as part of their professional résumé. One of them was Thomas Dowd, who ended up representing Senator McCain but seemed to take great pleasure in attacking me during the hearings. Dowd, who earlier represented baseball star Pete Rose in his efforts to avoid expulsion from major league baseball for gambling and later represented ousted Arizona governor Fife Symington for tax evasion and fraud, was a high-profile and prominent lawyer. I ended up hiring James Hamilton, who had broad experience in ethics trials and had written a fine book on ethics. Susie and I had dinner with Jim and his wife, Christine, at the Hay Adams Hotel. We enjoyed meeting them, and I discerned that Jim was a very serious lawyer, sympathetic to my situation, yet keenly aware of the political climate and the challenges we faced. I retained him, and his fees ran into the neighborhood of $400,000; I recall that he reduced his final bill by $20,000, a generous gesture on his part.

We commenced work on our case while the Senate Ethics Committee retained the services of Washington white-collar crime lawyer Robert Bennett. A well-known, savvy legal and political insider with strong Republican credentials and ties, Bennett had cut a colorful career path. He later represented President Bill Clinton in several of his travails during his second term, as well as embattled former congressman Don Rostenkowski (D–Illinois)—who fired him. Later, Rostenkowski told me that he terminated Bennett because he felt that Bennett had not represented him fairly in the process.[21] In addition to these high-profile cases, Bennett has represented numerous other political and business figures in and around Washington. He was charged with conducting an investigation and drafting a report on the Keating situation—not with serving as a prosecutor.

Yet Bennett persuaded the Ethics Committee to hold prosecutorial style hearings, and he launched a protracted effort to prosecute at least four of the five senators. I had prosecuted suspected criminals for many years, and the methods and style with which Bennett conducted the investigation resembled a criminal investigation being presented before a grand jury. Yet, significantly, there were no criminal allegations in the Keating situation. I recognized Bennett's prosecutorial approach from the outset. His opening statements, questions, and accusations appeared as actions of a prosecutor seeking to achieve a criminal conviction. Even Ethics Committee members recognized this approach. During the course of the hearings, I offered my observation that Bennett was serving as a prosecutor, and two U.S. attorneys with whom I spoke agreed that Bennett was attempting to seek convictions rather than reporting, investigating, and presenting evidence to the committee to help it make a determination about violation of ethics rules. The hearings lasted twenty-three days, and they included several closed depositions. They became a form of public entertainment, and some offices leaked information to the press. It was clear from information available to me (provided by personal contacts) that Senator McCain's office leaked some sensitive information.[22] Relations between our offices became almost frigid, and I found it difficult to discuss issues with McCain during this period. I defended myself aggressively and unequivocally. Cranston and Riegle also stood their ground. Glenn adopted a more cautious, contrite approach, and McCain responded to the charges in a politically pragmatic fashion.

It became clear to me, and it was later confirmed by Ethics Committee members, that Bennett was attempting to dismiss the charges against McCain, and in order to appear nonpartisan, he included Glenn in this effort. I also learned that Senator Warren Rudman, a member of the committee at this time, urged in the strongest terms that the complaints against McCain and Glenn be dismissed. The complaint against McCain differed from that against the rest of us because he had a longer relationship with Keating, including fund-raising, paid expenses, and use of airplanes and vacation property while he was in the House of Representatives. Some of these activities were reported, and some were not. McCain supporters argued that the Senate should not investigate McCain's relationship with Keating while he was in the House, though much of his alleged transgressions took place in that period. While in the upper House, McCain had received immense amounts of monies and used Keating's airplane but on a number of occasions failed to report these things.[23] I had used Keating's helicopter, but fortunately I had reported this activity. That difference notwithstanding, Bennett was determined to dismiss charges against Glenn and McCain. Thanks to the three Democrats on the committee and perhaps with the help of Senator Helms, however, the charges remained in place for all the senators under investigation. So all of us had to attend the twenty-three-day public hearing, which was indeed a trial, before the six-member Senate Ethics Committee. On the Democratic side were Chairman Howell Heflin of Alabama, a former state supreme court judge, who gaveled the hearings to order; Terry Sanford from North Carolina; and David Pryor from Arkansas. The Republicans were Warren Rudman from New Hampshire, who cochaired with Heflin; Jesse Helms from North Carolina; and Trent Lott from Mississippi.

Bennett played the key role in the hearings. Smooth and affable, he portrayed himself as fair and equitable. We made opening statements, and mine took two hours.[24] I argued aggressively that none of the senators, including me, had done anything improper. FHLBB chairman Ed Gray testified, each senator testified, and several of Keating's assistants appeared before the committee, although Keating himself did not testify. During this time, I seriously considered resigning from the Senate because I was so upset at being accused of unethical practices. I thought I had positioned myself appropriately when I fully disclosed my finances, issued press releases when I took overseas trips, and took steps to operate my Senate office as openly and honestly as possible. The hearings made me realize that no matter how sure I was that I had acted properly, nothing mattered except the perception of impropriety. Though Keating had misled me in several instances, he nevertheless employed many people in Arizona, and I represented Arizona. Further, I grew convinced that the regulators had been overzealous in pursuing him and that I had done my job as an elected official in looking into the situation and expressing my concerns. I dug in and confronted Bennett.

I accused him of unethical practices, playing the role of prosecutor in the hearings, and asked that the charges be dismissed. There was a question of fairness, and I wanted that point brought before the committee. The salient portion of my testimony, given on Monday, November 19, 1990, in Room 216 of the Hart Senate Office Building, pertained to Bennett's methods. "I wish I could tell you it was a pleasure to be here today," I began, "but, quite frankly, I'd much rather be sailing or playing golf, or doing . . . constituent service that we all do, but we're here. . . . We're here because a complaint has been filed by Common Cause . . . based on press reports, if you read their complaint. Common Cause has not been subject to any interrogation that I know, not that they are on trial or any charges have been filed against them. But I would submit that a good investigation would indeed ask a question or two of who filed the complaint. What was their motive? Did they have a Board of Directors meeting or an Executive Committee meeting, deciding let's file some complaints here. And what are we going to achieve by it? Well, I don't know the answers because nobody's asked them. But I can tell you what they are trying to achieve. They're trying to raise money. They're trying to damage the reputation of a number of Senators and they're trying to pass certain legislation. And I think it's a travesty in and of itself. And we will supply, before this hearing is all over, a stack of letters from Common Cause that have been mailed out that demonstrate that they have a motive here to raise money and do damage to Congress, in particularly, these five Senators.

"All of the evidence admitted, as I understand now that lies over there, some 44 volumes, I must make just a general comment about it. It is evidence that has been gathered over a long period of time under Mr. Bennett and his staff, with no right or no opportunity for any of the Senators to refute any of it, really, until today, though much of it was released in late September after Mr. Bennett released his report to the committee, only. Some of it has just come in recently, as recently as the 14th of this month. Now, that's not Mr. Bennett's fault, because he was trying to go ahead and expedite these hearings. But the point is that this information contains hearsay, which is not the best information that you can get. Somebody's thoughts or somebody, what they heard once upon a time, and it's there in [an] affidavit and different types of documents before you. It contains rumors, unfounded allegations about all the Senators, I dare say. . . . I cannot stand here, gentlemen, and not protest in the strongest terms that I resent [this man (Special Counsel Robert Bennett)] tying this senator to bribery, to a crook. . . . There's no evidence at all that that's what occurred. And yet he stands here as a prosecutor, not as a Special Counsel. . . . He wants a victory. He wants to nail somebody. He wants to get somebody, I'm sorry to say. He wants another trophy on the wall."[25]

I continued, ". . . there's been no cross examination on most of that information by any one of the Senators here today. Even a defendant in a criminal case, with the exception of going to the grand jury, has often an opportunity to have cross examination and sometimes before the trial. And certainly in civil cases in our justice system, you don't take depositions without the other counsel being there to cross examine and to be sure that both sides are on the record. . . . I have to mention and make reference to Mr. Bennett because of the manner in which he presented the case Thursday and Friday. It's very disturbing to me the way he presented that case. But having been a prosecutor myself, having understood what it is like to go into battle and want to get a verdict, you don't go into the court thinking, oh, well, I'm going to present a little case here. When I'm the prosecutor, I want a verdict. I want a judgment from the jury or judge in my favor.

"So, Mr. Bennett very skillfully, and he has been skillful, I must say, and he has a long reputation as a prosecutor, very skillfully brought up some very very interesting items in his presentation. He used the word 'bribery' twice. Now he qualified it. He said, now, you know, in all fairness to the Senators, we don't want any inference that they're involved in bribery here. He used the bondholders' losses incurred by Lincoln Savings selling and American Continental. Then he qualified it; oh, no, we're not going to make any inference or anything that would tie the Senators to that. The elderlys who were investors, the taxpayer who has to pick up the bill for the savings and loan crisis, the failure of Lincoln. But then he carefully says, no, we're not suggesting that they had anything to do with that. That is a technique of a very skilled prosecutor." Still, I was not finished, and I pressed forward with other arguments.

I proceeded to inform the committee that I considered constituent service of paramount importance. This aspect of my work as a senator, I asserted, was important to the people of Arizona. ". . . when I get involved," I told them, "I get involved personally. And I stay involved. I'm persistent. Some of you have observed me on committees on the Senate floor, whether it's [regarding] assault rifles or the war on drugs

I'm persistent and I stay there as long as I can possibly win my objective on legislation. And if I think there is a cause where the government has mistreated a constituent, I'm going to do all I can, within the bounds of ethical conduct, to see that government responds to this constituent. . . . I got a feeling that Mr. Bennett wanted to lay out this long history of Dennis DeConcini intervening and snapping to every time that Mr. Keating called. No more snapping to or doing things for Mr. Keating than I would not have done for Mr. [Jerry G.] Brown, the President of McDonnell Douglas, if I thought it was right. . . . there's no connection and there's no evidence in all that paper . . . between American Continental, Lincoln, or Mr. Keating, campaign funds regarding this sale, or anything that this senator did in their behalf."

I suggested campaign finance reform as a panacea because, I said, the current system "looks like hell. I don't like it. And I've supported campaign reform every year that I've been here. . . . quite frankly I don't want to have to go raise all that money and go through all this consternation. . . . public service has been my life. And it is important to me. . . . And to my reputation, Senator Rudman, I think, said it is on the line. Take your time. It's not on the line, it's fallen over. It's in a free fall. And it's unfair, it's unfair as it can be." I concluded with the statement: "This senator has done nothing wrong."[26] I still believe that to this day.

Gene Karp and Laurie Sedlmayr, my office staff who worked on banking and finance issues as they related to Keating, were not allowed to provide detailed testimony about communications among Senate offices. In addition, misleading statements and leaks were going out to the press during the process. This problem prompted the Senate majority leader to appoint a special counsel to investigate the leaks. Although the investigation was thorough and the report reached "no conclusions as to the sources of the many leaks,"[27] I am on the record as saying that I have "little doubt that McCain was responsible."[28]

McCain, as the country has learned through his autobiography *Faith of My Fathers: A Family Memoir* and his colorful run for the presidency, has a fascinating personality that can be at once charming and biting. When he was first elected to the House of Representatives in 1982, one of his first acts was to call me. He asked if my office could help him set up a constituent service office because my staff had gained a sterling reputation in this regard. We complied with his request. His staff came to our offices, and we taught his people our methods, and he applied them to his work in the House of Representatives. When McCain won the seat of retiring Senator Barry Goldwater in 1986, I felt he had difficulty assuming the role of junior senator (I was now the senior senator). At formal sittings, I sensed he resented this situation. I assumed that he was immensely competitive. Robert Timberg, in his excellent and insightful examination of five Vietnam-era military and political figures that include McCain, suggests that this competitiveness is an essential aspect of McCain's personality. He wanted to defeat the other side on any issue. This trait has been a double-edged sword for my former colleague.[29]

As a freshman senator in 1987, he was not selected to serve on the Appropriations Committee and therefore had little, if any, access to funding mechanisms, though he succeeded in gaining the introduction of highway legislation in northern Arizona—the Turquoise Trail—for which he deserves great credit. I was on the Appropriations Committee and therefore brought to Arizona millions of dollars in public benefits, and I am convinced that my position triggered his rhetoric regarding being "antipork." Over these issues and the Keating affair, a discernable distance developed between us.

In fact, at the time of the Ethics Committee hearings, the *New York Times* declared the relationship between McCain and me to be "a private war within public hearings." Some accounts claimed that McCain and I barely hid our mutual dislike, though we said "hello" when passing in the hallway. Others claimed we were tearing each other apart. I stated to one reporter from the *Times*, "I'm not a bearer of any ill will. I said hello to him this morning, shook his hand. But I haven't asked him to go to dinner or anything." McCain told the same reporter: "We say hello. But we don't stop and engage in any long conversation." Then he added, "When two people from the same state are under investigation and one has been exonerated, there's bound to be tension."[30] That exchange perhaps best illustrated the tenor of the time. Of course, we both received criticism from the committee, but neither of us was reprimanded.

It is my view that McCain received lenient treatment from the press and the Ethics Committee because of his cozy relationship with Bennett. I asked Bennett directly why he did not delve into such possible transgressions as the trips McCain took to the Bahamas with Keating. In the end, however, my questioning Bennett pertaining to McCain's transportation transgression mattered little because when public figures find themselves in political survival mode, they will do almost anything to protect themselves, even if the consequences of those actions hurt another elected official. And if the two figures are in opposing political parties, the survival tactic—and its consequences—make little difference. The upshot of my testimony was that a huge mistake occurred, but that none of the senators had violated the rules of the Senate.

The dynamics of my personal life were altered significantly during this period. My wife, equally distressed at the accusations of ethical transgressions, wanted to issue direct mailings to the people of Arizona; we spent more than $15,000 in one that featured a picture of my family and me that carried a written narrative with our side of the story. Susie became actively involved in my defense. We also ran some television ads in an effort to control political damage at home. I traveled to Arizona often and explained my position. The press, of course, had a field day, and the *Arizona Republic* ran negative articles about McCain and me. McCain held a press conference in Arizona, admitting he had made mistakes and promising to testify against Keating in the criminal case in Los Angeles. I held a series of press conferences but tempered my statements, avoiding comments about Keating's trial, though I allowed that I would testify if summoned to court.

I kept an active schedule in the aftermath of the hearings, and several weeks passed before the Ethics Committee issued its findings. It concluded that Senator Cranston had violated rules of ethics in his fundraising activities and in his capacity in the Banking and Finance Committee, and he was the only senator to be sanctioned by the Senate at the committee's recommendation. Cranston had already announced his retirement from the Senate because of prostate cancer, and he failed to attend a majority of the hearings. I was saddened immensely because through his impending retirement and absence from the hearings, he became an easy mark. The other four senators, including me, received a critical review of our aggressiveness in pursuing answers and solutions for Keating's troubled economic situation. Significantly, the report concluded that no rules or laws were broken, but our assertiveness caused an appearance of impropriety in dealing with Keating and Lincoln Savings and Loan.

In cases involving my constituents, I usually became aggressive when I discerned that some government official or agency acted improperly toward them. Whether the issue related to veterans' affairs, highways, education, the military, or any other public-policy area, I went after abuses with the utmost determination. I considered this determination a distinguishing characteristic of my service to constituents.

The entire Keating experience unnerved me. I came away disturbed that the press had somehow transformed this situation into a criminal case and that I had to defend myself. The Keating Five were "guilty" of something, and this notion spread quickly through Arizona, though we were not found guilty of anything. Thousands of letters flooded our offices. Many were critical and negative; some expressed support. Nelson Issleib of Tucson sent these words to my Senate office: "We wish to let you know that we, along with the vast majority of Arizonans, know that you are a man of high integrity and decency and we regret that you are being subjected to the current witch hunt in Washington, D.C. We are registered as Republicans but have always supported you and will continue to do so. We feel that you have always acted in the best interest of the people of Arizona."[31]

In the midst of this adversity, I heard from old family friends, whose expressions of support and friendship were invaluable. W. Michael Flood, an attorney for the Phoenix law firm Jennings, Strouss, and Salmon, sent a kind letter to Chairman Heflin. He wrote, "I have known Dennis throughout my life—from first grade and first communion through high school graduation, college, and law school. Though our career paths diverged when Dennis chose to enter public service, I have followed him carefully throughout. Although I am a Republican and not always in agreement with his views and decisions, I have never questioned or doubted Dennis's integrity, sincerity, and credibility. Despite all of the innuendos over the Charles Keating matter, I am convinced that Dennis at all times was acting properly and in the best interests of his country and state and in total fairness to an individual who had sought his assistance. I am further convinced that Dennis DeConcini cannot be bought or influenced at any price or for any favor. If Dennis has a flaw it is his willingness to hear out someone and act in reliance on one's good faith, until he has cause to question it. To me, this openness is not a flaw but a needed human quality which I would hope every one of our senators possesses. I appreciate the difficult task that your committee has and the mounting pressure to blame for the Savings and Loan industry debacle. I simply wanted you to know that to those who know him best, Senator DeConcini is honest, upright and worthy of belief and trust as a member of the U.S. Senate."[32]

When the hearings ended, I spoke to several Ethics Committee members and indicated that I felt the press had driven much of the hearings and their content. The Democrats informed me that because of my criticisms of Bennett, they would never again retain him. The Republicans, from what I learned, had a strong supporter in Senator Helms for more severe reprimands. He apparently believed that we had broken some rules, and he held hope that others besides Cranston would receive sanctions.

Helms was a man of contradictions. I knew him for years and have maintained cordial relations with him, though he was notoriously difficult. He took to me somewhat because I was a pro-life Democrat. I walked a fine line with him and disagreed with him on most issues. He wanted the United States out of the United Nations, refusing to allow us to pay our dues to that organization; he made derogatory statements about AIDS patients and victims who had contracted that virus through sexual contact; and his divisive and offhand remarks often offended me and others. I accepted Senator Helms as he was, though he wanted to punish me on the Keating issue. I later worked with him on several foreign-policy issues and found him to be congenial and friendly in that context. He was a unique piece of work and one of the most unforgettable characters in the Senate.

Others on the Ethics Committee left an indelible impression on me. Senator Lott, then the up-and-coming glamour senator on the committee, possessed some flash and wanted to befriend everyone. He also wanted to find a way out for everyone. He went along with Chairman Heflin's recommendation, and Cochairman Rudman, of course, followed suit and took great credit for the outcome. Rudman, however, went to the floor of the Senate and acrimoniously argued the case against Senator Cranston. As I witnessed this speech, it took all of my resolve not to stand up and defend Cranston from what I considered to be hypocritical and self-serving statements.

I had another reason for resenting Rudman's behavior. At the same time that the Keating hearings were taking place, the nomination of David Souter for the U.S. Supreme Court was being debated. Souter was from Rudman's state, New Hampshire, and Rudman escorted the nominee to meet with various senators. In an almost surreal visit, they came to my office and discussed the nomination process. As a member of the Judiciary Committee, I would vote on Souter's nomination, but it seemed particularly strange that I would receive this visit from a member of the committee that was at that very time conducting the hearings where I was being charged with ethics violations. Before leaving my office, Rudman emphasized to me how personally important this judiciary vote was to him and how he would never forget it if I supported Souter. During the same twenty-one-day period, Rudman came to my office again, seeking support for a courthouse in his jurisdiction. I was the chairman of the subcommittee that appropriated money for the courthouses. Again, he indicated how personally important this matter was to him. I strongly felt that Rudman was misusing his position on the Ethics Committee to lobby me for a judicial appointment and a courthouse during the ethics hearings. And he apparently was attempting to make a name for himself in these very public hearings by condemning an ill and retiring Alan Cranston.

Cranston was a veteran and a journalist, and he had helped many people. He was a decent human who cared about his fellow citizens. He worked hard, raised money for reelection, and suffered because one of the liabilities of public service is raising campaign funds. The press, depending on the issue, implied or insinuated that votes and influence were exchanged for contributions. As Rudman postured and posed, the hearings came to an end, the rulings were announced, and I experienced a sense of relief. I returned to my full-time duties in the Senate and demonstrated that I still worked constituent cases.

As I reflected on my testimony before the Ethics Committee, I recalled bringing to its attention that many constituents raised money for me and that I served them in a number of ways—intervening with regulators, acquiring legislative appropriations, and organizing meetings. That, I told the committee, was how the system worked.

I recalled working with the Environmental Protection Agency (EPA) on a number of issues and intervening on behalf of farmers and water users. In one case, Senator Goldwater and I worked together in gaining access to President Reagan's secretary of housing and urban development, Samuel Pierce, for help in funding a project in downtown Phoenix, Square One, which now forms a critical portion of Copper Square. In fact, after several rebuffs to my request for federal help on this project, I approached Senator Goldwater on the floor of the Senate and explained to him that I could get nothing from the secretary. Could Barry talk to him? Yes, he responded, "You get him on the phone, and I will talk to him right now." So I went into the cloakroom of the Republican Committee, called my office, wrote down Pierce's number, and called. His administrative assistant answered and asked who was calling. I did not identify myself but responded that Senator Goldwater would like to talk with the secretary. Sure enough, Pierce got on the line, and I still did not identify myself. I said, "Just a minute, Mr. Secretary, Senator Goldwater is outside on the floor, and he wants to talk with you." I hurried to the floor, and Goldwater followed me back to the Republican cloakroom. He got on the phone and unloaded on the secretary, and within a week Pierce approved millions of dollars for construction of a park and parking garage in downtown Phoenix.

My office, happily, generated a press release that cited Goldwater's efforts but also allowed me credit for this significant appropriation for the city of Phoenix. I took the release to his office so he could review the copy, and he said, "Oh, it's fine, Denny." That kind of intervention, I suggested to Ethics Committee members and others, was the kind that benefited constituents, and I believed that was a senator's job. Of course, the contractors donated money to both Goldwater's and my campaigns.

I realized that some disagreed with this approach to Senate duties. They disdained "getting their hands dirty" and hesitated when serious disputes emerged. I found, however, that a significant majority of senators took affirmative action on constituent issues and felt that it was, in fact, their job to intervene so that agencies were responsive and polite and served the public as mandated by law. I heard innumerable complaints about federal workers' arrogance, rudeness, and arbitrariness. Those problems, which also affect the private sector, were relatively small; I found the vast majority of federal workers to be dedicated, service oriented, and proud to work for the government. Still, when a constituent complained about a federal worker or agency that responded improperly to a request or question, I addressed the problem.

The personal consequences and political fallout from the Keating Five situation were numerous and in some cases profound. I will always be grateful to the many people who stood with me during this difficult period. We called a number of witnesses on our behalf, many of them from Arizona, ranging from a longtime friend who was a disabled veteran to Pima County sheriff Clarence Dupnik to teachers, lawyers, businessmen, ranchers, and miners. They testified how thankful they were to have me as their senator. Even Cardinal O'Connor of New York wrote a letter on my behalf. I had known the cardinal for many years, and we exchanged occasional greetings but were not close friends. Another remarkable human aspect of the hearings was that some senators came forward with written and verbal statements on my behalf.

Perhaps the best and most poignant statement of support came from Daniel Inouye. A Japanese American from Hawaii, Senator Inouye had lost a limb during his service in Italy in World War II. Smart, congenial, and fair in his judgments, he always comported himself in a principled and dignified manner. He was chairman of the Indian Affairs Committee, and I served with him on that committee. A great advocate for Native Americans, he truly believed that our government had failed them in many cases, so he initiated a great number of necessary reforms. I asked him if he would help me with my defense in the Ethics Committee hearings, and without hesitation he said, "Absolutely." Over the objection of some of his senior staff, he testified in my behalf for about one-half hour. He stated simply yet eloquently that I was doing my job serving my constituent and that there should be no penalties issued against me. His testimony left a strong impression because he was universally respected in the Senate. Other senators helped as well: Fritz Hollings and Strom Thurmond, South Carolina's senators, and Paul Simon, a Democrat from Illinois, penned supportive statements. Former attorney general Griffin Bell testified for all of us, stating that there were no improper actions taken in our efforts to intervene. Although some did not come forward, I held no grudges, but I remain thankful to those who stood up and testified on my behalf.[33]

Many times over the years my staff recommended that I should not testify or issue statements on behalf of potentially problematic people. In one instance, I said that I wanted to testify on behalf of a lawyer who was on trial in Arizona. He had been a friend a long time, and I knew him to be a decent guy who had made a mistake. I did not believe he should go to jail, and when I indicated that I wanted to testify, my staff responded, "Why do you want to do that?" In Keating's case, Laurie Sedlmayr had advised me not to intervene on Keating's behalf. In hindsight, she proved correct in her analysis. I took a risk for a constituent, and it turned out to be a huge mistake because eventually Keating was convicted of breaking the law, with Senator McCain as one of the star witnesses at his trial. Though Keating was freed recently, the felony convictions that put him in prison stand as a testament to his fiscal recklessness.

During Keating's trial in the early 1990s, the Justice Department contacted me, interviewed me, and asked if I would testify. I responded with a question of my own, "What would I testify about at Keating's trial?" They said that if I were called, they would ask if I knew that Keating had misled me and the other senators, if I had some knowledge that he was committing criminal acts, or if I were suspicious that he was committing crimes. I explained the history of my relationship with Keating—how I had intervened with FHLBB regulators, but that I did not know if he had criminal intent when he had sought out the five senators. Not surprisingly, I was not called to testify at the trial.

Life teaches difficult lessons. The Keating Five case taught me several important ones. First, I should have represented myself at the hearings. I respected Jim Hamilton greatly and had been recommended to hire counsel because lawyers make notoriously terrible clients. The Senate, however, provided a different environment than a traditional courtroom, even though I felt that in this case Bennett ran the hearings like a criminal trial, as I could easily see from my experience as a prosecutor in both civil and criminal court. I had relationships with the other ninety-nine members, and they had formed opinions about me. I had formed solid friendships and gained respect, and I concluded that the committee would have acted differently had I, rather than my very able counsel, been posing questions to witnesses. In 2002, Senator Max Baucus of Montana faced sexual harassment charges when one of his staffers filed a complaint against him. As the Senate Ethics Committee assessed the complaint, I spoke with Baucus and said, "Max, if you do anything, represent yourself. You know yourself. These people who are going to judge you know you, have worked with you, know you are an honest man, and that this person who has accused you has falsely accused you." The case ultimately was dropped, but I would advise any others in a similar situation to avoid hiring counsel.

I would also tell them to make an aggressive defense, not to hold back. I considered, for example, calling Alan Greenspan, at the time chairman of the Federal Reserve, as a witness, but counsel and staff convinced me otherwise. The prevailing wisdom was that Greenspan might be unpredictable. Good lawyers never ask questions of a witness without knowing the witness's answer. In Greenspan's instance, he had prepared his statement, and though he had been on Keating's payroll, he was a recognized, renowned economist with impeccable credentials, and he echoed exactly what the five senators said about Keating and Lincoln Savings and Loan. I had little trepidation about Greenspan and believed that he would have reiterated the previous statements made in his reports. Another economist, L. William Seidman, was a regulator from Arizona, and I wanted him called to testify. Seidman was a fair-minded Republican, but advisors talked me out of calling him for the same reasons outlined concerning Greenspan. The witnesses I hoped most to call, which would have raised eyebrows on the committee, were Robert Bennett, the Ethics Committee's counsel, and two former U.S. attorneys who were reviewing his statements and questions and writing a statement arguing that Bennett was acting as a prosecutor and not an investigator. Bennett played poker with some of his witnesses, had strong ties to Republicans, and, as I noted earlier, worked hard to excise McCain from the process. I wanted to question Bennett under oath. I suspected that the committee would have denied the request, but I wanted Bennett to testify, for the record, under oath.

Finally, I should have returned to Arizona early during the process, held press conferences, and explained my position more frequently. I was too defensive and took the issue personally rather than viewing it through a political prism. One cannot fight "City Hall"; as I learned, the press is "City Hall."

Many have asked if I bear grudges. I do not, and I have been around long enough not to stay angry for a long period of time. Bennett and others who, I thought, treated me unfairly also treated others in similar fashion, even John McCain. It took me some time to arrive at this place, but my religious beliefs helped me move on. I have not nursed any grudges, though clearly I have not forgotten people and events that affected my family and me during that most trying time in my Senate career.

9 A New Federalism for American Indians

The Navajo Nation at a Crossroad

While the Keating saga unfolded in the late 1980s and early 1990s, several other issues of great significance required my attention. In 1988, the longstanding struggle by American Indians for self-determination, a cause I had championed throughout my public career, was brought into sharp relief. Peter MacDonald, the controversial and longtime chairman of the Navajo Nation, became the focal point of this political and legal struggle, and I took actions that caused me no small amount of concern. In this regard, I faced a challenging philosophical choice. The intractable conflict of any democratically elected representative—whether to follow the popular will or act according to your own conscience—became an underlying theme in a particularly sensitive investigation that I chaired in the late 1980s. In effect, I was faced with the question: When the popular democratic will is specifically manifested by the election of one representative, under what circumstances does another democratically elected representative have either the duty or right to investigate the former?

Growing up in Arizona, I had a long-standing commitment to justice for our first citizens—American Indians. Serving on the Select Committee on Indian Affairs for more than fifteen years, I authored numerous pieces of legislation to benefit American Indians. This commitment to justice for them was reflected in the overwhelming support I uniformly received in each election from Arizona tribal residents, averaging more than 70 percent of their vote in each of my Senate races.[1] I received strong support from the Navajo Nation, located largely in northeastern Arizona, and from its longtime leader Peter MacDonald.

The Navajos are the largest American Indian tribe in the United States, both in population and area. The Navajo population is more than one-fifth the population of all reservation Indians in the country, and the landmass of the Navajo Nation is larger than West Virginia and eight other states.

The leading Navajo politician of the modern era—and some would say the most prominent American Indian leader overall—was Peter MacDonald. First elected tribal chairman in 1970, MacDonald was almost universally credited with ushering in the modern era of tribal government for the Navajos and indeed became an example for other elected American Indian leaders throughout the United States. His people elected him to four terms, amounting to almost twenty years as chairman and chief executive of the tribal government. For most of his time in office, he enjoyed widespread popular support among Navajos.[2]

During his mercurial career, MacDonald had always been an ardent and consistent supporter of me. In 1976, MacDonald urged all Navajos and all twenty-one Arizona tribes to vote for me in my first run for the U.S. Senate. He repeated these endorsements in subsequent campaigns. The percentage of the vote that I received on the Navajo Reservation was indeed overwhelming, averaging nearly 90 percent, well higher than the approximately 57 percent of voter support I received statewide. Clearly, the extraordinary percentage of Navajo votes for me reflected both my support for their cause and Chairman Peter Mac Donald's powerful backing.

In October 1987, the *Arizona Republic* ran an extensive series of articles on the state of American Indians and the failures of the federal government, of oil and other natural-resource companies, and of others to act in the interest of American Indians. Prompted by these reports, Senator Daniel K. Inouye of Hawaii, chairman of the Select Committee on Indian Affairs, decided to investigate fraud, corruption, and mismanagement in American Indian affairs. Chairman Inouye, who combined a long-standing commitment to Native American rights with extensive involvement in Senate investigations, moved quickly to establish the Special Committee on Investigations to uncover and root out the fraud and corruption that held back American Indians' self-determination.[3]

The Special Committee on Investigations, authorized by the full Senate in February 1988, had a unique mission in the annals of congressional and federal oversight of American Indian affairs. Congress itself, of course, has a long history of investigating the federal government's relationship to Indians. Yet never before in that history had a special committee been assembled whose sole task was to conduct a comprehensive and intensive investigation of the entire spectrum of the federal government's relationship with Native Americans. Moreover, unlike prior investigative committees, such as those for Iran-Contra or Watergate, which were designed to investigate a specific set of already established allegations, the Special Committee on Investigations was charged simply to investigate fraud, corruption, and mismanagement—the precise allegations were unknown ab initio.

In historical context, these investigations attempted to reassert our original congressional intent in our relationships with Indian tribes. At the birth of our constitutional democracy, the Founding Fathers recognized the original inhabitants of North America as independent, self-governing nations that long pre-dated European settlement. At that time, we began to sign treaties, under the Constitution, with American Indian tribes. In calling for agreements, President George Washington and the other founders pledged that the United States would deal with tribes on a consistent, honorable, and fair basis. In the century that followed 1789, however, western expansion unleashed economic and political forces that threw Indians on the defensive. During the nineteenth century, Congress abandoned the commitment to fair and honorable treatment. Indeed, throughout that century, the federal government prosecuted aggressive and brutal wars to subjugate recalcitrant tribes. Military campaigns led to conquest and forced removal of many tribes from their native territory; the Navajos' incarceration experience from 1863 to 1868 at Bosque Redondo, New Mexico, far from their homeland, served as a bitter reminder of those campaigns.[4]

During the investigations, I never lost sight of the fact that in exchange for vast lands that today compose most of the United States, the federal government had promised tribes permanent, self-governing reservations, along with federal goods, services, and fiduciary responsibility. Instead, government administrators, often the agents assigned to particular tribes, became corrupt and in some cases tried to substitute federal political power for self-determination. By the turn of the twentieth century, there seemed to be no limit to the federal government's paternalism. It was not uncommon for government officials to sever ties between parents and children by confining the children in government boarding schools. They undermined the authority of religious leaders and jailed them for holding traditional religious practices, and they destroyed indigenous economies by seizing lands and reneging on promises of support and financial assistance. Perhaps worst of all, in my view, was the fact that although the government had historically offered Indians equal membership in the United States, it had failed miserably in granting them basic freedoms to form their own governments and to live free from tyranny.

Although progress concerning rights to self-determination has been made in the past few decades, American Indians have remained trapped in nineteenth-century poverty. Essentials such as electricity, plumbing, and telephone were in many cases rare commodities when I undertook the investigation in the late 1980s. I had hoped that after two hundred years of life under the Constitution, our country might finally reject the errors of history. I thought it was time that the United States abolish federal paternalism but at the same time ensure full support. Congress intended to launch "a new federalism for American Indians," reaffirming our faith in those who created this Republic while redeeming promises made long ago to its first peoples.[5]

Senator Inouye appointed me chairman of the Special Committee on Investigations. Because I believed that the investigation must be conducted in a fully bipartisan—indeed, nonpartisan—manner, I chose Senator John McCain, my junior Republican colleague from Arizona, to serve as my partner and cochairman. I was fortunate as well in having Senator Tom Daschle, then the relatively new senator from South Dakota, serve as the third member of our committee. Again, rare in the annals of congressional investigations, Cochairman McCain and I decided to conduct the entire investigation in a completely bipartisan fashion and together hired one nonpartisan, unified professional staff without any Democratic or Republican designations.

Although the legal charge of the Special Committee was broadly formulated, the public expectation of its work was indeed narrow. All of the allegations set forth in the comprehensive *Arizona Republic* investigative articles concerned how non-Indians were exploiting the Native American population. From large oil and other natural-resource companies to the federal government's own inept Bureau of Indian Affairs (BIA), what unquestionably gave rise to this extraordinary investigation was continued outside exploitation of Native American citizens.

To ferret out this outside abuse, Senator McCain and I assembled a large and highly experienced investigative staff. The staff was charged with extensive outreach, visiting more than seventy tribes in more than sixteen states, conducting more than two thousand interviews, and gathering through subpoena and other methods some 1.1 million documents. The committee also held twenty days of extensive public hearings, taking sworn testimony from 172 witnesses. We indeed found substantial exploitation by natural-resource companies and federal mismanagement and incompetence, in magnitude and scope well beyond what the *Arizona Republic* had reported. However, it was our discovery of what had not been reported—corruption within the tribal leadership itself—that caused one of the most difficult tasks of any elected politician: following individual conscience over popular will.[6]

As suggested earlier, the federal government has a long and undistinguished history of overriding the will of Native Americans. Yet even as we enter the twenty-first century, federal policymakers are still held captive to the ghosts of paternalism and dependency. Given this sorry history of federal relations with Indian tribes, a Senate challenge to the legitimate will of the largest American Indian nation seemed a particularly daunting prospect. Could democracy truly exist if the democratically elected representatives were themselves corrupt? Political corruption, by its nature, vitiates democracy on the most fundamental level. This was the conundrum Senator McCain and I faced in the summer of 1988.

When Senator McCain and I had sent the staff out to several reservations to gather as many facts as possible, I sent my staff director and chief counsel, Ken Ballen, to the Navajo Nation because of its leading importance in Indian country. Ken was a distinguished former federal prosecutor, having successfully prosecuted major organized crime in

My father, Evo DeConcini, addressing a group of attorneys in Tucson, 1982.

Shaking hands with Poland's Lech Walesa shortly after he was awarded the Nobel Peace Prize in 1983.

My brother Dino and I meeting with Prime Minister Indira Gandhi of India at her Parliament home office during a Helsinki Commission trip, 1984.

TOP: Meeting with Soviet Refusenik Dr. Alexander Lerner during a Helsinki Commission trip, 1985.

MIDDLE: Meeting with Prime Minister Simon Peres of Israel on a tour of the Middle East, 1986.

BOTTOM: Greeting King Hussein of Jordan at a U.S. State Department function in Washington, D.C., 1987.

Shaking hands with President Hosni Mubarak, with Ambassador Said Hamsa looking on, during a Senate trip to Egypt, 1983.

With Governor Rose Mofford, Senator John McCain, and recently retired Senator Barry Goldwater at Arizona State University, 1988.

Campaigning for reelection in 1988 in northern Arizona.

At the Berlin Wall shortly after the reunification of Germany, 1989.

Meeting with former Soviet leader Mikhail Gorbachev during his visit to the United States in 1990.

In the Oval Office with President Bill Clinton, June 23, 1993.

Meeting President Nelson Mandela of South Africa in 1994, shortly after he was elected; he had been awarded the Nobel Peace Prize in the previous year.

With John Walsh of the National Center for Missing and Exploited Children, where I serve on the board of directors, 1995.

fraud and racketeering cases. Senator Inouye initially recommended Ken to Senator McCain and me because he had been one of the staff counsel on the Iran-Contra Investigative Committee, which Senator Inouye had chaired. According to Inouye, Ken was one of the finest investigative attorneys on the entire Iran-Contra staff. When Ken asked to meet with me alone, I knew that the matter was of some gravity. As a skillful and experienced prosecutor, he simply relayed to me the facts: how he had met with Chairman MacDonald, who had urged him to focus the investigation on the federal government; but also how scores of ordinary Navajo citizens had approached him on the street to ask for our help in freeing them from MacDonald's corrupt and oppressive regime; and, last, how in the middle of the night someone had slipped some documents under his door.[7]

The documents were simply public records: an advertisement in the *Wall Street Journal* offering land for sale in Arizona for $25 million and a record of the purchase of the land shortly thereafter by the Navajo Nation for more than $33 million. As an experienced prosecutor myself, I immediately understood the import of what Ken was telling me—and the crisis of conscience that now confronted the Special Committee.

The question before us was whether we should investigate MacDonald with the same vigor and diligence that we were investigating the oil companies and other outside interests allegedly exploiting Native Americans. The implications of such a decision extended far beyond our committee's work and threatened the progress American Indians had achieved during the second half of the twentieth century. There was no simple or even correct resolution to the sensitive problem. MacDonald had been democratically elected, just as I had been. Moreover, the responsibility for criminal investigation and enforcement rested with the Department of Justice and not with Congress.

Nevertheless, Congress maintains the ultimate responsibility for federal policy regarding American Indians. It should accept blame for not adequately overseeing and reforming Indian affairs. Rather than actively pursuing this responsibility, Congress has demonstrated an attitude of benign neglect. By allowing tribal officials to handle hundreds of millions of dollars in federal funds without stringent criminal laws or adequate enforcement, Congress left American Indian people vulnerable to corruption. Further, it tolerated administrative breakdowns of federal agencies, at the same time refusing to deal with tribes as responsible governments.

From my view, it is a fundamental tenet of American federalism that local governments have the responsibility to manage their own affairs unencumbered by inappropriate federal restrictions, but accountable for the funds they receive. Yet up to the time of this special investigation, Congress not only had neglected to hold corrupt tribal officials accountable, but also had instead imposed a stifling and duplicative layer of federal bureaucracy over all tribal governments. In effect, it micromanaged Indian affairs, deluging tribal governments with red tape and meaningless procedures. By imposing a double layer of government, it created a political no-man's-land, where responsibility shifted from one entity to the other. Tribal officials blamed federal officials for failings, and federal officials blamed weak tribal government for their shortcomings. No one was responsible, and no one was accountable. The American Indian citizens suffered the consequences of this political vacuum.

Our committee, therefore, had been charged with one of the most important investigations of American Indian affairs in congressional history. If the progress American Indians had achieved at so much cost were to continue, then the true problems confronting Indian country had to be exposed. There was simply no right or wrong answer. I knew, too, that this was fundamentally a matter of conscience, and not one where I could turn to polls or public opinion for an answer. It was clear from the outset as well that this decision to expose the corruption would be enormously unpopular among some American Indians and among their numerous allies in Washington.

Given the acute sensitivity of the MacDonald matter and the critical importance of the utmost secrecy in any potential investigation, I told Ken that I would not discuss the matter with any other staff and that he should brief Senator McCain and Senator Daschle in secret and without staff. That night had to be one of the most sleepless I spent in my entire Senate career. Weighing the issues of democracy and conscience, American Indian rights and the role of congressional investigative oversight, I came to the conclusion that we had to follow the facts, no matter where they led. In order to exercise full democracy and sovereignty, the Navajo people were entitled to the truth—and the facts ultimately would be less paternalistic than deciding for them the right course of action. I nonetheless hoped against hope that our investigation of MacDonald would exonerate him and his government. And I secretly hoped that Senator McCain, as my cochair and partner in this investigation, would have a different view of whether or not to investigate MacDonald.

But Senator McCain, after being presented with Ken's initial report, indeed came to the same judgment I had, and together we decided to embark down a road pitted with large potholes. The instructions I gave to Ken were clear: the investigation must be fair, secret, and thorough. If we were to go down this path, I knew that the evidence against MacDonald had to be conclusive, or we would risk damaging Indian country without any potential reward.

The investigation into MacDonald began in the same fashion as any thorough investigation: by the meticulous collection of thousands of documents through compulsory legal process and otherwise—bank records, business contracts, real-estate records, phone records, credit reports, and countless other documents. As the investigation proceeded, committee staff also interviewed and took sworn testimony under oath from more than sixty-five individuals. The committee, with the concurrence of the Department of Justice, also granted limited-use immunity to obtain the testimony of an additional twenty-six witnesses. Unique in the history of the Congress, the Special Committee took the extraordinary and unprecedented step of engaging in surreptitious audio recording of the subject of the investigation, Peter MacDonald.[8]

MacDonald was born Hashkesilth Begay in 1928 on the Navajo Reservation. A good student, he graduated from the University of Oklahoma and became an engineer with Hughes Aircraft in 1957. Returning to the reservation in 1963 to work for the tribe, he headed the Office of Navajo Economic Opportunity in 1965. Raising his public profile in that position, he ran for Navajo tribal chairman in 1970 and was elected. He served three four-year terms until 1983, throughout the era when tribal governments were transformed into modern governments supported by extensive federal funding. Although defeated in his reelection bid in 1982, he had helped usher in a new political era on the Navajo Nation.[9]

In consultation with his lawyer and the Department of Justice, the businessman who had served as MacDonald's closest cohort, Byron T. "Bud" Brown, agreed to be wired and placed under surveillance by Special Committee investigators while he was speaking to Chairman MacDonald. On at least ten different occasions between November 1988 and January 1989, in cooperation with the Department of Justice and the FBI, the committee taped conversations with Brown, Chairman MacDonald, and his son, Peter "Rocky" MacDonald Jr., in cars, restaurants, and airports and over the phone. These taped conversations as well as numerous documents and testimony by Brown, by other contractors in business on the Navajo reservation, and, in a poignant and dramatic day of public hearings, by MacDonald's own son, Peter Jr., constituted overwhelming evidence of Chairman MacDonald's extensive and massive corruption.

Without question, Peter MacDonald played a dominant role in Navajo political and economic affairs during the period 1970–90 and arguably was the leading Navajo politician of the modern era. He trumpeted an exciting vision of economic development and social progress for the impoverished Navajo Nation. By attracting private-sector capital to the reservation, he claimed jobs would be created for the 47 percent of the population that were jobless. "The Navajo Nation is one of America's last economic frontiers," he declared at his inauguration as chairman in 1987 (although defeated in 1982, he was reelected in 1986). "I see a wealth of opportunity for all of us. Let us, once and for all, share in the bounty of America!"[10] In fact, MacDonald created the Commission on Accelerating Navajo Development Opportunities to foster the establishment of shopping centers, tourism, gaming, and construction on the reservation. Senators Peter Domenici (R–New Mexico), John McCain, Daniel Inouye, and I attended an "economic summit" to support MacDonald's vision. His rhetoric promised a new era in Navajo economic development.

In reality, however, during his first three terms of office MacDonald ran the Navajo tribal government like a racketeering enterprise. The amassed evidence proved that after his reelection as tribal chairman in 1986, MacDonald received bogus "consulting fees," "loans," and "gifts" —and even persuaded the tribe to purchase for more than $33 million a vast track of desert land, the Big Boquillas Ranch, near Seligman, Arizona, which had no mineral or other resources and was valued for at most $26 million. Through a shell company, MacDonald could thus enjoy a secret share of the more than $7 million markup. He also devised a scheme where all private enterprises attracted to the Navajo Reservation had to "take care" of MacDonald first. Sham "consulting contracts," bogus "loans," and naked demands for cash and gifts were among the extortionate practices MacDonald employed, ostensibly along with his son, Peter Jr. But no matter what form the extortion took, the evidence before the committee overwhelmingly demonstrated that the unambiguous price of doing business on the Navajo Reservation was a kickback to the chairman of the tribe.[11]

This pattern of corruption became transparent with his reelection to the tribal chairmanship on November 4, 1986. As he sought to regain his position from Peterson Zah that year, who had defeated MacDonald in a bitter election four years earlier, MacDonald turned to his close friend Byron T. "Bud" Brown for help. Together they devised plans whereby Brown would act as a broker for future businesses locating on the Navajo Nation, assuring that in each instance the chairman would receive a secret cut.

Not content with milking kickbacks from outside businesses, MacDonald took funds directly from the Navajo Treasury to pay for his regal trappings and lifestyle. Although 46 percent of Navajos had no electricity, 54 percent lacked indoor plumbing, and 79 percent lived without a telephone, MacDonald used tribal funds to pay for private luxury airplane flights for personal trips and for his own remodeled executive suite with mahogany and gold-plated fixtures.[12]

MacDonald's corruption extended to a far grander scale. According to his son's testimony, the documentary evidence, Bud Brown's testimony, and, most tellingly, MacDonald's own words from countless surreptitiously tape-recorded conversations, the chairman had concocted a scheme to defraud his impoverished tribe of millions. Given that the Navajo Nation is more than three times the size of Massachusetts, the last thing its people needed was noncontiguous, desert land with no mineral or other resources. Yet together with Brown, MacDonald conceived a scheme where a shell corporation secretly controlled by Brown would buy this desert real estate on the open market and then sell it to the unsuspecting Navajo Nation after a substantial markup. Other payoffs and bribes—BMWs, cash payoffs, aircraft for personal use, vacations, gifts—added up to an endemic pattern of corruption. As the evidence proved also, MacDonald tried to blame all of the illegal activities on his son Rocky. It was a sad and regrettable situation. The committee forwarded evidence against MacDonald to the Department of Justice.

As a result of the committee's incontrovertible evidence, MacDonald's position became untenable, and the majority of the Navajo Tribal Council organized against him. At first, MacDonald promised to resign his position peacefully if the council would furnish him a defense fund. The council refused, and on February 16, 1989, MacDonald resigned. But the next day he reneged on his resignation, and the situation grew confused and violent.

As a result of this unusual political standoff, the Navajo Tribal Council, in an unprecedented and courageous step, voted forty-nine to thirteen to place MacDonald on involuntary administrative leave without the defense funds he demanded. One week later Navajo district judge Harry Brown, MacDonald's brother-in-law, ruled the suspension invalid. But on April 13, 1989, the Navajo Supreme Court upheld the council's action and placed MacDonald on involuntary administrative leave. Then, despite a series of court orders, MacDonald supporters forcefully occupied the chairman's opulently remodeled offices until tribal police removed them.[13]

In an untoward and ill-advised maneuver, MacDonald returned to the Navajo Nation brandishing a purported letter from the U.S. Attorney's Office claiming that on July 19, 1989, he had been cleared of all charges. He announced also that he was issuing an executive order reinstating his police chief and that he was reclaiming his rightful position as chairman of the Navajo Nation. He demanded further that his band of three hundred followers, many of whom were former bureaucrats in his administration, were going to retake the government. Armed with clubs, lumber, and baseball bats, the protesters approached tribal offices in Window Rock. Several grabbed a Navajo police lieutenant, handcuffed him, and beat him severely. Another officer rushed to his aid, but another protester grabbed the officer's gun and shot him in the leg. At this juncture, unfortunately, Navajo officers opened fire and shot the protester who had wounded the officer. Another protester was killed in the gunfire. No others were wounded in the melee. MacDonald, who was not with the crowd, claimed that the police, unprovoked, had opened fire on innocent supporters of the rightful Navajo chairman.[14]

MacDonald was ultimately removed from power, successfully prosecuted by the Department of Justice for his widespread crimes, and indeed served a long sentence in federal prison. However, the opposition to the committee's hearings exposing MacDonald was, as I had feared, vehement and fierce—and to a large extent based on legitimate concerns with which I empathized. MacDonald had been democratically elected, just as Senator McCain and I had been, and to hold hearings questioning his legitimacy was indeed a monumental step—especially for American Indians, whose self-determination had been so long in coming. The question of whether the committee's outside intervention in Navajo affairs was the correct course can easily be answered on one level. The Navajo people, through their democratically elected legislative body, the Tribal Council, quickly and decisively removed MacDonald from power once his illegal activities had been exposed. Democracy requires transparency, and political corruption, by its very nature, can flourish only covertly. Corruption at its very core fundamentally skews democratic government by rewarding the elite few who benefit from the corruption itself. Peter MacDonald manifestly proved that point by pursuing his own personal enrichment at the expense of his people.

Yet, on another level, particularly given the federal government's long history of paternalism toward American Indians, nagging philosophical questions remained. By intervening, did the committee set back the cause of self-determination and reinforce federal paternalism? Perhaps because McCain, Daschle, and I shared such doubts, and perhaps indeed to compensate for our difficult decision, the Special Committee came up with the most radical recommendations to reform American Indian affairs in more than fifty years. We proposed a full transfer of federal power to the tribes themselves, with increased levels of accountability to prevent the kind of systemic abuse that Peter MacDonald imposed.

Most observers throughout the country hailed the committee's revolutionary proposals. Leading newspapers hailed the call for a new era in Indian self-determination as innovative, courageous, and timely. They found the committee's work an outstanding effort that all Americans could point to with pride. Nevertheless, I knew that these proposals would be quite controversial. Of course, many western senators immediately opposed them, fearing the transfer of power to Native Americans at the expense of their other constituents. And, ironically, many American Indian leaders greeted the committee's recommendations with a degree of skepticism because of the committee's investigation of MacDonald. Perhaps they too could fall under the federal investigative microscope, so they not surprisingly expressed initial resistance to the committee's report, issued in November 1989.

Put another way, the MacDonald investigation raised the ugly specter of past federal paternalism. It prompted the committee to come up with the most radical transfer of power to American Indians ever proposed; yet, because of the investigation, the committee's recommendations elicited distrust among American Indian leaders even though they stood to benefit most.

I was convinced, however, that with time and debate the initial skepticism among American Indians would fade and be transformed into unqualified and enthusiastic support. I also believed that the opposition of other entrenched interests would be overcome with the firm and dedicated leadership of McCain, Daschle, and myself. But that was not to be.

The dark cloud of Keating and the savings and loan struggles seized daily news accounts within months of our bold proposals, robbing them of the unencumbered stewardship they so desperately needed to succeed. This set of political circumstances is one of the great regrets of my entire Senate career. The Keating affair clearly deprived Senator McCain and me of the ability to champion fully the radical reforms we proposed in the investigations into corruption on Indian reservations.

The most important task of any democratically elected official is to honor a matter of conscience over popular will. As an elected representative, his or her first and most sacred duty is to represent faithfully the people he or she has been elected to serve. Chairman Peter MacDonald, the duly elected chief executive of the Navajo Nation and a long-time political supporter of mine, expressed his people's collective will. Although the same voters had elected me, I was faced with the unenviable decision of calling into question their expressed democratic intent. This decision was inextricably linked to the dark history of the federal government's oppressive paternalism toward American Indians, something I was dedicated to reform as chairman of the Senate Special Committee on Investigations for the Select Committee on Indian Affairs. The choice I made and the reasons why I made it I have tried to explicate in this chapter as best I can. But the fundamental reality remains: any politician who truly believes in democracy can only be deeply troubled by any usurpation of the democratic will, no matter how seemingly justified. The fluid nature of democracy can occasionally be at war with itself: overriding democracy to further democracy shall always be a dangerous, though sometimes necessary, course.

The committee also investigated numerous other abuses in Indian country. Evidence existed that known pedophiles and poor teachers were hired in BIA schools, and oftentimes severe and cruel punishment was administered to Indian children. Besides the Peter MacDonald case on the Navajo Nation, the investigations also uncovered the fact that several major energy companies, including Coke Oil, committed significant frauds against tribes. Oil and gas leases on Indian land were regularly used as vehicles to exploit unknowing victims, and the falsification of documents regarding energy taken from various well fields and other facilities was legion. The Department of Justice initiated a series of investigations to address these abuses. Indeed, federal and state governments must remain vigilant in attempting to minimize the abuses in their relationships with American Indian tribes. In Arizona, the equitable division of Colorado River system water, health care, land exchanges, and education were key issues as I looked toward a third term in 1988, and these issues remain at the forefront of relations between the federal government and Arizona's twenty-one tribes today.

10 Transitions

Although when I was first elected to the U.S. Senate, I had stated that I would serve only two terms, circumstances changed: I decided to seek a third term and prepared for the political fallout. I knew my decision to run for reelection in 1988 was controversial, but I committed to it wholeheartedly and undertook an aggressive fund-raising effort. My stature had risen in the Senate to a significant degree, and retiring Senator Goldwater had nice things to say about me. "My friend Denny," he would say, "is our new Carl Hayden." Some leftist activists, however, displeased with my moderate-to-conservative voting record, considered me a Republican masquerading as a Democrat. Nevertheless, in 1988 I contended that drugs, crime, defense, and the deficit were the issues most important to voters.[1] In fact, in early 1988 New York's Senator D'Amato and I introduced a comprehensive $2.6 billion drug bill that we hoped would make a significant advance on the war on drugs. Nearly ten months of wrangling brought forth the notion in some circles that I had once again aligned myself with conservatives to pass "a campaign-year drug bill." Actually, it was the Democrats who forced the most significant changes in the bill, with 60 percent of the funds going for treatment and 40 percent targeted for law enforcement, a reversal of the figures in my original bill. The amendments notwithstanding, I was pleased to see Congress take decisive action on the war on drugs.[2]

With no serious challenge in the primary, my outstanding campaign fund-raiser, Earl Katz, helped raise more than $3 million—an amount that discouraged many potential candidates, but not my Republican opponent in the general election, Keith DeGreen, a thirty-nine-year-old financial planner with little political experience. An early poll placed me at a three-to-one advantage, and the Republican Senatorial Committee, the PAC charged with wresting control of the Senate from the Democrats, decided to expend its fiscal and human resources in other states. Washington insiders considered me a "shoo-in" for a third six-year term, even though I had changed my mind about limiting my service to two terms.[3] But in the context of the Keating revelations and an increasingly conservative electorate in Arizona, I knew that the race could tighten, and I had learned from my previous two campaigns that anything could happen.

In fact, late in the campaign, during the last week of October, reports emerged questioning my family's land holdings along the CAP route north of Tucson. DeGreen, who had gained little traction and had experienced difficulty generating campaign contributions, held a news conference on October 24 and charged me and my family with making substantial profits on sales of lands to the federal government knowing the land would be condemned for the construction of the CAP. Bob Maynes, my campaign spokesman, called DeGreen's allegations "gibberish" and responded quickly to this challenge.[4] The insinuations uttered in DeGreen's press conference irked me, and I issued a terse response: "I don't buy land to condemn it."[5]

The family company, 4-D Properties, consisting of my brothers Dino and David, my sister Danielle, and me, had bought 320 acres north of Tucson near Marana for $1,250 an acre in October 1979, a few months after the federal government, at public hearings, had focused on three possible CAP routes. In 1985, 4-D sold this land to the U.S. government for $8,000 an acre for use as part of the CAP route. In August 1983, 4-D had also entered a limited partnership in a venture called Lake Pleasant Associates, acquiring 12.5 percent interest in 630 acres northwest of Phoenix. The total cost of the property was $7 million, and owner Don Lee, of Phoenix, had sold the land to the limited partnership. Former Democratic Party gubernatorial candidate and businessman Lee Ackerman was the general partner of Lake Pleasant Associates and had become interested in the property in the fall of 1982 after the Bureau of Reclamation assured him that it would not be needed for any aspect of the water project, though federal officials had begun studying the area in 1979. As it turned out, after plans for construction of Orme Dam at the confluence of the Salt and Verde rivers fell through for a variety of political reasons, federal administrators adopted the so-called Plan 6, which called for building New Waddell Dam at the southern end of Lake Pleasant and just north of the land that Lake Pleasant Associates had purchased in 1983. On April 3, 1984, Interior Secretary William Clark approved Plan 6 as the Orme Dam alternative. The government needed 347 of the 630 acres held by the partnership for power lines and other facilities related to the New Waddell Dam, which would store CAP water. In 1987, the federal government purchased the 347 acres for $20,000 per acre.[6]

I knew that federal law prohibited the government from doing business with members of Congress, so I sold my 3.1 percent interest to my family as soon as Secretary Clark approved Plan 6. There was no way anyone could have known the federal government was going to condemn the land at the time 4-D invested in it. In addition to the complications I have already outlined, Lake Pleasant Associates submitted a master plan for the entire 630 acres to the Maricopa County Board of Supervisors on June 29, 1984. It called for a resort on the lake, a restaurant, commercial development, and clusters of single-family homes. Early the next year Lake Pleasant Associates sought to have its property rezoned for commercial use. The proposal was submitted to the Maricopa County Planning and Zoning Commission on January 17, 1985. The Bureau of Reclamation argued against rezoning, contending that such a move would inflate the value of the property. As a result of the impending controversy, I sent a letter to Bob Olsen, acting head of the Bureau of Reclamation, disclosing my small percentage interest in the property. I wrote that I had 3.1 percent interest in the 620 acres and that I had no management responsibility or authority regarding the land. I wanted to disclose this information to reclamation officials in order to avoid any appearance of a conflict of interest.[7]

In the 1988 reporting of the CAP land-sale controversy, factual mistakes, innuendo, and attack ads about alleged misdeeds brought forth the influence of the Republican Senatorial Committee and raised further questions about my integrity and family honor. I was not pleased. The most recent *Arizona Republic* poll had me leading DeGreen by a margin of 60 percent to 18 percent, but I was concerned by the way in which the issue was portrayed in the media. The Republicans, sensing political vulnerability, would doubtlessly turn their attention toward our campaign in an eleventh-hour attempt to defeat me.

On October 26, 1985, I opened the *Arizona Republic* and read the headline that ran with Sam Stanton's article, "GOP Panel May Aid Cash-Poor DeGreen." Three days later Stanton and veteran political journalist Don Harris cowrote a story, "GOP Group Donates $212,000 to DeGreen: Its TV Ad Targets DeConcini Land in Path of CAP." Before the campaign cash infusion, DeGreen had only $2,500 on hand. Even Republican Party presidential candidate George H. W. Bush sent $5,000 to the DeGreen campaign.[8] In the next few days, newspaper accounts claimed I had dropped as much as seventeen rating points in the two days since DeGreen's press conference leveling charges against me. To DeGreen, at least, the race was now in play.[9]

The infusion of last-minute campaign cash prompted the airing of several attack ads produced by the Republican Senatorial Committee; the commercials changed the dynamic of the campaign. They featured President Ronald Reagan urging Arizonans to stand with the Republican Party, but also, among other things, they claimed that I had given away the Panama Canal, had made millions of dollars on questionable land deals, and had voted with Ted Kennedy more than I did with Ronald Reagan. Contrary to DeGreen's and the Republicans' expectations, however, the tone and substance of the ads resulted in a host of public officials flocking into my camp. One headline read, "DeGreen Ad Prompts 300 in GOP to Back DeConcini."[10]

The negative campaigning, moreover, helped galvanize my political base. Arizona's Democrat governor Rose Mofford, for example, was so angered at what she called "eleventh-hour, unprovoked accusations against DeConcini" that she announced her support for my reelection. Calling me "an honorable man," she said, "As governor of our state of Arizona and a longtime friend of the DeConcini family, I felt that I really had to come forth after seeing what's been . . . shaping up in this race for the U.S. Senate." She said she had known my family for forty-eight years and had worked with me when I was an assistant to former governor Sam Goddard and when I was Pima County attorney. She "was shocked" at the unfounded accusations about my profiting from land deals. She turned to some of the inherent contradictions that marked my opponent's charges against me and questioned his commitment to the job, noting he had failed to vote in 1982, 1984, and 1986. The following day, at the state capitol, the governor attended a rally of fifty law enforcement officials, which featured one of my leading supporters, Pima County sheriff Clarence Dupnik. He announced his support and asserted that I had been a leader in law enforcement for many years and that Arizona could not afford to lose my services. He also predicted that the county attorneys association and the county sheriffs association would issue critical statements about DeGreen's attacks. I was touched by Governor Mofford's heartfelt statements and actions and welcomed the support of the law enforcement community.[11]

On November 4, I called what the press termed my "first news conference" of the campaign. I said that DeGreen had turned the race into one of the worst I had experienced: "In my opinion, this Senate campaign in Arizona, and I've been around here a few years, is the most negative, the most vicious, the most scurrilous that I have ever seen." To bolster my claim I released letters from two Republican friends and colleagues in the Senate, Paul Laxalt of Nevada and Orrin Hatch of Utah. Laxalt was an especially close advisor to President Reagan. They wrote letters condemning DeGreen's attacks about profiteering as fiction and affirmed that I was a man of integrity. Hatch said, "Dennis has brought honor and respect to himself and added immeasurably to the prestige of the U.S. Senate." "Personal attacks," like DeGreen's, Hatch added, "go beyond the bounds of legitimate political discussion." Laxalt wrote that I was "a man of integrity" and "a straight shooter who enjoyed the respect of other senators because of his honesty and integrity."[12]

Then, almost on cue, photographs of Joe Bonanno resurfaced en masse in early November and were distributed at convenience stores and public places throughout Arizona. The message, of course, was that as a person with an Italian surname, I was somehow a pawn of organized crime and the Mafia. This predictable and unfortunate tactic produced little, if any, advantage for the opposition. My campaign nevertheless countered these charges in print and in the electronic media. We ran one commercial touting my success at securing continued federal funding for the CAP and another that maintained as its central theme that drug dealers feared Dennis DeConcini.

As it turned out, my conservative opponent, besides alienating a major portion of the electorate with his negative campaigning, also made several public statements about raising taxes. This inherent contradiction for a Republican in the era of Ronald Reagan virtually doomed DeGreen from the outset of the general-election campaign. The allegations against my family's land holdings and regarding ties to organized crime disappeared from the political radar screen as voters flocked to the polls on November 8, 1988. I carried every county in the state and defeated my opponent 660,403 to 478,060.[13] I was pleased to see that my home county, Pima, supported me with a resounding 72.8 percent of the vote.[14]

The last two years of my third term coincided with President Clinton's first two years as president. When Bill Clinton was elected president in 1992, the United States had the largest peacetime budget deficit in the nation's history. Although he did not emphasize reducing the deficit in his campaign, early in his presidency he decided to make deficit reduction a major priority. I agreed with this basic premise, and in early May, only five months into his presidency, President Clinton presented to Congress the 1993 Budget Reconciliation Bill, also known as the Revenue Reconciliation Act of 1993. When the 263-page text hit the streets, Beltway insiders, K Street lobbyists, accountants, and attorneys spent days absorbing what seemed the hottest page-turner to hit Washington in a decade. Clinton proposed to provide tax incentives for business and raise $272 billion over the next five years. As it turned out, the congressionally modified version of Clinton's budget blueprint passed in August 1993 without one vote to spare. This bill was a sharp departure from the tax policies of the Reagan and Bush administrations, which stressed the economic benefits of reducing taxes on upper-level incomes. Significantly, I played a crucial role in the passage of this landmark tax policy revision.

The president asked Congress for a number of changes designed to eliminate the deficit. Among the most important called for raising the individual income tax rate to 36 percent for single taxpayers earning more than $115,000 per year and for couples earning more than $140,000 per year, as well as to raise the top corporate tax rate from 34 percent to 36 percent.[15] Indeed, the tax increases of the 1993 Budget Reconciliation Bill were not politically popular, and they doubtlessly played a role in the Democrats' dismal showing in the 1994 congressional elections. Yet the increases reduced the deficit, and by 1998 the federal government actually had a budget surplus for the first time in thirty years. In 1999, the surplus increased to $120 billion. The enhanced budget revenues were the most important reason for the reduction of the deficit and the transformation to a surplus during the late 1990s.[16]

I played a key role in this momentous and historically significant vote that laid the foundation for the Clinton economic plan for the years 1993–2001. Bill Clinton is a remarkable human being. I have never known anyone else like him. I had an opportunity to support him early in his campaign for president, but I did not because I concluded prematurely that he was going nowhere. Clinton looks directly at you when he speaks with you, and he is such a likeable guy one on one. He is pragmatic and accommodating, and he tries to please you. However, in 1993–94, I never assumed that Clinton had a core set of values regarding the ultimate direction and shape of his administration. That said, once he decided on something—such as his Middle East policy or his economic program in 1993—he was unafraid of political risk.

On June 25, 1993, I was one of six Democratic senators who voted "no" when President Clinton's economic plan passed the Senate fifty to forty-nine. Yet I allowed that I would "never say never" to the president, signaling to the administration that I would consider administration concessions. Still, when I left the Oval Office after a meeting with Clinton in July 1993, I was convinced that the president would not make changes I considered necessary for me to support the package. As I put it to David Broder of the *Washington Post*, "My guess is that they're going to get the votes from where they got them before; they just wanted to be sure that there wasn't something they could do for me."[17]

At the time, I was ambivalent. I would regret voting against the new president because I had been committed to debt reduction since I entered the Senate in 1977, and Clinton was the first chief executive to use honest figures and make a sincere effort for real debt reduction. Moreover, I knew that Jon Kyl, the likely Republican nominee for my senate seat in Arizona in the 1994 election, had informed the press that public sentiment in Arizona was against Clinton's tax plan. I knew the better vote was against it, and throughout the summer of 1993 I was comfortable with my intention to oppose the plan.

Yet I remained in touch with the White House, and in late July I reconvened talks with the administration. My first and most important demand was to strengthen the "trust fund" that the president had proposed to assure that new taxes would be used, by legal requirement, to reduce the deficit. I realized that the requirement was little more than symbolism, but I knew also that it was politically essential. Clinton contacted me and promised to see if my goal could be achieved by executive order, thus assuring my vote. I told him that I had two other problems: the gas tax and Social Security taxes. Although I realized that I had to compromise, I wanted more than just the deficit buy-down.

Within twenty-four hours, a draft of the executive order had arrived on my desk. But, as I stated at a news conference the following day, it was not close enough to the language I prescribed, and I repeated my calls for a higher threshold on Social Security taxes—a sensitive issue for retirees in Arizona—and I reiterated that if the gas tax remained at the Senate level (4.3 cents a gallon), I did not anticipate voting for the package. A reporter at the news conference quipped, "What if the president comes to you and says, 'I need your vote'?" I replied, "The Republican campaign committee is here, hoping that is what happens and I change my vote so they can make the most of it." I knew the political ramifications of my situation, and so too did the media.

The punditry in fact used all the predictable clichés during the ensuing news cycle. I was a top Republican Party target in the 1994 elections, and the "Keating Five" moniker continued to attract readers to the print media and viewers to television news. Plus, rumors of a primary challenge in Arizona surfaced at this time as Richard Mahoney, the Arizona secretary of state and son of a longtime supporter, began testing the political waters among Arizona Democratic activists. I knew also that Congressman Kyl,[18] if he were the Republican nominee for the Senate seat, would prove a formidable opponent to any Democrat in the running.

Other pressures were brought to bear on the 1993 Clinton tax vote. My failing to support the president had a down side among liberal activists in my primary. I had already garnered significant disfavor with that wing in the party for my votes in support of placing Clarence

Thomas on the Supreme Court and for my backing of some abortion restrictions. Former Arizona governor and recently appointed secretary of the interior Bruce Babbitt entered the debate over my vote. He stumped Arizona in July urging me to back Clinton's budget. "It is time for courage," he stated publicly, seeking to build pressure on me. The Democratic National Committee ran ads backing the bill, and President Clinton added that he shared my desire for "the strongest possible controls to guarantee that all the tax dollars go for deficit reduction."[19]

In spite of this effort, I had to consider the broader electorate and its conservative character. My offices received a flood of phone calls from antitax groups. As I pondered my dilemma, Democratic senator David Boren of Oklahoma switched to the opposition, thus making my vote absolutely essential to the president. Treasury Secretary Robert F. Rubin was immediately back in my office, offering modified language on the executive order. On that same day, I recall, House and Senate conferees contacted me about an improved threshold for higher Social Security taxes. But the gas tax remained at a level I could not support.

On Tuesday, August 3, President Clinton called my office and read the final language. It included all I had asked of the president. That night he went on national television and made public my commitment to the order. I was the only senator he mentioned by name. I still had not committed to vote for the bill, but Clinton, the consummate persuader, forced the issue, and one of his officials uttered to the press that the administration was "very optimistic" about my support.[20] But I was still uncommitted. In this context, Congressman Kyl saw a political opportunity with Arizona voters. He derided Clinton's concessions as "gimmicks" and warned against the political fallout from a "DeConcini flip-flop."[21] I met with Clinton again and was satisfied with the compromise struck on Social Security and the gas tax. On August 4, 1993, I decided to support the Clinton tax bill of 1993.

Speculation ran rampant on my decision to support the president's initiative. My vote resulted in a tie vote in the Senate, broken by Vice President Al Gore. Some said my support depended on President Clinton's persuading Dick Mahoney—who came out against the Clinton economic package—not to run in the primary. That was not the case. Kyl chimed in that my vote went against popular sentiment in Arizona. In the end, I concluded that voting for the package was the right thing to do, and, as it turned out in the long term, this bold initiative had a beneficial impact on the nation's economy.

Shortly after the vote, President Clinton said, "I will never forget what you did for me and this country, Dennis." He stated it twice, and it has remained with me. Long after the vote, Clinton expressed his gratitude, and while I was still a U.S. senator, he invited me twice to fly on Air Force One with him. Once we traveled to the Middle East and the other time to Europe. During these flights, he asked what he could do for me, and I responded that I hoped he would consider positions for some of my staff people. I had determined by then that I would not seek reelection, so I asked for several considerations. One, for which I am extremely grateful, was the appointment of Michael Hawkins to the U.S. Ninth Circuit Court of Appeals. A longtime friend, supporter, advisor, and outstanding jurist, Judge Hawkins has served his nation with distinction in his position. I also asked to be appointed to the board of directors of the Federal Home Loan Mortgage Corporation, and the president came through in that regard. Perhaps I overstepped boundaries when I asked him for an ambassadorial appointment to Italy, but I believed at the time that he was asking what he could do for me. As it turned out, for a variety of reasons, including Al Gore's presidential aspirations and internal politics in the state of Pennsylvania, I was not appointed as ambassador to Italy, though I was under consideration for some time. In this case, the administration let me down without much explanation.

Bill Clinton, I have concluded, would be considered one of the outstanding presidents of his era had it not been for the sexual scandals. In his terms, our nation had one of the most prolonged economic expansions in history. We balanced the budget after three decades of red ink, and we had a strong military, though many Republicans would take issue with that assessment. During the Clinton presidency, the military budget actually increased, though not at quite the rate of the first George H. W. Bush administration. Clinton's health-care legislation got mired in political turmoil, and his foreign policy in Bosnia, Serbia, Africa, the Middle East and other parts of the world caused much debate in Congress, but overall he was a nice guy, although not always consistent. His endgame appeared to center on any possible impact on him and his administration.

Even if we consider all the pluses and minuses, Bill Clinton remains one of the most popular public figures in American politics. I have marveled that he commands hundreds of thousands of dollars per speech. In 2003, I watched him on CNN's *Larry King Live* as King asked him if he was embarrassed about taking huge sums for speeches now that he was no longer the president, in light of the fact that he had assured the nation that members of his administration would not use their former positions of power to enrich themselves. His response, of course, disarmed King and the majority of viewers: "Well, you know, Larry, I now own a United States senator, and they are very expensive, and I just have to make money to support that senator." Even though I knew that was not the case—Hillary Clinton maintains her own substantial economic resources—his humorous and "Clintonesque" answer to King's departure from softball questions secured the desired result and highlighted the former president's unmatched political tools.

In Clinton's second term, as Congress impeached him, I could not help concluding that it was one of the most partisan events I ever witnessed in my years in Washington, D.C. Though I had retired from the Senate and was well situated in my new role as a lobbyist on Capitol Hill, I could not remember such vitriol from Republicans both in and out of Congress. This type of extreme partisanship has resurfaced as President George W. Bush experiences extreme political opposition from Democrats. This unhealthy atmosphere ill serves the American public and offers a sharp contrast to the more cordial atmosphere of my early years in the Senate.

Bill Clinton's election in 1992 coincided with my ascension to ranking member on two committees: Intelligence and Veterans Affairs. On Intelligence, Senator David Boren of Oklahoma left the chairmanship because of the "eight-year rule." William Cohen (R–Maine), the ranking Republican member, also left the committee and the Senate. Senators cannot chair two committees, so I had to make a choice.

I consulted my staff, political advisors in Arizona, and several colleagues. The consensus was that I should choose to become chairman of the Veterans Affairs Committee. I had a long history with veterans' organizations, and many thought I could make a difference. The political advantages were obvious, and at that time I intended to seek a fourth term in 1994. Yet I chose to chair the Intelligence Committee because of my commitment to the subject matter, and I maintained the naive notion that I could bring about consolidation of the various agencies involved in this important aspect of our government. In December 1992, I informed my colleagues that I intended to assume the chairmanship of the Intelligence Committee.

In preparation, I began forming a staff and developing a working relationship with the ranking Republican member of the committee, John Warner.[22] We overcame some initial differences in staffing—Warner wanted to appoint several of his people to the committee, and I wanted to keep those professionals who were already on staff—and soon settled into a productive working relationship. For chief of staff of the majority, I selected Norman Bradley, the Chief of the Customs Air Branch in Tucson. I had known him and worked with him for years, and he brought prestige and professionalism to the position. For deputy chief of staff, I chose Tim Carlsgaard, who had been working in my Senate office as deputy press secretary. He was smart and loyal and had matured quickly in the position.[23] With a lean, efficient, and talented staff, we formed our Intelligence Committee as Bill Clinton ascended to the Oval Office.

The new administration nominated James S. Woolsey to head the Central Intelligence Agency (CIA). In briefing papers, it seemed his résumé was exaggerated, but he was a successful Washington insider and had already accomplished much in public policy and government service. Born in Tulsa, Oklahoma, in 1941, Woolsey attended Tulsa public schools, graduating in 1959. His college and graduate school backgrounds were distinguished: Stanford bachelor's degree (1963), Oxford master's degree (Rhodes Scholar) 1965, and Yale University law degree (1968), where he was managing editor of the *Yale Law Review.* Before his nomination as CIA director, Woolsey had served in the U.S. government in several positions: ambassador to the Negotiation on Conventional and Armed Services in Europe, Vienna, 1989–91; undersecretary of the navy, 1977–79; general counsel to the U.S. Senate Armed Services Committee, 1970–73; and advisor on the U.S. delegation to the Strategic Arms Limitation Talks (Salt 1), Helsinki and Vienna, 1969–70. In addition to this distinguished service, he had been appointed to serve as delegate at large to the U.S.–Soviet Strategic Arms Reduction Talks and the Nuclear and Space Arms Talks in Geneva in 1983–86. Indeed, he seemed the ideal candidate to lead the CIA in the 1990s and the new century.

I first met Woolsey at a reception for the nominee at Brit Snyder's home. I was impressed. He had a distinguished academic background, and he appeared to be committed to making changes at the agency. His confirmation went smoothly, and his initial appearances before our committee were congenial and professional. He briefed Senator Warner and me on a number of sensitive issues and provided us with information that would shape his tenure. He worked well with our staff and helped a number of qualified people gain interviews at the CIA.

Just as soon as he had ingratiated himself to the Intelligence Committee and the staff, however, he became enamored of the CIA culture and quickly grew defensive about the agency. Many said, "That's his job," but he embraced the agency with an unusual zeal. In that vein, he prepared a budget that increased substantially the amounts for computers, foreign-language expertise, and technical intelligence gathering. It is important here to note that the CIA director does not control the National Security Agency (NSA), the Defense Intelligence Agency, or many other intelligence-gathering agencies under the purview of the Intelligence Committee. Though several past presidents considered cabinet status for the CIA director, it has become quite evident, especially after 9/11, that it should not have that position.

That administrative conundrum notwithstanding, Director Woolsey found himself an isolated bureaucrat who argued for more funds. He failed to penetrate Clinton's inner circle, which, during the early years of that administration, was focused on domestic issues. Shortly after a disturbed soul crashed a plane on the White House grounds in 1994, a joke made the rounds in Washington that it was Woolsey trying to see the president.[24] Indeed, Woolsey's influence with the new administration was minimal at best.

One of the areas on which the Intelligence Committee disagreed with Woolsey was the lack of emphasis and money placed on human "on-ground" intelligence—individuals who secured intelligence and brought this information to the agency for analysis and interpretation. Senator Warner agreed with my priorities and supported this concept. Woolsey approached the White House to trump the committee. He lobbied Tony

Lake (Clinton's national security advisor), Vice President Al Gore, and several others. I asserted that just to add more money for a few priorities and not to increase human intelligence substantially was an error. Both new at our respective jobs, Woolsey and I were on a collision course.[25]

As our budget markup approached, I advised Director Woolsey to secure tangible support from the White House. I asked that White House staff contact me, but nothing transpired. He apparently garnered no support. I called National Security Advisor Lake and Vice President Gore, but they neither indicated support for Woolsey nor renounced his budget request entirely. I called Gore again. I told him that I was going to fund my priorities—more human intelligence, but no additional amounts for other items—unless I heard from the White House. There was no response until the day of the markup. Lake called and said the White House supported Woolsey's priorities, but his call was too late. The markup had been printed, and the Intelligence Committee's priorities—with additional monies for human intelligence—were put forward for funding. The bill was passed. In fact, Senator John Kerry (D–Massachusetts) offered an amendment to cut the funding by $6 billion, an action that Republican campaign advisors exploited in the 2004 general elections. In defense of Kerry, there probably was some waste, but Senator Warner and I thought the amendment was too draconian, and we fought it. Kerry's amendment, in the end, was defeated. After the traditional route in conference committee, the Intelligence Committee markup bill for 1993 was signed into law.[26]

Thereafter, my relationship with Director Woolsey cooled to a significant degree. Relations were, at best, strained. Soon after our budget conflict, Woolsey told two senators that I had disclosed classified information. The information, actually forwarded to a reporter by Tim Carlsgaard and Brit Snyder, was not classified. After a thorough investigation by our committee, I asked for an appointment to see President Clinton about this allegation. I met with the president and Tony Lake at the White House and told him what had occurred. If, in fact, Director Woolsey had falsely accused me of disclosing classified information, I would ask for his resignation on the floor of the Senate. Tony Lake called me the next day and said that President Clinton was shocked and disturbed about this situation and that he would advise the two senators that I had not disclosed classified information. The situation ended there, but, clearly, this relationship had undergone irreparable damage. Woolsey "resigned" shortly after this incident.

The other significant issue that shaped my chairmanship on the Intelligence Committee was the Aldrich Ames case. Ames was a career, high-ranking CIA agent who spied on behalf of the Soviet Union and Russia from April 1985 through February 1994. His espionage caused severe damage to U.S. national security and undermined and compromised clandestine operations worldwide. From the earliest days of the republic, the United States has recognized the need to collect intelligence. And, as I suggested in my discussion of James Woolsey, this collection was conducted with human agents for much of our history. Technology, of course, has increased exponentially our ability to gather information, but these technical developments cannot eliminate the need for human sources of information. Concerning the Ames case, information from inside the Soviet Union gave us important insights into their intentions and capabilities. I am convinced also that when a comprehensive history of the Cold War has been crafted, human intelligence will be recognized as playing a significant role in winning that conflict.[27]

Ames's betrayal was profound and pernicious. In June 1985, he disclosed the identity of numerous clandestine agents in the Soviet Union, at least nine of whom were summarily executed. These agents, as it turned out, were at the center of our efforts to collect intelligence and counterintelligence against the Soviet Union. As a result, the United States lost opportunities to better understand internal Soviet operations at a crucial time in history. Over the next decade, Ames disclosed the identity of many U.S. agents, as well as the techniques and methods of double-agent operations. He in fact went to extraordinary lengths to learn details of our clandestine trade craft, communications techniques, and agent validation methods. Moreover, he disclosed information about U.S. counterintelligence activities that not only compromised our efforts at the time, but also made us more vulnerable to Soviet intelligence operations against us. Beyond these serious transgressions, Ames provided finished intelligence reports, current intelligence reporting, arms-control papers, and selected Department of Defense and Department of State cables.[28] Taken together, his activities enabled the Soviets and later the Russians to engage in "perception-management operations" by feeding selected information to the United States through agents they controlled without our knowledge.[29]

We held hearings, of course, and the resulting report foreshadowed the suggestions embraced in the 9/11 Commission investigation. Our investigation of Ames concluded that the FBI, the CIA, and other intelligence agencies were not working together and that this administrative obstacle enabled Ames and others to compromise sensitive information. The problem persisted until recently.[30] In 2005, President George W. Bush appointed John Negroponte to be director of national intelligence operations, responsible for multiple agencies, including the FBI and the CIA.

In the context of these troubling events that preoccupied the Intelligence Committee, the political calculus in 1994, coupled with profound changes in my personal life, provided an entirely different set of challenges and sent me into weeks of soul searching. In mid-1993, I began thinking about ending my career in the U.S. Senate, though, at first, it was an unconscious notion. It took time to make a decision, and during that process I reflected on many issues. I considered it a privilege to retire on my own volition rather than being voted out of office. Having spoken to many defeated representatives and senators, I can state with assurance that political defeat is more than a letdown.

How did I retire from the U.S. Senate? Some look at it as escape or freedom. Others suffer withdrawal or depression because they have lost the attention and notoriety that becomes part of a senator's daily life. I always recalled my father's admonition never to get carried away with yourself and think you are greater than others. So when I pondered retirement, I had much to consider. My personal life had reached a critical juncture; in 1993, I was in the midst of a separation and headed for divorce from my wife, Susie, after more than three decades of marriage. The Keating episode placed enormous stress on my family and me, caused me a significant amount of trauma, and cost a significant amount of money. Moreover, my children, who suffered much through this trying period, were understandably upset with me. Almost imperceptibly, I grew to long for relief from the strain and stress of the Senate. As I ruminated about life after the Senate, I never lost sight of the fact that it was the best job I had ever experienced in my life. I thought of Louisiana senator Russell Long's statement that it was the best job in the world. I would ask him, "You mean, Russell, that being a senator is better than being president of the United States?" He would smile and say, "You betcha." As president, he admonished, "you have to carry out the law as it is passed whether you agree with it or not. You have pressures that you cannot put off until next week or the next press conference." I thought about these comments, but still concluded that anyone involved in politics at this level would aspire to the presidency.

As I further contemplated retirement, I thought about the diversity of tasks I had performed and the gratification derived from helping constituents. Being one of a select one hundred people was indeed a distinction and an honor. My father's admonition to me that hard work was an indispensable component of virtue had influenced me greatly in my work ethic in the Senate. Being the second son, I had wanted to gain recognition from my father, so I worked hard. If I retired, I would miss the satisfaction of that hard work.

For three consecutive terms, beginning in January 1977, I had represented Arizona in the U.S. Senate and become a respected, influential, and effective public servant. I played major roles in shaping the Panama Canal Treaty and in securing Sandra Day O'Connor's appointment to the U.S. Supreme Court. My stance in the Clarence Thomas hearings, which confounded Democratic Party regulars, and my key vote in the Clinton administration's 1993 Budget Act had certainly left their marks.

From 1984 to 1995, I served as a member of the Committee on Security and Cooperation in Europe, also known as the Helsinki Commission, serving as its chairman from 1989 to 1994. The commission, established in 1976, monitors and encourages compliance between the United States and more than thirty countries that have participated in the Helsinki Final Act and in the subsequent human rights agreements and issues that compose the Helsinki Accords. The period in which I served on the commission saw the fall of the Berlin Wall, the rise of Glasnost and Perestroika, freedom for Nelson Mandela, and the elections of Lech Walesa and Vaclav Havel. Events in Angola, Bosnia, China, Czechoslovakia, El Salvador, Poland, and South Africa dominated the Helsinki agendas. I traveled the world hearing testimony regarding refugees' plights, their persecution, and their struggles for freedom. My work on this commission, I suggest, paved the way for human rights legislation at home and abroad. In particular, my work on behalf of

Soviet Jewish Refuseniks—Soviet Jews who were refused exit visas or other rights such as freedom of religion and expression (many of whom now call Tucson home)—and on behalf of others persecuted for their religious or ethnic affiliation has been a source of personal pride. As I thought further, I realized that my efforts to spread human rights ultimately took me to some of the world's most politically volatile nations, and during my watch the term *human rights* became part of the national lexicon.

My body of legislative work reflected the labor of a national figure—a senator—who was bound to regional interests. One commentator suggested that I was one of the most prolific and successful legislators to have served in Congress.[31] Some legislation I introduced received little attention, but bills addressing airline safety, antiterrorist training at airports, and the sale of missiles to Afghanistan today might seem prescient in light of the events of September 11, 2001. I sponsored more than four hundred original bills and cosponsored hundreds more as a member of the Judiciary, Appropriations, Veterans, Indian Affairs, Intelligence, and Rules and Administration committees. Rose Mofford, in introducing me at my 1994 retirement dinner in Scottsdale, estimated that legislation I introduced between 1977 and 1995 infused more than $50 billion into the Arizona economy. At the regional level, in fact, my legislation supported everything from telescopes and drug enforcement to wilderness preserves and military cemeteries. Largely through my efforts, Arizona was spared sharper military cuts and base closures during the 1980s. The troubled copper industry saw tariff protection and received a boost from government purchases thanks to some legislative handiwork.

After years of dispute with the federal government, the first resolutions were reached with American Indians on water rights and other settlements. Moreover, during an era of retrenchment of federal funding, all three Arizona state universities received funds for new building construction, including $4.57 million for the University of Arizona's Biotechnology and Insect Science Center, $25 million for the Engineering Building at Arizona State University, and $20 million for the Forestry Building at Northern Arizona University. I was proud to secure more than $2.46 billion for the CAP. The fact that the CAP, a seventy-year legislative odyssey and the dream of my distinguished predecessor Senator Carl Hayden, was finally completed in 1990 was a testament to teamwork, skill, persistence, and commitment.[32]

These reflections about foreign travel, fascinating people, intellectual stimulation, and the whole range of benefits gave me pause about retirement. I hesitated, tempted to stay on and run for reelection in 1994. As the election drew nearer, I remember well a critical period in making my decision. In late summer 1993, I was sitting in an apartment in Roslyn, Virginia. I had separated from my wife and was living alone. I was going over the calendar of functions for the campaign, which included fund-raising, political speeches, and dinners. This schedule would take me through January 1994, and as I analyzed the travel schedule, I realized I was looking at a formidable amount of campaigning and fund-raising: nearly twenty fund-raising functions between September 1993 and January 1994, and doubtlessly more to be added. I needed to raise a great deal of money, probably around $4 million. And the Keating affair, as I indicated earlier, made me a Republican target. Congressman Jon Kyl, the putative Republican nominee, had begun organizing his campaign. He was a competent congressman with a solid following on the right wing of his party. He did not, however, appeal to women, minorities, and blue-collar workers, who were among my core constituencies. Nevertheless, he posed a significant challenge because he could raise money. The Keating situation would have been a campaign issue because Kyl received more than $20,000 from Keating. As I looked at the general election, I knew it would be a difficult race. I was still confident I could prevail because I knew how to campaign and I had good people with experience committed to me.

In addition, Dick Mahoney, the Arizona secretary of state, indicated that he wanted to challenge me in the Democratic primary.[33] Earlier in the year, Mahoney, his chief of staff Sam Vagenas, my state director Barry Dill, and I met for breakfast at the Pointe Hotel and Resort on Seventh Street in Phoenix. Dick indicated that he was thinking about running for the Senate and wanted to find out whether I was going to run. At that time, I intended to seek reelection. I recalled vividly that Dick expressed great support for me and stated that he would never run against me. But if I chose not to run, he would declare his candidacy. Barry Dill and I have discussed this 1993 meeting several times in recent years, and he came away with the same interpretation of it that I did. Dick had committed to support me if I decided to run. Long before I announced that I would not seek reelection, however, he abandoned his commitment and announced that he would run for my seat in the U.S. Senate.

The Mahoneys, as most longtime Arizona residents knew at the time, maintained a prominent profile in Democratic and Catholic circles. The family patriarch, William Mahoney, knew my parents well, had been elected Maricopa County attorney, ran for the U.S. House of Representatives and barely lost, worked hard to elect Democratic candidates, served as a national committee man, and, with the election of John Kennedy in 1960, was selected to serve as ambassador to Ghana.[34] His wife, Alice, was part of the Phelan family of San Francisco and was one of the nicest people I had met in politics. Many of my friends had worked with Bill Mahoney, both professionally and politically, and when Dick announced that he would run against me in the primary, many of these people attempted to discourage him. I remember that one of these people, Dan Cracchiolo, a prominent and successful lawyer and long-time family friend, called me and said, "I can't believe Dick Mahoney is doing this. Are you really going to run, Dennis?" he asked. "Because if you are, the Cracchiolos are on your side." At the time, I assured Dan that I was running for reelection. I knew he probably had spoken with Bill and Dick Mahoney, and though Dan had worked for Bill when he was county attorney, he had also clerked with my father when he was on the Supreme Court.[35] Like the Cracchiolos, other longtime friends from my earliest campaigns stood ready to support me in this reelection effort.

In September 1993, I finally arrived at a conclusion. I had recently been to New York and raised $60,000 in an hour at the home of a luggage magnate. I knew only one person in the room. I thought to myself for the first time, "I just don't want to do this anymore."[36] I had already raised a total of $1.4 million and had to raise another $3 million to run a solid campaign. My mind filled with reasons, pro and con, about running, and within a forty-eight hour period, entirely on my own, I decided that I would not seek a fourth term. I do not know how my decision was leaked to the press, but I assume some people in Phoenix began telling political insiders that I was not going to run. I told only Gene Karp, my chief of staff. By the next day, my decision was on the streets in Phoenix. Upon learning that rumors were on the streets, I called Ron Ober and other trusted advisors and friends and told them that I intended to announce that I would not seek reelection. Dick Mahoney was already busy running, unfortunately by making negative statements about me. Another young, bright Democrat, Sam Coppersmith, who had been elected to the House, expressed interest in running for the Senate. Sam was a good congressman, and I liked him. On the Republican side, Jon Kyl was planning his campaign, though he had not made an official announcement.

I flew to Phoenix and called a press conference for September 16, 1993. I announced that I was sorry to leave the Senate, but that I did not want to go through the fund-raising efforts necessary to finance an expensive reelection effort. "I detest that part of it," I told the press. My announcement was, for the most part, a surprise. I had already raised more than $1 million and put together a political and fiscal organization thanks to my finance chairman, Earl Katz, and my campaign chairman, Ron Ober. We had rehired Ray Strother as our media consultant. He had helped immensely in my reelection campaigns of 1982 and 1988. We had also hired an opposition research analyst and were deep into research on John Kyl and Mahoney, and we had employed a pollster and telephone bank firm. When I made my announcement, I am sure many who were looking forward to the excitement of another statewide campaign were let down. I was relieved. I was young enough, at fifty-seven, to do many things I had thought about in the eighteen years I had served in the Senate. I was in good health. As my final act in calling off the campaign, I returned donations to each contributor on a pro-rata basis, an unusual move that I was not required to make.[37]

As I faced my final fifteen months in office, I determined to work as hard, or even harder, than in my first fifteen months. I was chairman of the Intelligence Committee, one of the ranking members of the Appropriations and Judiciary committees, and a senior member of the Veterans Committee. I was third in line on the Rules Committee and chairman of the Helsinki Commission. In short, I was in a very influential position to shape legislation and aid in constituent service. Moreover, I had a seasoned and motivated staff who understood me and my commitment to constituent service. It was one of the most rewarding phases of my Senate career.

When it came time to leave, I packed up my own boxes and closed down the office.[38] When my term officially ended, January 5, 1995, I took a couple months to myself and contemplated the future. My former legislative assistant, Romano Romani, had formed a public-affairs firm with Tom Parry, former chief of staff and legal counsel for Senator Hatch of Utah, and he asked me to join them. Romano, who had established a bipartisan lobbying and consulting firm in 1984, had approached me previously about this option, and I had considered it a possibility. They had demonstrated good success, with clients such as the Motion Picture Association of America, pharmaceutical companies, and a host of others. In fact, while I was in the Senate, I had formed a good relationship with Jack Valenti, president of the Motion Picture Association of America, because I chaired the subcommittee that had jurisdiction over copyrighted patents.[39] This industry had great interest in patent protection, and I played a crucial role in seeing that laws were passed, implemented, and enforced that achieved this goal. I was leaning toward working with Parry and Romani on a part time basis.[40]

During this transition, I would have considered an ambassadorship to Italy. Unfortunately, obstacles from within the Department of State, combined with a short and selective political memory at the White House, derailed these hopes. When Clinton assumed office in 1993, I pushed hard for Enzo DeChiara, a prominent Italian American businessman who had run restaurants and consulting businesses in Washington, D.C., to be appointed ambassador to Italy. He had raised significant sums for Clinton's election campaigns in his races for both governor and president. DeChiara had even taken Governor Clinton and some Arkansans businessmen to Italy on a trip that later afforded Clinton access to Italian business opportunities. That effort notwithstanding, my support for DeChiara fell on deaf ears.

President George H. W. Bush had earlier offered me the position as the first director of national drug-control policy (drug czar), but political realities—the appointment almost assured election of a Republican in my place in the Senate—dictated against that possibility. Although I would have considered working with the first President Bush, I was not as anxious to work with the Clinton administration. However, an ambassadorial post remained an attractive position to me.

I liked Bill Clinton personally, but I discerned that the concept of loyalty was not important to him. As noted earlier, I wondered if this was because he seemed willing to do almost anything necessary to succeed in gaining his objective. He could easily burn a bridge or discard a person in achieving his ends. He nevertheless maintained a coterie of longtime staffers from Arkansas. Some were competent, others not.

Ultimately, I decided to join Parry and Romani, though I elected not to buy into the firm as a partner. My friend Ron Ober gave me sound advice at the time: "Dennis, why do you want to buy into a consulting firm and have to take on some of the responsibilities of being an equity owner?" He continued, "You don't want to do that; you want to enjoy life and make a few dollars." Ron knew me well, and I took his advice. I truly enjoy my semiretirement. As a part-time lobbyist, I travel a great deal, something I have always liked. I have worked with Parry and Romani in the ten years since I left the Senate, and the experience has been both economically rewarding and professionally challenging. This decision has helped me retain ties to the federal government and continue to participate on issues of political importance to Arizona and the nation.

11 Memories and Reflections

Some members of the Senate, House of Representatives, and others not discussed earlier deserve mention here because they influenced my political career. Also, my travels throughout the world on behalf of the United States bear some consideration. This meditation is not intended to be comprehensive, and not all members of the House and Senate receive proper consideration or comment.

As noted at the outset of this volume, during the final quarter of the twentieth century I served with some of the nation's political "giants." When I entered the Senate in 1977, many of these members were referred to as "old bulls": John Stennis (D–Mississippi), James Eastland, Barry Goldwater, Ted Kennedy, Daniel Inouye, Ted Stevens, Robert Byrd, Russell Long, Jacob Javitz (R–New York), Warren Magnuson, Henry "Scoop" Jackson, Herman Talmadge, and Edmund Muskie (D–Maine). Among them, Byrd was by no means "one of the boys." He maintained a distance from most senators and was relatively humorless, though during my eighteen-year tenure he assumed the role of scholar and historian of the U.S. Senate. And though I mentioned Senator Inouye prominently earlier, I want to reemphasize that he was a quality person and perhaps the most outstanding senator I had the pleasure of serving with during my years in Washington. He was intelligent, dignified, and able.

A second tier of younger senators included Sam Nunn, Lloyd Bentsen, Alan Cranston, Robert Packwood, Mark Hatfield, Thomas Eagleton (D–Missouri), Joe Biden, Dale Bumpers (D–Arkansas), and David

Pryor (D–Arkansas)—they were the most prominent, anyway. I grew to know and admire most of these younger senators, who were for the most part my contemporaries.

Ted Kennedy truly represented the liberal wing of the Democratic Party. A charming, smart man and a great speaker, he always had a great sense of humor and was unfailingly gracious to me. Though we had our political differences, Kennedy seemed never to be without something nice to say about me. He came to Arizona and spoke on my behalf when the political winds were right. He felt deeply about his liberal positions, and I enjoyed him immensely during the eighteen years we spent together on the Judiciary Committee. When a left-of-center bill would emanate from Judiciary, Kennedy, with a smile, would say, "Come on, Dennis, you can vote for this one, no one will know in Arizona. . . . When we put out a press release, we will leave your name off of the bill." We would laugh, and sometimes I would support him, but sometimes I would not. When Kennedy, Metzenbaum, and other liberals went after William Rehnquist in the Judiciary Committee, I opposed them, but we never had a bitter exchange. Indeed, our relationship was and is one of mutual respect.

Another great senator was Ted Stevens of Alaska. He was tough and could be nasty as hell, but he delivered for the people of Alaska. Forceful and brazenly candid, he offered no apologies. Fortunately for me, he helped Arizona on a number of occasions. I returned the favors by voting for or persuading others to support measures coming from Senator Stevens for Alaska. His three-decade career and his position as chairman of the Appropriations Committee placed him in a very powerful position.

Some of the "old bulls" delivered well for their states. Byrd was legendary for all of the federal jobs and appropriations he secured for West Virginia. Magnuson and Jackson of Washington utilized their influence for luring federal funds and projects for defense contractors such as Boeing. Mississippi's senators Stennis and Eastland similarly used their seniority and clout to attract defense industries and the jobs that went with them to their comparatively less prosperous southern state.

Of course, my senior colleague Barry Goldwater achieved national prominence, and when there was a Republican in the White House, he was unafraid to exercise his deserved prestige to deliver for Arizona.

Goldwater was a legend, and, with the exception of Carl Hayden, few Arizona lawmakers have approached his influence. As my successor Jon Kyl put it, Goldwater "could be as tough as the Petrified Forest; as memorable as the Grand Canyon; as unyielding as the Sonoran Desert; and sometimes, as prickly as an ocotillo."[1] Goldwater was much more than these metaphors suggest; he could be humorous, difficult, and profane. He was the first and probably the last person to address me as "Denny," a moniker that never really agreed with me. Yet, for some reason, I never tried to dissuade him from using it. He was not an establishment Republican, and his famous comment to his friend Senator George McGovern (D–South Dakota) in 1968 echoed humorously his own landslide loss to Lyndon Johnson eight years earlier: "George, if you've got to lose, lose big." Certainly, the numerous books, articles, and documentaries that trace and analyze the career of this conservative icon serve as testament to his enduring influence in Arizona, the United States, and the world.

Like Goldwater, Wendell Ford (D–Kentucky) represented his state with dignity. He became my neighbor when I received my first permanent office space. A former governor, Ford was good-natured, humorous, and very smart. Our staffs grew to appreciate each other, and our proximity promoted our personal friendship. My mother especially liked Wendell Ford. As governor and senator, Ford had met her while she served on the Democratic National Committee as national committeeperson from Arizona. She and Ford had served together when Ford was governor. When she was ninety-two years old, my mother asked me, in response to my request for a donation to my own campaign, "What about my friends Wendell Ford, Scoop Jackson, and Fritz Hollings?" She was always anxious to contribute to those three particular senators, especially Ford. Hollings would often kid me in front of others, "My gosh, Dennis's mother, Ora, gives more money to my campaign than she gives to her own son." Although a lighthearted exaggeration, it made a good story because it was extraordinary that someone from as far away as Arizona sent checks of $1,000 or $2,000 to someone she had met only a few times. Hollings always let me know that he appreciated my mother's commitment to the Democratic Party.

I cherished the true, close friendships I developed in the Senate. New York's Alfonse D'Amato served with me on the Appropriations

Committee. We enjoyed each other's company and forged a strong friendship. We shared a love of fine Italian wines, discussed our mutual heritage, and worked diligently on several programs, including the Center for Missing and Exploited Children. Our friendship was forged in 1986 while I delivered a speech to a group of bankruptcy lawyers at the Grand Hyatt Hotel atop Grand Central Station in New York. An old friend from Tucson and San Diego, Bud Grarette, the CEO of Bowery Savings, attended the event, and we planned to get together after I completed my speech. He asked if I would go to a D'Amato fund-raiser at the same hotel with him. For a few seconds I hesitated, wondering if I should attend a Republican fund-raiser, but quickly I decided that I wanted to go. Besides, I liked D'Amato, and we were already developing a friendly working relationship. We joined a throng of two thousand people that included several Republican senators. I was immediately asked to speak, and I affirmed that Senator D'Amato was an outstanding public servant. I emphasized the remarkable accomplishments that benefited the state of New York.

D'Amato never forgot my impromptu talk and in an act of inspired generosity offered to host a fund-raiser for me. The notion of a senator from the other party hosting such an event, though not unprecedented, was rare. Held at the exclusive East River Club in New York City, it garnered $65,000 for my 1988 reelection campaign, which seemed like a windfall to me, though Lloyd Bentsen of Texas raised $280,000 at a "Democratic" fund-raiser in New York City at the same time. Still, for an East Coast Republican to host a fund-raiser for a southwestern Democrat appeared incongruous, but in this case friendship and respect trumped party allegiance.

Another good friend to this day is Pennsylvania's Arlen Specter. A Republican with a brilliant legal mind that made him a renowned prosecutor, he served as the lead attorney in the John F. Kennedy assassination investigation. In that role, he arrived at the "one bullet theory," which says that only one bullet ricocheted through Kennedy's body and bounced around several other places, killing Kennedy and injuring Governor John Connelly as well. Though many ridiculed his theory, I read his treatise on the topic and was convinced he was correct in his analysis. We shared gossip from our respective parties, protected our sources of information, and formed a solid working relationship. When traveling as chairman of the Helsinki Commission, I was accompanied by Senator Specter. Though not a member of the commission, he would request to travel with our congressional delegation. During these lengthy trips, he was not shy about offering his opinions on any number of issues. I always tried to allow members who traveled with me to express their views to any world leader. Senator Specter took full advantage of this opportunity. It was during these trips especially that I grew to like and admire him. He and his wife almost always had a suggestion or two about how to improve on the various logistical challenges created by long flights. One idea that struck a chord was to travel during the day instead of night when going to Europe or the Middle East. He asked, "Why leave in the afternoon and fly all night?" so that one had to sleep upon arriving at the destination. I took his suggestion, and we modified our departure times; it turned out to be a much better way to travel. Although in his never-ending efforts to do things the right way, he rubbed some people the wrong way, and although he was not the most popular member among the Republican caucus, he became a friend to me and garnered my respect as a good lawyer and legislator.

Yet another Republican with whom I formed a good friendship was Iowa's Chuck Grassley. We served together on the Judiciary Committee, and though a very conservative businessman and farmer, Grassley was great fun in social settings. He cultivated a reputation for being stingy and tightfisted—a kind of latter-day Fibber McGee, who scrimped to save every dollar. His "aw shucks" persona scarcely disguised a keen intelligence that served well his constituents in Iowa.

New Mexico's Pete Domenici and I became good friends. Four years my senior in the Senate, he was very hardworking and conscientious. He traveled seldom and remained focused on his jobs in the Appropriations and Budget committees. On Appropriations, he served as ranking member of one of the subcommittees I chaired. We worked together for Arizona and New Mexico and pushed through some tough law enforcement programs that impacted our border states. Customs, the Secret Service, INS, ATF, Border Patrol, and numerous other criminal investigation agencies benefited from our cooperative approach. He bargained hard for his state, and as we worked together, we socialized in Washington, D.C., from time to time. Yet, when I left the Senate, our relationship changed, and Pete had little time for me. I would occasionally see him on an airplane, and he would ask how I was doing or if I was making money. I would respond appropriately, but it was clear I was no longer in the inner circle. When you leave the Senate, you leave. Senators, in fact, are too busy to have a life of their own, and personal relationships, which take time, seem to drift away when one leaves office. The perquisites of elective office disappear as well, though I still have access to the Senate floor, parking, use of elevators, and the ability to travel to funerals with an official delegation.

Another Republican, Bill Cohen of Maine, who later became secretary of defense in the Clinton administration, lived two blocks from me. For a number of years, we would commute together, though I usually drove him home because his wife would drive him to the Capitol in the morning. An interesting guy, a conscientious senator, and a moderate in his political views, he, like me, oftentimes found himself at odds with his party. This was especially true during the Reagan years. Through diligence and hard work, he emerged as one of the most influential members of the Armed Services and Intelligence committees. He and Oklahoma's Democrat David Boren worked in bipartisan harmony to help raise the level of professionalism of that committee. Based on this productive precedent, John Warner, the ranking member, and I worked well together after I became chairman of the committee. Warner, I recall, was a deep-thinking, methodical senator who was careful in his approach to problem solving. As a former secretary of the navy in the Nixon administration, he was predisposed to trust the Department of Defense in almost all matters. We had one memorable standoff concerning staff appointments (noted in chap. 10), but in that situation good friend Wendell Ford helped me persuade Warner that we should build on the bipartisan example established earlier. We never subsequently had any substantive or partisan disagreements on that committee. We felt strongly about the sanctity of our national security; we concurred that intelligence operations were a fundamental threshold to effective military policy; and we were of the same mind concerning the CIA and its shortfalls, especially during the directorship of James Woolsey. We investigated the Aldrich Ames espionage case and others, and in these delicate matters I became convinced that John Warner was an outstanding American and a great senator.

Mark Hatfield of Oregon was another truly outstanding Senate Republican. A deeply religious moderate, he, too, experienced the trauma of an ethics probe. Significantly, it did not diminish his capabilities as a lawmaker, and he was one of the finest people I met in the Senate. His moderate political views caused traditional Republicans no small amount of consternation, and my experiences of being at odds with mainstream Democrats caused me, at times, to identify with him.

Ben Nighthorse Campbell (R–Colorado) came to the Senate after serving three terms in the House of Representatives (he was originally elected as a Democrat). He and I became fast friends. A jeweler by trade, a Harley Davidson motorcycle aficionado, and a black belt in judo, he was the only American Indian in the Senate.[2] On one occasion, when I visited his jewelry shop and walked around his hometown, everybody I saw told me they supported his election to the Senate. He did things the people of Colorado wanted and expected. He changed parties, but he remained an outstanding legislator and a fascinating person.

Vermont's Pat Leahy made a distinct and favorable impression on me from the outset, and I consider him a friend. I met Pat when he was a prosecutor in Vermont and I was a prosecutor in Arizona. I first became acquainted with him at a national district attorneys meeting, where he was in line to become president of the National Association of District Attorneys (NADA). It was during this time that he decided to run for the U.S. Senate, and some of his friends in NADA asked both Republicans and Democrats who were members of the association to contribute to his campaign. These contributions, Leahy's supporters suggested, would illustrate his national and bipartisan appeal to voters in Vermont. I think I gave $100 because I had met him only once and did not really know him at the time. As it turned out, he and his wife, Marcel, became good friends to our family. All of us lived in McLean, Virginia, and our children attended the same schools. He held liberal views on most issues of public policy, and our differences were most evident when we served together on the Judiciary Committee.[3] Senator Leahy was a joy to know, and I admired his work and dedication in the Senate.

Another New England senator, Claiborne Pell (D–Rhode Island), was one of the most gentle, kindest people I served with in the Senate. Considered an "old bull," Pell maintained great interest in Arizona because his grandchildren lived in the Grand Canyon State. His work in the area of human rights was fair, balanced, and instructive to me; and access to higher education became associated with "Pell grants," one of his most important legacies.

A handful of other Democrats made life in the Senate a pleasure. Max Baucus of Montana and Jeff Bingaman of New Mexico were wonderful colleagues with whom I worked on western issues. Bill Bradley of New Jersey was a brilliant thinker whose athletic background helped him in numerous ways—though, as I indicated earlier, I felt he often placed political expediency ahead of loyalty.

Female members of the Senate were relatively rare when I arrived in Washington in 1977. In fact, when I was inaugurated, there were no women members. Paula Hawkins (D–Florida) was elected in 1980, and after her arrival, two women won election to the Senate from their respective states: Barbara Mikulski (D–Maryland) and Nancy Kassebaum (R–Kansas) served with distinction. Later, Carol Mosley Braun (D–Illinois) defeated a very popular incumbent, Alan Dixon, in the primary—in large part due to his vote in favor of Clarence Thomas. I found Senator Braun a quick study and an exceptionally bright person. I liked her as soon as we met. We became nominal friends and worked together well on legislation. I admired the way she operated within the Senate. Unfortunately, she committed a political mistake, accepting questionable contributions and travel monies, and was defeated in her bid for reelection. Still, I thought she brought a fresh voice to the Senate and at the time had a bright future.

Senator Mikulski was a firebrand liberal and former House representative from Baltimore. My mother, in fact, had met her before I did, when Mikulski served on the Baltimore City Council and both had attended Democratic National Committee events. I recall my mother telling me about this feisty, tough person and finally met her when she was elected to the House of Representatives. I witnessed her work indefatigably for Walter Mondale in 1984, Mike Dukakis in 1988, and Bill Clinton in 1992. In 1984, while I worked closely with Mondale and attended most strategy sessions, Mikulski headed the Women's Political Caucuses, and I remember how she fought to get her points of view across and raise the many women's issues that she thought President Reagan had ignored. Coming from a conservative western state, I thought that some of her ideas would not play well, but she was determined to have her way. Unfortunately for our effort, Reagan won reelection in one of the most lopsided elections in U.S. history. Representative Mikulski nevertheless moved forward, running for the U.S. Senate in a contested primary and spirited general election. She became a friend and, like me, was able to secure an assignment on the Appropriations Committee during her freshman term. She was assigned to my committee, which, as I noted, had jurisdiction over various law enforcement agencies, the Treasury Department, White House expenditures, the Internal Revenue Service, and the General Services Administration. While in the House, she had worked to bring outstanding federal buildings to the state of Maryland, and on the Senate Appropriations Committee she worked to construct outstanding structures for federal agencies in Maryland. She secured millions of federal dollars for her state and protected the jobs of federal workers who lived there.

Her House colleague Stenny Hoyer (D), who hailed from Maryland's Fifth District, served on the same Appropriations subcommittee in the House of Representatives. He chaired the subcommittee on the House side, and I chaired it on the Senate side. We were the most effective law enforcement team that Congress had in many years. We also alternately chaired the Helsinki Commission. We agreed on human rights issues, worked closely on law enforcement issues as they pertained to the Helsinki Commission, and through it all Hoyer continually demonstrated his political acumen. He twice tried to become majority leader in the House. I lobbied my Arizona colleagues, but he could not override his opposition. That defeat notwithstanding, Hoyer and I have remained friends.

Tom Lantos (D–California) of Los Angeles, another House member, became a friend through our work together on the Helsinki Commission. He was born in Hungary and escaped with his parents as a young boy. As a Jew, he experienced the discrimination of both the Nazis and Communists in his formative years. In fact, the Nazis targeted his family for extermination, and his stories concerning his fight for survival were inspiring. Tom and I traveled through Europe and the Soviet Union several times, and I enjoyed his numerous contacts and his insights into European political affairs.

Pennsylvania's Jack Murtha, whom I mentioned earlier, was another House member who impressed me with his work ethic, knowledge, and dedication. A moderate to conservative Democrat, Murtha worked closely with me on Appropriations Committee business, especially as it related to Defense Department issues. He was direct, usually saying, "I need this. Can you help me?" His word was his bond, and as I worked on joint committees with him, I grew to respect him.

Representative Bob Stump (R–Arizona), who began his career as a conservative Democrat and soon found his philosophical home on the conservative wing of the Republican Party, knew me and my family long before we served in Congress together. We were friends and remained so during our tenures. He was very influential in Arizona's delegation and served his state and nation with distinction.

Washington's Norm Dicks was another House member with whom I developed a solid working relationship. He had served as chief of staff for Senator Warren Magnuson, the longtime Washington senator who was chairman of the Appropriations Committee when I came to the Senate. Dicks's successful run for the House also included a freshman appointment to the House Appropriations Committee. This unusual committee assignment was testament to his political skill and the numerous contacts he developed during his years on Magnuson's staff. Representative Dicks was a staunch proponent of national defense and national security, and he served on the House Intelligence Committee when I was chairman of the Senate committee. We had a few disagreements, of course, particularly concerning the early Clinton budget proposals, but Dicks stood out, like a few others, as an outstanding legislator.

Another influential House Republican whom I admired was Henry Hyde from Chicago. He served in the House for well more than thirty-five years and at various times chaired the Judiciary and Foreign Affairs Committees. A big man with a somewhat intimidating bearing, Hyde never downplayed his staunch conservatism. I found him to be a wonderful person—both astute and diplomatic in terms of working both inside and outside his party. When the House and Senate Judiciary Committees worked together on issues, I oftentimes found myself on the same side with Hyde, even though we were in opposing political parties.

This list of senators and their strengths and weaknesses could go on for several pages. Democratic Senator Frank Lautenberg of New Jersey, for example, was an outstanding lawmaker and friend, who returned to the Senate after the resignation of Robert Torricelli. He was a multimillionaire who had sold his computer chip company and then run for the Senate; we had many memorable foreign trips together and worked for better treatment from the State Department. Howell Heflin of Alabama, a conservative Democrat with a judicial temperament—he was a judge in Alabama—became a friend. Richard Lugar (R–Indiana), Paul Laxalt, Mitch McConnell (R–Kentucky), Connie Mack (R–Florida), Joe Lieberman (D–Connecticut), Joe Biden, and Carl Levin (D–Michigan) were dedicated public servants who made significant contributions while I served in the Senate. Whether my fellow public servants were Republican or Democrat, liberal or conservative, I rarely, if ever, let partisanship get in the way of friendship or working relationships. Almost all were hardworking and dedicated to their states and their nation.

Orrin Hatch, the Republican senator from Utah, was elected to the U.S. Senate in 1976, the same year as I. A relatively unknown transplant from Pittsburgh, Pennsylvania, he was a good attorney who held deep religious beliefs. A determined individual, Hatch overcame formidable odds to win his race for the Senate. Prior to his election, he had held no public office and was thus a political outsider and dark horse opposing three-term Democratic incumbent Frank E. Moss.[4] Campaigning on a platform of limited government, tax restraint, and personal integrity, he upset Moss in the general election with 54 percent of the vote and has never looked back. When he first arrived in Washington, he demonstrated his very conservative political ideology, and many of us referred to him and others of his ilk as "bomb throwers." During President Carter's term of office, Hatch and other ultraconservatives found themselves in the minority and had great difficulty stopping any Democratic initiative. I watched Hatch with interest as he took the offense, offering amendments to any legislation and thus forcing the Democrats to vote an all kinds of issues, many of which were not directly related to the legislation under consideration. He became particularly adept at this form of obstruction, and I admired his tenacity and effectiveness.

In 1980, when Ronald Reagan won the presidency and the Republicans took control of the Senate shortly thereafter, Hatch no longer was considered a "bomb thrower," but instead a constructive legislator. He worked with Democrats such as Kennedy, Biden, Eastland, and many others. He and I worked extremely well together on multiple issues in the Judiciary Committee. We also served together on a number of subcommittees and passed much legislation. Orrin Hatch was and is a skillful lawmaker, albeit a very conservative one, possessing the ability to work with anyone and to compromise for the benefit of the American people.

Harry Reid (D–Nevada), who has risen to the position of minority leader in the Senate, is a very unassuming, quiet man, but smart and effective in many ways. Born in the small mining town of Searchlight, Nevada, Reid was raised in a small cabin without indoor plumbing. He attended law school, served as lieutenant governor of Nevada, then won two terms in the U.S. House of Representatives in 1982 and 1984. In 1986, Nevadans elected Reid to the Senate, where he quickly gained a reputation as a consensus builder and an effective lawmaker. He never hesitated to move toward Democratic Party leadership, and he often found it difficult to reconcile the party's position with his more conservative constituents. A testament to Reid's political acumen was his solid 2004 reelection victory in a Republican state, although Tom Daschle of South Dakota could not navigate the perilous political waters in his state.

After Reid was first elected to the Senate in 1986, I helped him secure a position on the coveted Appropriations Committee. I liked him as soon as I met him, and I welcomed the presence of another westerner on Appropriations. I also convinced my colleagues that we needed another westerner on the Steering Committee and succeeded in this effort. Gene Karp, my chief of staff, called Reid to offer advice on one of several issues, and the Nevadan told Karp, "I may be a Democrat, but I have a memory like an elephant." He said that he would never forget my efforts on his behalf, and to this day he calls me to thank me. He is a fine person. Although he leads an even smaller minority in the Senate today and faces enormous challenges, I believe he is most qualified to lead the Democrats back to the majority.

Finally, I want to offer observations on the presidents with whom I served. They were distinct individuals who served their nation and the world with, for the most part, dignity. Jimmy Carter was the first president with whom I served. Although he had been governor of Georgia, he seemed a politically naive individual. When I first met him, I thought to myself, "This is a nice guy." He was sincere, almost sweet, when he spoke with you. Unfortunately for Carter, he truly believed he had a mandate from the American people to arrive in Washington and change everything. And when I say everything, I mean everything. No longer were special interests going to dictate policy or to influence legislation. No longer would powerful members of the Senate or House control or bottle up initiatives. Worse for some, no longer were state dinners and functions at the White House to have hard liquor served. He even sold the *Sequoia*, the presidential yacht. His proposed $50 tax cut was laughed out of town. His manner alienated many at the outset of his term. He presented proposed legislation in such a haughty fashion, as if to say, "I know what is best, and you guys on Capitol Hill need to just do what I want." Shortly after I arrived in Washington, I learned the level and degree of his weakness. In introducing his legislative plan to House and Senate leaders Tip O'Neill (D–Massachusetts), Robert Byrd, and others, he lectured this veteran group and never sought their input.

When Carter placed the CAP on a hit list of western water projects, I became outwardly critical of him and ultimately did not vote for his reelection in 1980, instead voting for the other guy (Reagan). My anger with the president of the United States, a member of my own party who wanted to wipe out the most important fundamental water project in the history of Arizona, prompted this vote. In another instance, I recall meeting with President Carter regarding an issue that pertained to Davis Monthan Air Force Base in Tucson. We were attempting to put Kolb Road underground in the area where it crossed through the air base. The Department of Defense raised objections, so I went to the president to address this problem. I came away from this meeting astounded that he knew a great deal, even the minutiae, about Davis Monthan that I didn't know. Despite my often negative views of Carter, he was a decent man and a religious person, and when he left office, it was a great personal defeat. But he has risen now to a different calling.

His work with Habitat for Humanity reflects accurately his moral and spiritual commitment to humankind, and the construction of this low-cost housing and the volunteerism inherent in that process sets an example for all of us. He also established the Carter Peace Institute in Atlanta, Georgia. He won a Nobel Prize for his efforts to bring about peaceful settlements to international conflicts. He was, as I discussed earlier, the president who put through the Panama Canal Treaty. A truly refined and remarkable individual, President Carter unfortunately was unable to discern the difference between the statehouse in Georgia and the White House in Washington, D.C.

Ronald Reagan was a stunningly popular president. He appeared to be one of the boys. I enjoyed thoroughly going to see him at the White House, whether he called on me or if I asked to see him. He was a great storyteller. One time he called me down with a group of other senators to discuss the prayer-in-school amendment. I supported the idea. He began to talk about the days when he played high school football, and he would pray before the game. He wondered how anyone could object. After all, he mused, praying was voluntary; inevitably someone would just say, "Let's say a prayer," and everyone would hold hands and pray. When he was asked, "Was it always a Christian prayer?" he would answer yes, that it was the Lord's Prayer or some similar prayer. I thought to myself, "How interesting that the president would equate this issue to a high school football game rather than see it as the constitutional issue that it is." Although I was surprised at his simplification of this complex and emotional issue, I thought he was remarkable in his persistence in national-security goals. He wanted to outmatch the Soviet Union with weapons that would bury them—not militarily, but economically. In retrospect, Reagan proved to be correct in his assessment of the situation, and the nation is indebted to him because of that resolve, although not for his efforts to eliminate the Department of Education and legal services for the poor or to cut aid to welfare mothers by 40 percent.

Vice President George H. W. Bush succeeded Reagan to the presidency. I thought he was a fine president, and I liked him. Though I did not cross over and vote Republican, as I did in 1980, his election in 1988 was no surprise to me. He was defeated after one term in part because he let the Democrats, primarily George Mitchell, talk him into raising taxes despite his now infamous proclamation, "Read my lips, no new taxes," a contradiction that promoted questions about his ability to lead and caused his base within the Republican Party to abandon him. I agreed with his handling of the Gulf War, though his son would not have been saddled with the Iraq issue today—as it is currently configured—had he moved on Saddam Hussein at the time.

I would rate Reagan highest as a president because of his resolute stand on national-policy issues. Clinton and Bush were good presidents. Clinton's economic policies and political instincts distinguished him from many others, but Bush's solid approach was unfortunately disrupted by an economic downturn and his inability to adjust. As I noted earlier, Carter, though an admirable person, failed to understand the subtleties and nuances of the executive office.

These reflections and opinions touch on the careers of these distinguished Americans in an impressionistic rather than exhaustive fashion. Innumerable others who served in the House and Senate also impacted me in profound ways. These impressions and observations are forever part of me. These men and women added substance, texture, and joy to the most memorable eighteen years of my life.

Foreign travel as a U.S. senator differs significantly from travel as a private citizen. In 1978, two years into my first term, I took my first and one of my most eventful foreign trips as a senator. Senator Abraham Ribicoff (D–Connecticut), chairman of the Government Affairs and Operations Committee, decided to take a congressional trip to the Soviet Union. I was one of thirteen senators who, with their wives, took this trip. I suspected that my work on behalf of human rights in the Soviet Union—particularly my efforts in the area of religious freedom and my opposition to jailing those who desired to practice religion—attracted his attention. Most cases involved Jews, though Christians and Muslims also suffered from Soviet repression.[5] My deep involvement in Arizona's Jewish community and in various national groups brought me into contact with a number of remarkable activists. Religious oppression caused me great concern and motivated me to take action. I spoke to groups throughout the United States and became deeply involved in antipersecution movements. This trip to the Soviet Union enabled me to contact several important Refuseniks in Leningrad and Moscow. In fact, I brought along a number of items that were considered contraband objects: Jewish religious icons, clothing, grooming accessories, magazines, and cigarettes.

The plane and flight were noteworthy. We boarded what was once President Johnson's Air Force One plane, took off, and headed for

Shannon, Ireland, where we refueled. Seniority took precedence as the senators were seated from front to back in their pecking order. I sat near the rear of the plane. From Shannon, we departed for Helsinki, and I read my State Department and Intelligence Committee briefings with great interest, enjoying the hot food and drinks, and relishing the first-class accommodations. We disembarked in Helsinki, met various dignitaries there, and then headed to the Soviet Union, where our first stop was in Leningrad.

We checked into the government-run hotel and attended a welcoming ceremony that took several hours; then, with our evening free, my press secretary Bob Maynes, Susie, and I commenced looking for Refuseniks. Bob had several addresses and a set of directions, and we secured a taxi. I was sure the driver was a government informant. He took us on a long, circuitous route to the neighborhood. We found the street, but the address was at a building that had been demolished. The driver helped find some alternative addresses, and we entered another building. There we looked up several individuals who had received information that we were going to contact them. They told us to step outside so our conversations could not be overheard. They told us of their plight; we took notes and left them some items. The following night we did the same and came away with testimony regarding numerous violations of the Helsinki Accord.

The Helsinki Accord, drafted in 1975, was signed by Leonid Brezhnev on behalf of the Soviet Union and by President Ford on behalf of the United States. This international accord stated, in part, that all governments would abide by human rights and standards of freedom in terms of selection of leaders, freedom of religious practices, and a variety of other related issues. Of course, the Soviets violated all of these tenets, and we pressed them hard every time we met with their leaders.

The trip continued to Moscow, where we met with Brezhnev and other leaders. These meetings were marked by a great deal of listening on our part, which was difficult for thirteen senators. I recall vividly the Soviet leaders expounding for hours about the enlightenment of Soviet rule, Soviet economic prosperity, the superiority of their society and culture, and, of course, the inferiority of the United States. After three hours of interminable and predictable pronouncements, I addressed Brezhnev directly about his country's refusal to allow people out of the country. I provided him a list of names; he was not impressed. He responded with recrimination, emphasizing that the United States itself violated the rights of African Americans, Native Americans, and other minorities.

We then took pictures with Brezhnev.[6] During the photo session, I handed Brezhnev an envelope with more than two dozen names of Refuseniks. The list included the period of time they had been waiting to leave the Soviet Union and where they had been detained or incarcerated, and an accompanying note asked if, as a gesture of goodwill to the United States and the Helsinki Accords, these people could be released. I never knew if he read the envelope's contents.

As the trip progressed, we settled into a pattern: dinner, opera or ballet, then visits to as many Refuseniks as possible. I remember one distinguished medical doctor who wanted to practice his Jewish faith. His participation in "underground activities," practicing Judaism, had caused him to be jailed on several occasions. When we went to visit him—we needed flashlights to navigate the darkened stairways—we were greeted with a cake decorated like an American flag. There was a picture of President Kennedy on the wall. The doctor and his family had expected Senator Ribicoff to attend this meeting, but Ribicoff had been asked to decline because the Carter administration did not want to confront the Soviets on these issues. That nonconfrontational policy notwithstanding, I had decided to meet with the doctor.

The meeting lasted until 4:00 A.M., and when we left, there were no taxis and no traffic. The doctor and a friend walked us down the street, and he could tell that we were not going to find any transportation. However, when a car with its parking lights on appeared suddenly, the doctor said, "I imagine that this car will take you to your hotel." When the doctor asked the driver if he could take us to our hotel, he said that he would take us where we wanted to go. I tried to pay the driver, but he refused. There was no meter in the car.

The following afternoon we went to see another Refusenik at his apartment. We talked briefly and agreed to return the following day so he could give us some information to deliver to a son who lived in Richmond, Virginia. The persecution he himself had suffered was disturbing: on occasion, he would hang out a sign that said, "Long Live Israel," but he was arrested, of course, and he lost his job as a teacher.

When we returned to meet with him the next day, his wife said that he had gone to the public gymnasium but was detained by the police. We tried to contact the police. That afternoon our embassy took our request that he be released to the foreign ministries office, and we were assured that he was being asked questions only about his employment and membership in the gym. In time, I learned that he was held in captivity for three days and questioned severely about our visit. I did not wish to cause this man any pain or distress. Two years later he and his wife were granted visas to travel to the United States. They have become U.S. citizens and now live in Richmond, Virginia, with his family. For many years, he sent me a Christmas card, always thanking me for my role in changing his life. It never ceases to be a moving experience to receive this type of message.[7]

I took many trips to other countries, usually in behalf of the Helsinki Commission. We would often stop in London to meet with Prime Minister Margaret Thatcher, her successor John Major, or members of Parliament. Six times I traveled to Israel. I visited Egyptian president Hosni Mubarak on a number of occasions. In fact, one time, when Senator Specter was traveling with me, we met with Mr. Mubarak and were advised that Yasir Arafat was in the country. We asked for a meeting, and the president arranged it. The next day, there was Arafat, adorned with weapons and wearing army fatigues. As we talked, I reflected on the numerous times Senator Specter and I had denounced his terrorist activities on the floor of the Senate, and there we were together, pondering peace in the Middle East.

We traveled to Syria on two occasions, Saudi Arabia three times, and Jordan four times. We also visited Qatar, Dubai, and Turkey. In most cases, we would meet with the head of state. In Israel, we always met with the prime minister, foreign minister, defense minister, and head of the opposition party. I was always deeply impressed with Simon Peres. Benjamin Netanyahu was also a great leader, but he had trouble with the art of political compromise. Menachem Begin, in contrast, saw the light—compromise was the only way to get some sort of peace—and, of course, Camp David was a remarkable success for President Carter, the Palestinians, the Israelis, and the Egyptians.[8]

I also visited Taiwan twice, as well as Pakistan and India. In India, I first went to New Delhi and met Prime Minister Indira Gandhi shortly before she was assassinated in 1984 by two of her Sikh bodyguards who claimed to be avenging the insult heaped on the Sikh nation. She was kind to my wife, the rest of our group, and me. We discussed U.S.–Soviet relations for more than an hour and later conferred with the foreign minister. Afterward, we met the prime minister's son, Rajiv Gandhi, and his wife. He later became head of the Congress Party and prime minister, and his wife was recently elected head of the Congress Party and is a leader in her own right. Although born in Italy, she spoke English fluently and had a great command of domestic and foreign affairs.

India was among the most fascinating countries I encountered during my tenure in the Senate—highly technical and advanced in parts, but poor and degraded in other sections. In Calcutta, I visited Mother Theresa's orphanage, a most impressive expression of humility and caring. In the evening, I attended a dinner at one of the government officials' homes; it was in an area that was deemed luxurious, but one would never know it. The streets teemed with people sleeping on the roadsides, and in the mornings the authorities would pick up those who had passed away during the night. Calcutta, the cultural center for South Asia, supported an opera, high-technology manufacturing, and automobile and jet engine factories, but at the same time grinding poverty provided an overarching theme to this democracy with horrendous problems.

From India, we flew to Pakistan and met President Zia-ul-Haq, who a few months later was killed in an airplane crash. Zia, though optimistic about the U.S.–Pakistan relationship, wanted F-15 airplanes that Pakistan had paid for yet had not received, and I carried his message to the State Department. We pressed him on human rights, and he listened better than Brezhnev had a few years earlier. After meeting Zia, I flew to Peshawar on the border with Afghanistan. At the time, the Soviets were entrenched in their disastrous occupation, and the United States was supplying the Afghan freedom fighters—the Mujahadeen—with stinger missiles. I objected to this policy. For years, I had attempted to stop the proliferation of stinger missiles, but my efforts succeeded only in one instance in the Middle East. The Mujahadeen drove my entourage about three kilometers into Afghanistan and pointed out some combat areas where they had engaged Soviet forces. We returned to Peshawar and flew back to the United States via Dubai and London.

As noted earlier, I served on the Helsinki Commission for more than twelve years and was chairman for about half that time. I traveled to eastern Europe and to all the republics of the former Soviet Union. With the fall of the Berlin Wall in the late 1980s, we suggested to the leaders of these republics that they must move in a more democratic direction. Some of them, especially those in Uzbekistan and Tajikistan, had difficulty incorporating democratic values into the new political order. For years, if they provided troops and resources for distant Moscow, they were left alone and controlled their region in autocratic fashion. On one trip to the capital of Tajikistan, Dushanbe, we encountered a riot, and our motorcade took a circuitous detour around the disturbance. Opponents and dissidents to the new regime objected to corruption in government, and several leaders experienced the wrath of the populace. These leaders, though committed Communists, nevertheless were anti-Moscow and anti–Soviet Union. Many had been forced to relocate to fit within the system, thus creating ethnic problems in many different republics. As members of the Helsinki Commission, we would review the situations and make suggestions from a human rights perspective. In the former Soviet Republics, we would often stay in government housing—which was nice—but good food and other western amenities were lacking. Good restaurants and fine hotels were the exception to the rule. In the mid-1980s, for example, I visited the Republic of Georgia. Tbilisi, the capital, had a beautiful, tightly secured, modern hotel built by the Germans, but the surrounding area and the city's infrastructure were a wreck; buildings, sewers, and streets were in disrepair. Indeed, the Helsinki Commission exposed me to some unique problems in all corners of the world.

Perhaps one of the most impressive trips I made was to South Africa in 1992, when Nelson Mandela was released from prison at Robben Island. We traveled to Johannesburg, Pretoria, Cape Town, and some of the townships in the outlying areas. We met with recently installed President F. W. DeKlerk and his predecessor Pieter W. Botha, a strong and lifelong supporter of apartheid. DeKlerk, whose religious upbringing influenced his style of governance, modified his views on apartheid and delivered a famous speech that proclaimed the end of this form of institutional and cultural separation. I thought it remarkable to meet this man who, because of worldwide political pressure, instituted such profound change. Mandela was pardoned and released, and his National African Party gained political recognition. Before leaving South Africa, I gave DeKlerk a proposal for the creation of an African Helsinki Commission process for human rights. Though interested, he took no immediate action.[9]

I also had the opportunity to travel with the U.S. president's party to several countries, including Israel, Saudi Arabia, and Jordan. On several occasions, I accompanied the president as chairman of the Helsinki Commission, which reflected the U.S. commitment to justice, individual rights, and freedom. I was proud to represent the United States, its people, and the moral compass we possess.

After my retirement from the Senate in January 1995, I was busy, but had not fully determined exactly what work I wanted to do. The personal and professional crises I had been through took their toll, and I went through a difficult divorce. I stayed in Washington and joined the firm of Parry and Romani and Associates, which has become Parry, Romani, DeConcini, and Symms. Steve Symms of Idaho, a great friend and senator, joined the firm in 2000. In addition to carrying out specialty projects for the firm, I tend to personal business with 4-D Properties in Tucson and La Jolla, California.

Besides the lobby firm, I sought out, happily, a role in the National Center for Missing and Exploited Children. Ernie Allen, the president and CEO, asked me to serve on the board of directors. As many know, this organization was started twenty years ago by John and Reva Walsh of Broward County, Florida, near West Palm Beach. Their son Adam was kidnapped and murdered by someone who was believed to be a sexual predator. Adam was never found, but in his memory the Walshes established the Adam Walsh Foundation. They lobbied Congress with alacrity, and the center quickly gained congressional recognition thanks to the legislative efforts of Senator Paula Hawkins and Senator Paul Simon.[10] In fact, after eight years on the board, I was nominated to serve as chairman for the year 2004–2005.

In addition to this board, I serve on the boards of a few small public companies and just recently left the board of Nyumbani "Children of God Relief, Inc." This organization, founded by Father Angelo d'Agostino, a Jesuit priest at Georgetown University, is dedicated to fighting AIDS in Africa and runs an orphanage in Nairobi, Kenya. I visited there several times. My brother Dino took my place on this board, and to his credit—he is always doing good works—he volunteered during the Christmas season.

My life has been full in many ways. In August 2003, I married Patricia Lynch, who has brought tremendous joy and happiness to my life. Today I spend my days lobbying on a part-time basis, traveling, enjoying my family and friends, and keeping involved in public-policy issues of importance to Arizona, the nation, and the world.

12 Conclusion

As I survey the historical landscape, I return repeatedly to the strength and love provided by my family—my parents, brothers, sister, aunts, uncles, cousins, wives, and children. I grew up in a nurturing environment that exposed me to rural life, strong religious values, and respect for the land. At the same time, my Tucson boyhood inured me to the dynamic changes taking place in a rapidly urbanizing and suburbanizing civilization that demanded public involvement and participation. My parents, Evo and Ora, worked hard to find answers in dealing with my academic challenges, placed me in the most beneficial learning environment, and guided me through these early days. In spite of my childhood shortcomings, my bouts of adolescent rebelliousness, and my less than stellar early academic career, they demonstrated a familial perseverance, resolve, and love that transformed me and helped shape my values and character. By the time I entered high school, I knew the importance of public service. I thank them for this.

In many ways, Dino, my elder brother, and others such as my high school teacher Danny Romero became contemporary role models in these early years, influencing me in the right direction. I emulated Dino's academic bearing and ability and listened to the constructive criticism and guidance that Danny Romero provided when I most needed it. Several outstanding professors at the University of Arizona, such as Dr. Neil Houghton, encouraged my progress and helped refine my critical thinking at a time when I realized that a formal education, as my father counseled, was the key to achieving one's goals in life.

Exposure to my father's legal career and its culture prompted me toward law school. Moreover, his political activism and leadership attracted me to the public realm and, though I became hooked in high school, I continued indulging this passion through college, law school, and my early legal career. Working on Ernest McFarland's Senate campaigns in 1952 and 1958, observing carefully the changing political culture in Arizona in the 1950s and 1960s—as the state moved decidedly to the right of center—and working on grassroots organizing in Tucson prepared me well for what lay ahead. My life became a life of law and politics. Gaining a foundation in the legal community was a godsend, and I thank my father for this influence. He provided hundreds of introductions into Arizona's growing legal community at the outset of my professional career, and words cannot describe the help these introductions provided.

Meeting and marrying my first wife, Susie, and having three beautiful children created a solid foundation for my professional and political development. At this time, my father played a critical role in shaping my early political choices and saved me from some early missteps. Patience, a disciplined approach, and organization were his hallmarks for political success, and I took his advice about when and how I should take on a campaign. As I entered electoral politics, I was also fortunate to come into contact with Ron Ober, Gene Karp, Michael Hawkins, Judy Abrams, Mike Crusa, and Barry Dill. They and so many others provided the guidance, knowledge, and passion that enabled me to distinguish my campaigns from others.

As I embarked in earnest on a political career, I met some outstanding public servants and elected officials. Democrats Sam Goddard, Raul Castro, Ernest McFarland, and Rose Mofford knew my family and encouraged me at every turn in the early years. I learned and listened, worked diligently when called upon, and served in gubernatorial administrations without reservation. These fine people and countless others, such as Clarence Dupnik and Joe Arpaio, came to my aid when I declared my run for Pima County attorney in 1972 and were there when I ran for the Senate the first time in 1976.

By the time I ran for county attorney, I had developed a consistent political philosophy that could best be described as "centrist." Throughout my career, I was labeled a "moderate to conservative" Democrat or, as

Governor Mofford put it in her foreword to this volume, a "vigilant centrist." Though by predisposition I was a Democrat, there were many issues throughout my career—such as law enforcement, antidrug policy, abortion, and, in some cases, tax policy—regarding which I had more in common with Republicans. Thus, when I became a U.S. senator, I moved easily between and among Democrats and Republicans. I could be as comfortable engaging in dialogues with conservative Republicans Barry Goldwater, Orrin Hatch, and Paul Laxalt as with liberal Democrats Ted Kennedy, Patrick Moynihan, and Tom Daschle. The bottom line was that I was interested in working for the people of Arizona and the nation. I voted for countless Republican judicial appointments, and though I took heat from my fellow Democrats, I never apologized because I felt I had thoroughly examined the person's legal qualifications. I opposed Reagan's tax policies once I saw they were deleterious to our country, and, of course, my vote on the Panama Canal riled conservatives. I sought to reform policy regarding Native Americans in the later twentieth century, but these efforts were subverted to other forms of political entertainment—namely, the Keating Five affair.

As a practical matter, I knew well that a Democrat from Tucson had to attract conservative votes to remain in office. Thus, my centrist position on the political spectrum served as a kind of political life support in Arizona. In my three statewide elections, in fact, I won voter-rich and increasingly Republican Maricopa County each time. In many ways, my career served as a kind of political barometer of Arizona in the late twentieth century.

I served with presidents, senators, congressmen, judges, administrative officials, Capitol Hill staffers, and countless others—all of whom possessed talent, strengths, and weaknesses. Some were brilliant, others not so, and they often had great senses of humor. Presidents Carter, Reagan, Bush, and Clinton, each distinct in his manner and ability, treated me well. I tried to work with each of them to the best of my abilities. My working relationships with my fellow senators mirrored relationships to be found in other work environments: some were excellent, others average, and still a few others poor. I have tried to portray my perceptions and views of the Senate and the senators in a candid and forthright fashion.

Although I voted on thousands of issues, introduced myriad legislative bills, and cosponsored incalculable numbers of laws, I have focused my attention in this volume on issues that best illustrate and reflect the nature and direction of my eighteen years in the Senate. My vote to return the Panama Canal was obviously one of historic proportions, and I will forever be identified with that action. I parted ways with Carter over his western water policies and with Reagan over his draconian and ill-advised fiscal policies. My opposition on these issues and others served as a centerpiece to my reelection campaign in 1982, though the Panama Canal vote continued to be the eight-hundred-pound gorilla in the room.

I enjoyed immensely the camaraderie developed in and the satisfaction of my three successful Senate campaigns. Each had its own distinct personality. The 1976 campaign against Sam Steiger in many ways was historic and demonstrated that the Arizona electorate had indeed matured by voting a Tucson-based Democrat to statewide office. That first campaign also produced some enduring political anecdotes that will resonate among historians for generations: burros, the attempt to mix religion and politics, and an angry Barry Goldwater stepping into the race.

In the 1982 race, the Panama Canal was brought up, of course, but so too were Bonanno and organized crime, and we had fun with the Torrijos tape recordings. Ron Ober still chuckles when discussing the televised debate on KAET and my opening comment about the score of the 1982 World Series, ruining Pete Dunn's chances at gaining any type of political traction through television viewers. Likewise, 1988 brought forth an underfunded and undisciplined candidate, Keith DeGreen, raised the specter of the Panama Canal—again—and included more negative campaigning that challenged my patience and my staff's resiliency. I am convinced, however, that Arizona voters elected me to the Senate three times based on representation, constituent service, and political performance.

Although there were successes, there were also setbacks. The Keating Five debacle took a great deal out of me personally and professionally, demoralized my staff, and placed immense pressure on those around me. Unlike some of my fellow senators involved in this controversy, I took the charges as a personal attack on my integrity. Perhaps I should have viewed the investigation as a purely political matter that had to be dealt with on the political playing field, but I chose another course.

Convinced that I had done nothing wrong, I fought the charges at every turn. History will judge whether or not that was the right course, but today I maintain that it was the correct one to take.

My choice not to seek reelection in 1994, shortly after I voted to support President Clinton's 1993 tax bill, came about after much deliberation and thought, and my move into the private sector has been, in retrospect, one of the best decisions I have made. The lobby work for Parry, Romani, DeConcini, and Symms continues to be rewarding and keeps me in touch with friends and families from my days in the Senate. And, as I indicated earlier, my recent marriage to Patty Lynch has added an incalculable dimension to my life; together we can look back on mutual careers of service, accomplishment, and good friends. My eighteen years as U.S. senator were humbling, rewarding, and unforgettable, and for them I am thankful.

NOTES

Acknowledgments

1. Tim Roemer was a former congressman; Karen Robb was my chief counsel, along with Dennis Burke, on the Judiciary Committee; and Ed Baxter and Romano Romani remain partners with me in our Washington, D.C., lobby firm. Nancy Suter was my executive assistant who made life good in times of crisis.

2. My mother passed away in 2004. Morris, who still lives at the Tucson family home, and my mother knew one another for only three months before they were married. My mother was taking her third African safari trip, which included her grandchildren and a dear friend from Tucson. Considering her own morals and wanting to provide a good example for the grandchildren, she felt she could not travel with a man even though they were engaged, so she and Morris married a few weeks before the African trip. They had many fine years, traveling to Europe, San Diego, and elsewhere, and Morris's knowledge of history always added a fascinating dimension to their trips. When my mother was in her early nineties, and I visited the family home in Tucson, she informed me that it would be best that I not go swimming in the evening with them as I often did. They had a very private indoor pool, and I leave it to the imagination as to why she did not want me swimming with them. Morris lives an active life in the home he and my mother occupied during their life together. He is very much like a father to many in our family, and he has enriched so many lives. With generosity and warmth, he has embraced the large extended family he inherited.

Chapter 1. First Days

1. Four days prior to the election, an uninsured motorist hit the DeConcini campaign car at the corner of Forty-fourth Street and Van Buren in Phoenix, breaking three of my ribs. I was elected while recovering from injuries at St. Joseph's Hospital and, fortunately, was able to attend the inauguration ceremonies. Shortly after the election, I spent about one and one-half weeks flying around the state thanking people. The calls from Democratic Senate leaders surprised me as well; they treated me as if I were one of their buddies, but they were lobbying for my support in their efforts at gaining the position of Senate majority leader.

2. Ron Ober, "Dennis DeConcini Oral Histories," oral history interview by Jack L. August Jr., November 20, 2002, Phoenix, Arizona; Michael Rappaport, "Dennis DeConcini and the Central Arizona Project," oral history interview by Jack L. August Jr., September 18, 2002, Tempe, Arizona. Both in Dennis DeConcini Congressional Papers Collection, Special Collections, University of Arizona Library, Tucson.

3. Joann Piccolo did not stay on very long and left during my first term.

4. *Arizona Republic* (Phoenix), March 11, 1976; *Arizona Range News* (Willcox), March 11, 1976; *White Mountain Independent* (St. Johns, Arizona), March 11, 1976; *Arizona Daily Star* (Tucson), March 11, 1976.

5. Goldwater's support for Democratic candidates was not unprecedented. In fact, he endorsed Democrat Carl Hayden over Republican nominee Evan Mecham in the 1962 U.S. Senate election. Later in his career, he endorsed Democrat Karan English over her opponent, Douglas Wead, for election to the U.S. House of Representatives.

6. *Arizona Republic,* March 10 and 11, 1976; *Arizona Daily Star,* March 10 and 11, 1976. I resigned my position as Pima County attorney a week after my announcement that I would be running for the Senate. Ron Ober reconfirmed that the Wisconsin primary became a kind of "due date" for our announcement for either the House or Senate. Ron Ober to Jack L. August Jr., February 21, 2005.

7. *Arizona Republic,* March 10, 1976; "DeConcini Announcement: Candidate for U.S. Senate," Dennis DeConcini Congressional Papers Collection, Box 18, File 9.

8. Arizona Secretary of State, *Primary Election, Official Canvass* (Phoenix: State of Arizona, September 7, 1976); *Arizona Republic,* September 8, 1976;

Phoenix Gazette, September 8, 1976; *Arizona Daily Star,* September 8, 1976. I received 121,423 votes in the primary, Carolyn Warner garnered 71,612, and Wade Church mustered 34,266.

9. *Arizona Republic,* August 18, 1976.

10. *Arizona Republic,* August 18, 1976; *Phoenix Gazette,* August 18, 1976.

11. *Arizona Republic,* August 25, 1976.

12. *Arizona Republic,* August 19, 20, 1976; *Arizona Daily Star,* August 20, 1976.

13. *Arizona Republic,* August 20, 1976.

14. *Arizona Republic,* September 8, 1976.

15. *Arizona Republic,* August 20, 21, 22, 1976; *Arizona Daily Star,* August 18, 19, 20, 22, 23, 1976; *Arizona Daily Sun* (Flagstaff), August 19, 20, 21, 1976.

16. See, for example, "Dem Claims Her Foe Is Weak," *Arizona Republic,* September 3, 1976.

17. *Arizona Republic,* September 8, 1976; *Arizona Daily Star,* September 8, 1976.

18. *Arizona Republic,* September 8, 1976.

19. *Arizona Republic,* August 25, 1976; Sam Steiger, "My 1976 Campaign Against Dennis DeConcini," oral history interview by Jack L. August Jr., November 19, 2002, Prescott, Arizona, Dennis DeConcini Congressional Papers Collection, Special Collections.

20. *Arizona Republic,* September 9, 1976; "Politics from the Pulpit: Meat Ax versus Scalpel," *Newsweek* (August 21, 1976): 34–36.

21. See *Arizona Republic,* September 3, 1976. Eaton was president of something called Eaton International, Inc., and Bradley was a Phoenix-area home builder.

22. *Arizona Republic,* September 3, 1976. The newspaper published the letter in its entirety.

23. *Arizona Republic,* August 25, 1976.

24. *Washington Times,* September 4, 1976; *Arizona Republic,* August 25 and September 5, 1976.

25. All quotations from *Arizona Republic,* September 5, 1976.

26. *Arizona Republic,* August 26 and September 4, 1976; *Daily Courier* (Prescott), October 10, 1975, and September 4, 1976.

27. Udall, after Jimmy Carter wrested the presidential nomination from him, easily won reelection to his seat in the House of Representatives in

District One. Steiger defeated Conlan in the Republican primary, 102,843 to 93,033. See Arizona Secretary of State, *Primary Election, Official Canvass* September 7, 1976. A record 442,270 votes were cast in the primaries, representing 50.2 percent of registered voters in both major parties.

28. *Arizona Republic,* September 9, 10, 11, October 27, and November 3, 1976; *Arizona Daily Star,* September 9, 11, 1976.

29. *Arizona Republic,* September, 8, 11, 12, 1976.

30. *Arizona Republic,* September 22, October 25, 1976. My first campaign staff included five key players. Ron Ober, my campaign manager, was a veteran from my 1972 campaign for Pima County attorney. By this time, Ron had graduated from the Business College at the University of Arizona and oversaw all facets of the campaign. John Evans, former head of the Arizona branch of the AFL-CIO and former governor Samuel Goddard's appointee in 1965 to the Arizona Employment Security Commission, was one of my chief advisors. Dino DeConcini, my brother, helped with strategic decisions and fund-raising. He took a leave of absence from his work as executive assistant to Governor Raul Castro. Phoenix attorney Michael Hawkins helped with scheduling, policy issues, and statewide contacts. And Gene Karp, Tucson attorney and former Pima County Democratic Party chairman, provided critical input at all stages of the campaign. In addition to these key people, former Arizona Supreme Court judge Lorna Lockwood served as honorary chairwoman, and Tucson businessman Sam Sneller contributed his considerable skills as treasurer to the campaign.

31. *Arizona Republic,* November 6, 1976.

32. Arizona Secretary of State, *General Election, Official Canvass* (Phoenix: State of Arizona, November 2, 1976). Steiger won Yavapai County 12,251 to 9,182 and Mohave County 7,091 to 6,959. Minor-party candidates Allan Norwits, William Feighan, and Bob Field pulled in approximately 19,000 votes combined. See also *Arizona Republic,* November 3, 4, 1976; *Phoenix Gazette,* November 3, 4, 1976; *Arizona Daily Star,* November 3, 4, 1976; *Tucson Citizen,* November 3, 4, 1976.

Chapter 2. And We Danced for Fifty Years

1. See Leonard Arrington and David Bitton, *The Mormon Experience: A History of the Latter Day Saints* (Knopf: New York, 1979); Walter Nugent,

Into the West: A Story of Its People (New York: Vintage Books, 1999), 80–83. During these summers on the farm, I spent anywhere from three to six weeks with my relatives, and, of course, on occasion my mother and father traveled to Graham County to check on my welfare.

2. Ora Webster DeConcini, oral history interview by James F. McNulty, December 9, 1986, Evo DeConcini Oral History Project (EDOHP), Arizona Historical Society (AHS), Tucson; Dennis DeConcini, oral history interview by Jack L. August Jr., July 10, 2001, Tucson. Ollie Damron was born April 5, 1872, in Kanosh, Willard County, Utah. He was the fourth child of eleven born to William Damron and Elizabeth Hester Ray Damron.

3. Thomas George Webster, date of birth unknown, came to the United States from St. Ellens, England, and, according to family accounts, never lost his British accent. He apparently converted to Mormonism in England, and on November 12, 1864, he married Mary Elmer, who was born on August 2, 1844, in Parlet, Illinois. Oscar was their fifth child, born June 29, 1872, at Levan, Juab County, Utah (near St. George).

4. In fact, Oscar and his brother Frank built brick farmhouses about two hundred yards apart, and in those houses they brought up their families. The children, including my mother, remained there until they married and went their separate ways.

5. William Damron died October 2, 1898, and was buried in the Thatcher cemetery. Graham County was formed in 1881 by the Eleventh Territorial Legislature and was created from parts of Apache and Pima counties. The territorial legislature broke with the tradition of naming Arizona counties after local Native American tribes when it named the new county after the 10,516-foot Mt. Graham, the highest peak in the area. The mountain, in turn, had been named after Lt. Col. James Duncan Graham, a senior officer in General Stephen Watts Kearny's U.S. Army Corps of Topographical Engineers. Graham County's early history was one of exploration more than settlement. There were no noticeable Mexican or Spanish communities, and most inhabitants were Apaches. Camp Goodwin was established in 1866, but it was abandoned when the troops moved north to establish Fort Apache in 1871. In the 1870s, farming communities began appearing along the Gila River, which bifurcates the county from east to west. Munsonville, now San Jose, was established in 1873; Safford followed in 1874; Solomonville in 1876; Smithville, now known as Pima, in 1879. In the next decade, Thatcher, Eden, Central, and Bryce were settled—all within a few miles of

each other. This part of Arizona was and is today a rich agricultural area. Safford was the first county seat, but the seat was moved to Solomonville after two years. In 1915, after an election, the county seat was returned to Safford, where it remains.

6. McNulty interview with Ora DeConcini, EDOHP; Ora Webster DeConcini, "Oscar and Ollie Webster," unpublished manuscript, n.d., Dennis DeConcini Congressional Papers Collection, Family Papers. The ranches Oscar purchased after the demise of the freighting business were located southwest of Highway 70 about twenty-five miles from Old San Carlos and Coolidge Dam. The main ranch house was about fifty miles from the Gila Valley ranch house. Oscar made frequent trips to the ranch by wagons and teams and later by Dodge truck. Hawk Canyon Ranch, named after the canyon, was later renamed the UB Ranch. The last five miles of the road was up the canyon, where raging waters often washed out the road. According to my mother, Oscar always helped the ranch hands rebuild the road. It was the narrow, dangerous roads that caused Oscar's untimely death at age sixty-one. Several times in Oscar's life, the date June 21 occurred as a date of adversity. On June 21, 1911, a fire destroyed the Webster Brothers flour mill in Thatcher, and Oscar was seriously burned. Three years later, on June 21, 1914, the feed fuel and supply store owned by the brothers burned in Globe. And the accident that took Oscar's life was on June 21.

7. At this time, Thatcher did not have a high school, and all high school students in the area went to Gila Academy—now Eastern Arizona College. The Mormon Church ran the school. All of Ora's brothers and sisters attended Gila Academy. See McNulty interview with Ora DeConcini, EDOHP.

8. Ibid.

9. Ora recalled that her mother would not let her go to Los Angeles by herself even though she had turned eighteen during the process of attending Woodbury. So her sister, Zola, with two children in tow, went with her. Every morning that first summer, she took the streetcar to downtown Los Angeles to Eighth and Hill, where the business college was located. She needed a portion of the following summer to complete the units for her business school diploma. Her stint as student, teacher, and secretary lasted roughly from 1926 to the end of 1927.

10. Ora took a few other part-time jobs during 1925–27, including working as a secretary in North American Life Insurance Company and as

a secretary to a purchasing agent for the Ambassador Hotel Corporation while she was in summer school in Los Angeles.

11. McNulty interview with Ora DeConcini, EDOHP.

12. Ibid. She taught night school at Tucson High School from 1927 to 1930, taught two and one-half years at Tucson School District One from 1930 to 1932, and served as registrar at Mansfield Junior High in 1932.

13. Just before his death, my grandfather planned to return to Europe for his first visit since emigrating to the United States. See Evo Anton DeConcini, *Hey! It's Past 80: A Biography of a Busy Life* (Tucson: Sunrise Graphics, 1981), 37. My grandfather was born on January 16, 1876.

14. Ibid., 55, 63. In addition, he had a winter income of $5.00 per week that he earned washing windows at the Commercial Bank.

15. Ibid., 1–4; McNulty interview with Ora DeConcini, EDOHP.

16. My mother described his "piecemeal" approach to law school. "Evo was always doing different kinds of things like getting into some mining thing or into some water thing or buying a duck pond, and so he started taking law piecemeal, like contracts, water law, mining law. And how he arrived at a degree was by chance. The dean called him in one time and said, 'Evo, do you realize you have enough units for a law degree, if you'd go back and fill your prelaw?' So that's how he became a lawyer." McNulty interview with Ora DeConcini, EDOHP.

17. Ibid.

18. E. DeConcini, *Hey*, 43; McNulty interview with Ora DeConcini, EDOHP.

19. Dennis DeConcini, oral history interview by Jack L. August Jr., June 8, 2004, La Jolla, California.

Chapter 3. Gaining Political Literacy

1. Ernest McFarland won election to the U.S. Senate in 1940 and gained reelection in 1946, but lost a third-term bid in 1952 to political upstart Barry Goldwater. He served two terms as governor of Arizona from 1955 to 1959. He was later elected as a justice of the Arizona Supreme Court in 1964, becoming chief justice in 1968 and serving until 1970. My father presided over McFarland's second inaugural as governor. See James Elton McMillan Jr., *Ernest W. McFarland: Majority Leader of the U.S. Senate* (Prescott, Ariz.: Sharlot Hall Museum Press, 2004).

2. Thomas Sheridan, *Arizona: A History* (Tucson: University of Arizona Press, 1995), 274–75. Sheridan's lively account suggests that seventy-five business leaders grilled then-mayor Newell Stewart and his city commissioners in the card room of the Adams Hotel. After hours of pressure, most of the exhausted commissioners finally agreed to fire the city manager, clerk, magistrate, and chief of police. Frank Snell later recalled, "It was kind of like a coup, and we called it the 'Card room Putsch.'" See John Rhodes, *I Was There* (Salt Lake City: Northwest, 1995), 22–23; Robert Alan Goldberg, *Barry Goldwater* (New Haven, Conn.: Yale University Press, 1995), 67–118.

3. Stephen Shadegg to Barry Goldwater, April 14, 1952, Stephen Shadegg Collection, Box 8, Folder 10, Arizona Historical Foundation, Hayden Library, Arizona State University, Tempe.

4. Goldberg, *Barry Goldwater,* 92.

5. Ibid., 92–93; *Arizona Republic,* April 25 and September 19, 1952; Barry Goldwater, oral history interview by Ed Edwin, June 15, 1967, Dwight David Eisenhower Presidential Library, Abilene, Kansas.

6. *Arizona Republic,* September 23, 1952. Also, the *Phoenix Gazette* and Tucson's *Arizona Daily Star* endorsed Goldwater for the Senate in 1952.

7. Goldberg, *Barry Goldwater,* 67–92.

8. Most of my University of Arizona friends supported Goldwater, but we were twenty years old and could not vote. See also McMillan, *Ernest W. McFarland,* 370–71, for a concise discussion of the 1958 Democratic primary election for the U.S. Senate.

9. Professor Neil D. Houghton was a distinguished scholar on the politics of water resource development in the arid Southwest.

10. Goldberg, *Barry Goldwater,* 124–25; speech by Ernest McFarland, "Campaign Materials," 1958, Box 142, Ernest McFarland Papers, McFarland State Historical Park, Florence, Arizona. In this speech, McFarland pointed to Goldwater's frequent absences from the Senate, missed roll-call votes, opposition to federal programs that benefited Arizona, and neglect of the state's pressing water issues. Goldwater, McFarland now claimed, was a luxury Arizona could not afford. "Barry Goldwater is the sound effects man for the U.S. Senate. . . . He is less a political figure than entertainer. Like any entertainer, he is more concerned about how he is received than about what he says."

11. Raymond Moley, "Test in Arizona," *Newsweek,* March 24, 1958, 14.

12. Ibid.; Goldberg, *Barry Goldwater,* 129. "These men and women," Goldwater announced, "by individual initiative, by energy and by sheer grit and courage, brought civilization to a wilderness, established well-ordered society in a lawless land" (Goldberg, *Barry Goldwater,* 129). This was soaring rhetoric for modern Arizonans, who, Goldwater suggested, were cut from the same cloth.

13. Paul Healy, "The Glittering Mr. Goldwater," *Saturday Evening Post,* June 7, 1958, 39, 116; "Personality Contest," *Time,* September 29, 1958, 15; *New York Times,* October 13, 1958, 32; *Arizona Republic,* March 24 and October 19, 1958.

14. For a thorough accounting of McFarland's two terms as governor, see McMillan, *Ernest W. McFarland,* 257–400.

15. *Arizona Republic,* October 25 and November 1, 2, 4, 1958; Goldberg, *Barry Goldwater,* 130.

16. Roy Elson, "Dennis DeConcini and the Democrats," oral history interview by Jack L. August Jr., October 5, 2003, Sonoita, Arizona, Dennis DeConcini Congressional Papers Collection.

Chapter 4. Road to the Senate

1. Jack L. August Jr., "Old Arizona and the New Conservative Agenda: The Hayden-Mecham Senate Campaign of 1962," *Journal of Arizona History* (winter 2000), 407.

2. Kleppner quoted in ibid., 408.

3. Goddard's term, from 1964 to 1966, was the last time that the Arizona governor served a two-year term. Thereafter, due to a change in the state constitution, governors served four-year terms.

4. Dennis DeConcini, oral history interview by Jack L. August Jr., November 11, 2002, Tucson, Arizona.

5. Bilby's father was the senior partner in this firm, which was located on the top two floors of the Valley Bank building in downtown Tucson. My father's office was in that building, as was our law firm at the time: DeConcini, McDonald, and Brammer. Of the twenty-four attorneys in the Bilby firm, only two were Democrats, Marvin Cohen and William Dolph. Cohen was active in Democratic Party politics but removed himself from consideration for county attorney early in the process and supported my candidacy. Bilby decided with no consultation that the Republicans would not

put forward a candidate, which, of course, aided my campaign significantly.

6. Ron Ober and Barry Dill, "Dennis DeConcini Oral History Interviews," oral history interviews by Jack L. August Jr., June 6, 2003, Phoenix, Arizona, Dennis DeConcini Congressional Papers Collection.

7. David Dingledine became my deputy after the election.

8. *Arizona Daily Star,* June 12, July 18, August 5, 1972.

9. During this period, Dupnik and Dave Dingledine would play golf together early in the mornings during the summer, and we developed close personal and professional relationships. I became a member of the Fraternal Order of Police.

10. This position was then known as administrative assistant.

11. Governor Castro surprised the experts by winning this spirited campaign for the governorship. In 1977, two years later, President Carter appointed him ambassador to Argentina. Castro had a varied and inspirational career prior to his election as governor of Arizona. A former Pima County attorney (1954–58) and Pima County Superior Court judge, this native of Cananea, Sonora, Mexico, earned a reputation as a man of keen mind and deep compassion during six years on the Superior Court bench. His stature grew over the years, and President Lyndon Johnson appointed him as U.S. ambassador to El Salvador in 1964. That four-year service was followed by an ambassadorial assignment to Argentina. He returned to Tucson in 1969 to specialize in international law and entered Arizona Democratic Party politics.

12. These offices were separate and distinct from the county attorney offices.

13. Arpaio served in the army for three years from 1950 to 1953 and from there built a federal law enforcement career that took him throughout the world.

Chapter 5. The Panama Canal Dilemma

1. The DeConcini Reservation, its official name, is also referred to as the DeConcini Resolution.

2. From the 1850s until the turn of the twentieth century, most Americans agreed that the Nicaraguan route was preferable. It became an almost enjoyable excursion as passengers from New York and New Orleans landed

at Greytown, proceeded in boats of light draft up the San Juan River to Lake Nicaragua, crossed the lake in steamboats to a point on the western shore called Virgin Bay, and from there were conveyed in carriages over a macadam surface road to San Juan del Sur. From there, a steamship sailed travelers to San Francisco.

3. See David McCulloch, *Path between the Seas: The Creation of the Panama Canal, 1870–1914* (New York: Simon and Schuster, 2002); Irwin Unger, *These United States*, vol. 2 (Boston: Little Brown, 1978), 610; H. W. Brands, *TR: The Last Romantic* (New York: Basic Books, 1997), 474–80. Soon after the Panama railway was completed, the Panama Railroad stock was the highest-priced stock on the New York Stock Exchange. To build a fifty-one-mile-long ship canal seemed an easy matter to some investors, but the construction project came to involve the efforts of thousands of workers over forty years. At first, these workers toiled under de Lessep's direction; soon, however, de Lessep saw his dream of extending French influence in the Americas fade away because of bankruptcy.

4. The first Hay-Pauncefote Treaty was never ratified because it prohibited the United States from fortifying the canal.

5. McCulloch, *Path Between the Seas*, 31.

6. Gerald Nash, *The American West in the Twentieth Century: A Short History of an Urban Oasis* (Albuquerque: University of New Mexico Press, 1977), 21–22.

7. Dennis DeConcini, oral history interview by Jack L. August Jr., September 20, 2002, Tucson, Arizona.

8. Clinton proved to be a political operative far superior to Carter, sensing the mood of the country and, frankly, championing policies that benefited the American people.

9. The *Phoenix Gazette* folded its operations into the *Arizona Republic* in the 1990s, and John Kolbe finished his journalistic career there.

10. John Kolbe's disdain for me was confirmed to me by his friends and by numerous mutual acquaintances.

11. At this time, no one in the U.S. government suspected Noriega as a conspirator in drug trafficking.

12. Romano Romani attained a Ph.D. in political science from Indiana University and came to work for me when I first arrived in Washington, having worked with retiring Senator Vance Hartke (D–Indiana).

13. Romano Romani, "Dennis DeConcini Oral History," interview by

Jack L. August Jr., September 19, 2002, Washington, D.C., Dennis DeConcini Congressional Papers Collection.

14. I asked Senator Sasser to speak at a Carolyn Warner dinner in Phoenix during the time he was going to Panama with Senator Byrd. Warner had been one of my opponents in the 1976 Democratic primary, and after the election she became a very strong supporter. She asked if I could help get a speaker so she could retire part of her campaign debt. To Sasser's great credit, he cut short his trip to Panama by one day, flew to Los Angeles and Phoenix, delivered the talk, and made innumerable friends in Arizona as a result of his effort.

15. At this juncture, I was still not prepared to vote for the treaty because I still had a second amendment that dealt with another issue.

16. The recall effort against me did not succeed due to a lack of sufficient number of signatures. If one runs for office in Arizona, the candidate must sign a statement indicating that he or she must stand for recall if enough signatures are obtained.

17. *Arizona Republic*, October 6, 1982; *Arizona Daily Sun*, October 7, 1982. The third stage of Reagan's tax-cut plan called for a 10 percent across-the-board reduction.

18. *Arizona Republic*, September 8, 1982.

19. "U.S. Senator Dennis DeConcini and Issues for the 80's," *Arizona Republic*, November 1, 1982.

20. *Arizona Republic*, September 8, 1982; *Arizona Daily Star*, September 8, 1982.

21. *Arizona Republic*, September 9, 1982.

22. Dean Sellers, unlike John Conlan in 1976, chose to support Dunn in the general election, even allowing himself to be named cochairman of the Dunn for Senate campaign. *Arizona Republic*, October 8, 1982.

23. *Arizona Republic*, September 17, 20, 21, 1982; *Arizona Daily Star*, September 17, 1982. In addition to Arizona, the NCPAC targeted races in Massachusetts, Texas, North Dakota, Maryland, Montana, Nevada, and West Virginia. Giordano, who picketed our campaign offices as a paid political employee, was rumored to have ties to the Reverend Sun Myung Moon and the conservative *Washington Times*.

24. *Arizona Republic*, September 20, 1976.

25. *Arizona Republic*, September 17, 20, 21, 1982.

26. *Arizona Republic*, September 25, 1982.

27. *Arizona Republic,* September 21, 1982; *Arizona Daily Star,* September 21, 1982.

28. Jack Pfister, "Dennis DeConcini and Phoenix Republicans," oral history interview by Jack L. August Jr., October 12, 2004, Phoenix, Arizona, Dennis DeConcini Congressional Papers Collection; "Why Is This Man Smiling?" *Arizona Republic,* September 19, 1982.

29. *Sacramento Bee,* September 24, 1982; *Arizona Republic,* September 28, 1982. Alfred S. Donau III, Bonanno's lawyer, claimed that the *Bee* had obtained the manuscript illegally and that he and other lawyers were preparing to file suit against the paper.

30. *Arizona Republic,* September 28, 1982. Gene Karp did an excellent job with the press, providing information and quotes to the media on this issue.

31. In fact, Ron Ober tied the NCPAC to Dunn with an excellent television commercial that prompted viewers to call Pete Dunn if they did not agree with his position on these three controversial issues.

32. *Arizona Republic,* September 8 and October 9, 19, 1982. I won the primary 140,328 to 25,909. Meanwhile, Pete Dunn and Dean Sellers ran a hard-fought race in the Republican primary, garnering 97,391 and 79,375 votes, respectively. Arizona Secretary of State, *Primary Elections, Official Canvass* (Phoenix: State of Arizona, September 20, 1982).

33. *Arizona Republic,* October 14, 27, 31, 1982; *Phoenix Gazette,* October 27, 31, 1982; *Arizona Daily Star,* October 14, 1982.

34. Arizona Secretary of State, *General Election, Official Canvass* (Phoenix: State of Arizona, November 2, 1982). Randall Clamons, the Libertarian candidate garnered 20,100 votes, and Socialist Worker Party candidate Rob Roper attracted 66 votes statewide. *Arizona Republic,* November 3, 1982; *Phoenix Gazette,* November 3, 1982; *Tucson Citizen,* November 3, 1982; *Arizona Daily Star,* November 3, 1982; *Arizona Daily Sun,* November 3, 1982.

35. *Arizona Republic,* November 3, 1982; *Phoenix Gazette,* November 3, 1982.

Chapter 6. A Day in the Life: Senate Culture, 1977–1995

1. There are several excellent sources of information concerning U.S. Senate history and culture. See, for example, Richard A. Baker, *The Senate*

of the United States: A Bicentennial History (Melbourne, Fla.: Krieger, 1988); Richard A. Baker, *First among Equals: Outstanding Senate Leaders of the Twentieth Century* (Washington, D.C.: Congressional Quarterly, 1991); Barbara Sinclair, *The Transformation of the U.S. Senate* (Baltimore: Johns Hopkins University Press, 1989); Donald Bacon, Roger Davidson, and Morton Keller, eds., *The Encyclopedia of the United States Congress* (New York: Simon and Schuster, 1995). Also the U.S. Senate official Web site, www.senate.gov, has a link that enables researchers to access an institutional bibliography of the Senate with more than six hundred books and articles.

2. On average, it actually took twenty-two minutes to get to the floor to cast a vote. If I was not in the Senate building, I had to take the train car to the Senate floor.

3. Kimmit was a longtime staffer in Mike Mansfield's (D–Montana) office.

4. In addition to these examples, I served at various times on the Intelligence Committee (later as chairman of the full committee), the Rules Committee, and the Veterans Committee, as well as on joint committees and commissions such as the Helsinki Commission and the Special Committee on Investigations set up to investigate the situation on Native American reservations (see chap. 9).

5. Each of these members served as chairman of the Defense Appropriations Subcommittee, but they also served on several other committees and were experts on numerous issues.

6. Though the situation differed in the Senate, new senators could influence key legislative areas because they were assigned to more committees, subcommittees, or chairmanships of subcommittees than their counterparts in the House. An especially aggressive senate newcomer, for example, might shape legislative issues early in the first six-year term.

7. Over the years, I gained the impression that those members with prisoner-of-war backgrounds received lenient treatment from the press and their colleagues.

8. See Warren B. Rudman, *Combat: Twelve Years in the U.S. Senate* (New York: Random House, 1996).

9. *Congressional Record,* 101st Cong., 2d sess., May 23, 1990, s 6789–s 6801; U.S. Congress, Senate, Committee on the Judiciary, *Review of the*

Second National Drug Control Strategy, Hearings, 101st Cong., 1st and 2d sess., 1990.

10. Osha Gray Davidson, *Under Fire: The NRA and the Battle for Gun Control* (Henry Holt: New York, 1993), 17.

11. Ibid., 211–12; Dennis DeConcini, "Outline of Legislative Subjects," n.d., Jack August's files, 2005.

12. Davidson, *Under Fire,* 201.

13. *Washington Post,* February 9, 1989. Senators John Chafee (R–Rhode Island) and Clairborne Pell (D–Rhode Island) were original cosponsors of the Metzenbaum legislation. Less than a month later Senators Edward Kennedy, John Glenn, Christopher Dodd (D–Connecticut), Patrick Moynihan, Brock Adams (D–Washington), and Frank Lautenberg placed their names in as cosponsors to the Metzenbaum bill on April 6, 1989.

14. *Washington Post,* March 15, 1989. The issue had grown hot. On February 6, the Stockton City Council voted nine to zero to outlaw assault weapons. One day later the city of Los Angeles took similar action. Within weeks, at least thirty states and countless municipalities had addressed this issue. See Davidson, *Under Fire,* 206.

15. Quote to a *Washington Post* reporter given in Davidson, *Under Fire,* 211.

16. James J. Baker to Dennis DeConcini, n.d., DeConcini Congressional Papers Collection, Box 11, File 14.

17. Dennis Burke to Jack L. August Jr., August 17, 2005, Phoenix, Jack August's files.

18. Senator DeConcini, Statement of Senator Dennis DeConcini Introducing the Anti-Drug Assault Weapons Limitation Act of 1989, April 11, 1989, 101st Cong., 1st sess. (April 11, 1989), DeConcini Congressional Papers Collection, Box 11, File 14.

19. McCain News Memo, "April 28, 1989," DeConcini Congressional Papers Collection, Box 11, File 14.

20. See, for example, *Arizona Republic,* June 3, 1989; and Dennis DeConcini to editor, *Arizona Daily Star,* August 23, 1989, DeConcini Congressional Papers Collection, Box 11, File 1.

21. Nothing of significance came of the "DeConcini Recall" over my introduction of S747.

22. See Davidson, *Under Fire,* 214. All over the country, gun stores were

finding it difficult to keep semiautomatic rifles in stock. Even with prices inflated 50 percent, buyers were placed on waiting lists.

23. Dennis Burke had many duties, but he was really in charge of all of my work concerning the Judiciary Committee.

24. Dennis Burke to Jack L. August Jr., August 26, 2005, Tempe, Arizona, Jack August's files.

25. Sarah Brady to supporter, September 8, 1989, DeConcini Congressional Papers Collection, Box 11, Folder 9.

26. Senator Dennis DeConcini to Honorable George Bush, President of the United States, May 22, 1990, DeConcini Congressional Papers Collection, Box 11, File 14.

27. Dennis Burke to Jack L. August Jr., August 26, 2005, Jack August's files.

28. James Baker to NRA members, June 26, 1990, DeConcini Congressional Papers Collection, Box 11, Folder 4.

29. Dennis Burke, "Summary of Final Bill," July 6, 1990, and Dennis DeConcini, press release, July 11, 1990, DeConcini Congressional Papers Collection, Box 11, File 3.

30. Dennis DeConcini to colleague, April 18, 1989, DeConcini Congressional Papers Collection, Box 67, File 12.

Chapter 7. Judicial Politics

1. As noted in chapter 1, former U.S. senator, governor, and Supreme Court justice Ernest McFarland of Arizona called Senator Eastland when I was elected and told him that "some guy with a funny-sounding name is heading back there from Arizona; treat him right because he is a good man." Eastland took this suggestion to heart and reiterated the story to me with pleasure. In 1977, Eastland and his fellow senator from Mississippi, John Stennis, possessed as much political power as any two people from one state. Stennis, as chairman of the Armed Services Committee, made sure that more ships and ports were built in Mississippi during his tenure than in any other period in history.

2. Mathias was a true fiscal conservative but moderate and even liberal in areas of individual rights and abortion rights.

3. Senator Eastland viewed me as a moderate, and he certainly tried to encourage me to vote with him on most issues concerning the committee.

4. This process could even lead to recommending to an appropriate body—which, of course was the Congress—to have a judge removed for just cause.

5. I had wanted to establish a commission that was composed of judicial and nonjudicial members that would listen to complaints and investigate them. This commission would have the authority to dismiss the claim, to investigate further, and to report to the court or Congress whether or not there was a basis for disciplinary action. This commission could even recommend expulsion from the bench. This idea ran into strong opposition from judges. They felt this oversight went too far and would compromise the judiciary.

6. In the course of conducting these hearings, I met many judges from around the country. After the nomination process was completed, I was often asked to speak at the various appellate conferences around the country.

7. I confirmed my suspicions with Republican attorneys that Dick Bilby had discouraged any and all from running for Pima County attorney in 1972.

8. John Frank had been nominated previously, during the Lyndon Johnson administration, and had been rejected by the U.S. Senate.

9. Mary Schroeder now serves as chief judge of the Ninth Circuit Court of Appeals.

10. I hired Mahoney's daughter, Mary, in my Senate office staff, where she worked for about eighteen years.

11. Mary Schroeder's husband, Bill, a professor at Arizona State University College of Law and a distinguished lawyer in his own right, was pleased and supportive of her appointment and confirmation.

12. John Collins, not surprisingly, went to battle with the Pima County Board of Supervisors in his efforts to secure economic resources for his special programs for juvenile offenders.

13. After his nomination died in the White House, John moved to California and opened a law practice with this son.

14. In fact, Rehnquist was appointed after the Democrat-controlled Senate turned down several of Nixon's nominations.

15. I never participated in polling-day legal battles, but Ed Morgan, the Democratic activist lawyer in Tucson, was one of the more aggressive challengers of these activities. A dedicated civil servant and civil rights leader, Ed was a model of the "liberal lawyer" in the best sense.

16. This was a contentious area in these hearings. Rehnquist's strict interpretations regarding due process and where it might or might not be applied to equal rights of citizens struck a chord with liberals on the Judiciary Committee.

17. Bennett Johnston (U.S. Senate retired) to Jack L. August Jr., January 3, 2005.

18. One of the witnesses against Collins was an African American judge who was disciplined for his activities; he was granted limited immunity for his testimony, which focused on Collins's paying for votes for a particular political candidate.

19. In chapter 3, I related how Governor Goddard wanted to remove certain members from a commission. We took the position that the governor had the power to remove members; the Office of the Attorney General took the opposite view. We sought an opinion from the attorney general, which triggered my first professional contact with Sandra Day O'Connor.

20. O'Connor's only real problem came from the political right. The president of the Right to Life organization testified against her appointment, and while O'Connor was in the Arizona state senate, she had cast some votes that raised questions about whether or not she was pro-life. I never asked her directly about this issue because I did not think it was relevant.

21. Bork sailed through with unanimous votes in his hearings for the appeals court.

22. My recollections of Thomas at the EEOC are that he was not especially sensitive toward African Americans and that his commitment to civil rights was lukewarm.

23. See Ken Foskett, *Judging Thomas: The Life and Times of Clarence Thomas* (New York: William Morrow, 2004).

24. For information by and about Anita Hill, see Anita Hill, *Speak Truth to Power* (Doubleday: New York, 1997); David Brock, *The Real Anita Hill: The Untold Story* (New York: Touchstone, 1997).

Chapter 8. Keating Five

1. See, for example, James R. Adams, *The Big Fix: Inside the S&L Scandal: How an Unholy Alliance of Politics and Money Destroyed America's Banking System* (New York: John Wiley and Sons, 1990); Michael Binstein and

Charles Bowden, *Trust Me: Charles Keating and the Missing Billions* (New York: Random House, 1993); Kathy Calavita, Henry N. Pontell, and Robert H. Tillman, *Big Money Game: Fraud and Politics in the S&L Crisis* (Berkeley: University of California Press, 1997); Kathleen Day, *S&L Hell: The People and the Politics Behind the $1 Trillion Savings and Loan Scandal* (New York: W. W. Norton, 1993); Martin Mayer, *The Greatest Ever Bank Robbery: The Collapse of the Savings and Loan Industry* (New York: Charles Scribner and Sons, 1990); Stephen Pizzo, Mary Fricker, and Paul Muolo, *Inside Job: The Looting of America's Savings and Loans* (New York: McGraw Hill, 1989).

2. In fact, the first meeting took place at a speech I delivered at the Flagstaff Country Club on January 9, 1981. According to one press account, I supposedly met Keating when he moved to Arizona in 1976, though I have no recollection of meeting him before 1981. See *Washington Post*, February 28, 1991.

3. His brother, a gregarious, good-looking man, was a member of Congress who was defeated when he ran for the Senate. In fact, I took him to lunch in the Senate dining room.

4. I later learned that Keating had run afoul of the government in 1979 and had signed a consent decree with the Securities and Exchange Commission arising out of insider loans; he acknowledged no wrongdoing and agreed to abide by securities laws in the future. See *Washington Post*, February 28, 1991.

5. I estimate that more than five hundred people attended this event.

6. Quoted in Pizzo, Fricker, and Muolo, *Inside Job*, 1–2.

7. *Arizona Republic*, February 3, 2002.

8. See, for example, *Arizona Republic*, February 3, 2002.

9. Pizzo, Fricker, and Muolo, *Inside Job*, 16–17.

10. According to Binstein and Bowden in *Trust Me*, Gray was a noble crusader who was much misunderstood by the Washington power structure.

11. Gray had an ill-starred tenure as chairman of the FHLBB. In the next four years, until his term ended in 1987, the FBI and the Ethics Committee investigated him; representatives and senators, including the speaker of the house, on behalf of their constituents, badgered him. Even Reagan and the administration ultimately hung him out to dry. The thrift industry, which had promoted him for the job, also vilified him for his efforts.

12. See, for example, Michael Binstein, "Ed Gray," *Regardie's* (October 1988): 12–15.

13. Legislation enabling savings and loan investment in real estate was introduced in the House, with more than two hundred cosponsors, and was embraced in the Senate. I cosponsored this legislation in the Senate.

14. *Arizona Republic*, October 3, 1999. Keating, Grogan, and other assistants legally solicited these funds. Earl Katz, my chief fund-raiser and treasurer, kept names and amounts contributed. Katz was one of the finest fund-raisers I have witnessed—a hard-charging and determined individual. He was a friend to my family, and we worked closely on other issues besides fund-raising.

15. See Pizzo, Fricker, and Muolo, *Inside Job*, 290.

16. Each of us could claim Keating as a constituent. Lincoln was based in California, Senator Cranston's home. American Continental Corporation, Lincoln's parent company, had been incorporated in Ohio, Senator Glenn's home, and had its headquarters in Phoenix, Arizona, my and Senator McCain's home. Keating had a hotel in Michigan, where Senator Riegle had him as a constituent. He also owned a newspaper and property in Ohio and numerous other business enterprises in Arizona.

17. See Pizzo, Fricker, and Muolo, *Inside Job*, 291.

18. See "The Five Senators Meeting," in ibid., 392–404. The meeting lasted two hours, with the four regulators and four of the five senators in attendance for the entire time. Cranston left for other business, although he indicated that he shared the other four senators' concerns.

19. Ibid., 293–94.

20. *Report of the Select Committee on Ethics, United States Senate, Together with Additional Views*, vol. 1, November 19, 1991, 34. DeConcini Congressional Papers Collection, Box 401. *Mesa Tribune*, October 29, 1989.

21. Rostenkowski, chairman of the House Ways and Means Committee, had been charged with using the Postal Service in the House of Representatives to take draws of cash, which, in essence, were credit even though the House was paid back. Put simply, he took stamps and converted them into cash.

22. See also *Boston Globe*, February 29, 2000, "Pluck, Leaks Helped McCain to Overcome S&L Scandal." *New York Times*, November 20, 1990, November 21, 1990. *Washington Post*, November 21, 1990.

23. *Open Session Hearings before the Select Committee on Ethics, United States Senate, One Hundred First Congress, Second Session, Part 1 of 6, November 15, 1990 through January 16, 1991.* Preliminary Inquiry into Allegations

Regarding Senators Cranston, DeConcini, Glenn, McCain, and Riegle, and Lincoln Savings and Loan, 4, 85. The hearings are on videotape. Warren B. Rudman, *Combat: Twelve Years in the U.S. Senate* (New York: Random House, 1996).

24. Ibid.

25. Ibid., 2–4, 8–9.

26. Ibid. 5, 6, 12, 13, 24, 78, 80, 88; see also *Arizona Republic,* November 20, 22, 1990; *New York Times,* November 20, 21, 1990.

27. *Report of Temporary Special Independent Counsel, Pursuant to Senate Resolution 202.* 1992, 70.

28. *Boston Globe,* February 29, 2000, "Pluck, Leaks Helped McCain to Overcome S&L Scandal." See also *New York Times,* November 22, 1990, "Washington Talk: Private War within Public Hearing." *Washington Post,* November 21, 1990, *New York Times,* November 21, 1990.

29. See John McCain and Robert Salter, *Faith of My Fathers: A Family Memoir* (New York: Random House, 1999); Robert Timberg, *The Nightingale's Song* (New York: Simon and Schuster, 1996).

30. *New York Times,* November 22, 1990.

31. Nelson Issleib to Dennis DeConcini, November 15, 1990, DeConcini Congressional Papers Collection, Box 214.

32. W. Michael Flood to Howell Heflin, November 15, 1990, DeConcini Congressional Papers Collection, Box 214.

33. I regretted that before the Keating situation exploded on the national scene, I had not supported Daniel Inouye for majority leader. The Senate Caucus held an election, and several strong candidates emerged for this important post, notably Senator Inouye, my friend and neighbor Bennett Johnston of Louisiana, and Senator George Mitchell of Maine. Mitchell had done a remarkable job running the Senate Campaign Committee, raising an unprecedented amount of money and quickly becoming a popular figure. He gained a reputation for his brilliance as well. I instinctively supported Inouye because of the kind of man he was, but I eventually went with Johnston because of the close ties and friendship. Johnston would have been a good majority leader, but the most competent candidate was Inouye. Both Johnston and Inouye went down to resounding defeat with Mitchell's rising popularity and fund-raising abilities. Later, I explained my vote to Inouye, and he said he understood those kinds of ties; he could not have been nicer.

Chapter 9. A New Federalism for American Indians: The Navajo Nation at a Crossroad

1. Dennis Burke to Jack L. August Jr., September 18, 2005, Phoenix, Arizona, Jack August's files.

2. For information on the Navajos, see Peter Iverson, *The Navajo Nation* (Albuquerque: University of New Mexico Press, 1983); Peter Iverson, *The Navajos* (New York: Chelsea House, 1990); Peter Iverson, *The Navajos: A Critical Bibliography* (Bloomington: Indiana University Press, 1976); John Upton Terrell, *The Navajos: The Past and Present of a Great People* (New York: Harper and Row, 1970); Gerald Thompson, *The Army and the Navajo* (Tucson: University of Arizona Press, 1976).

3. See *Arizona Republic,* October 4, 11, 18, 25, 1987.

4. See U.S. Senate, "Part One, Executive Summary: New Federalism for American Indians," in *Final Report and Legislative Recommendations: A Report of the Special Committee of Investigations of the Select Committee on Indian Affairs of the United States Senate,* 101st Cong., 1st sess. (Washington, D.C.: Government Printing Office, 1989), 3–5; Richard White, *It's Your Misfortune and None of My Own: A New History of the American West* (Norman: University of Oklahoma Press, 1993), chapters 2–5.

5. Ken Ballen, DeConcini staff director and chief counsel, "Dennis DeConcini and the Senate Select Committee on Indian Affairs," interview by Jack L. August Jr., September 20, 2002, Washington, D.C., DeConcini Congressional Papers Collection.

6. See "New Federalism for American Indians," 6.

7. Ballen interview by August, September 20, 2002. Tribal officials on other Native American reservations also blatantly sought improper payments.

8. Ibid.

9. See "New Federalism for American Indians," 182.

10. *Gallup Independent,* February 20, 1987. The largest American Indian tribe in the United States is the Navajo Nation. It includes a population of more than 250,000, and its land mass is larger than West Virginia and eight other states.

11. Ballen interview by August, September 20, 2002; "New Federalism for American Indians," 13–14.

12. As the costs of MacDonald's corruption began to weigh on the tribe,

he shifted the blame to the BIA in the Department of Interior. Because of the blur of overlapping responsibilities and duplication of bureaucracies, MacDonald maintained that Navajo prosperity was subverted simply by the overbearing presence of the BIA, or as he labeled it, "Boss Indians Around." As it turned out, many of MacDonald's wrongdoings fell between the cracks of existing federal law, which made his prosecution extremely difficult. Significantly, his conduct was not unique. While targeting the BIA as a scapegoat, he profited at the expense of his people.

13. *Los Angeles Times*, February 18, 1989; *Arizona Republic*, February 20, 21, 1989; *Arizona Daily Star*, February 20, 21, 1989; *Gallup Independent* (New Mexico), April 14, 1989; *Albuquerque Journal*, April 8, 1989.

14. *Washington Post*, February 17, 1989; *Arizona Republic*, July 21, 22, 1989; *Gallup Independent*, April 8, 14, 15, 1989.

Chapter 10. Transitions

1. See "DeConcini: Advice to Dukakis on Winning the White House," *Arizona Republic*, October 16, 1988.

2. *Arizona Daily Star*, October 15, 1988.

3. *Arizona Daily Star*, November 6, 1988.

4. Dill interview by August, June 6, 2003; Ron Ober, interview by August, May 8, 2004. My staff put together background material about three separate CAP routes in Pima County and distributed this material to the press. Unfortunately, this information was inaccurate, and the situation spiraled out of control. We dropped seventeen points in the polls in three days. We called on Ray Strother, a seasoned media ad man, who shot a commercial with me looking straight into the camera. As Ron Ober put it, "That ad stopped the bleeding."

5. *Arizona Daily Star*, October 25, 1988; *Arizona Republic*, October 25, 1988.

6. *Arizona Republic*, October 29, 1988. Lee Ackerman, general partner of Lake Pleasant Associates, told reporters that the government's decision to acquire the land near Lake Pleasant killed plans that he and the other investors, including 4-D, had for constructing a private resort. He went on to say that the federal government, in conjunction with Maricopa County, planned to build its own resort in competition with the private sector.

7. Dennis DeConcini to Bob Olsen, February 8, 1985, DeConcini Con-

gressional Papers Collection, Box 121, Folder 14; *Arizona Republic*, October 29, 1988.

8. *Arizona Republic*, October 26, 29, and November 1, 1988.

9. *Arizona Republic*, November 4, 1988; *Phoenix Gazette*, November 4, 1988.

10. *Arizona Daily Star*, November 2, 1988. Hugh Caldwell, a Republican attorney from Tucson, issued a statement to the press: "We are disappointed that the Republican Senatorial Committee has sent money to air distorted, negative commercials."

11. *Arizona Daily Star*, November 4, 1988.

12. *Arizona Republic*, November 5, 1988. Orrin Hatch, press release, November 4, 1988; Paul Laxalt, press release, November 4, 1988, DeConcini Congressional Papers Collection, Box 118, Folder 8.

13. Arizona Secretary of State, *General Election, Official Canvass* (Phoenix: State of Arizona, November 8, 1988).

14. DeGreen received 24.9 percent in Pima County, whereas Rick Tompkins garnered 1.6 percent, and the inveterate irritant Ed Finkelstein convinced 718 Pima County residents—only 0.7 percent—to vote for him.

15. In addition to these increases, the 1993 tax bill included other salient features. President Clinton proposed to add a 10 percent surtax to the top rate of individuals earning $250,000, to expand the earned income tax credit for families of the working poor and some lower-income workers with no children, to create a broad-based tax on energy that the administration said would be borne entirely by consumers, to cut the deductible share of business meals and entertainment from 80 percent to 50 percent, and to eliminate the tax deduction on club dues. Beyond these modifications, he also wanted to create a permanent investment tax credit for equipment purchases by small businesses and a temporary investment credit for stepped-up equipment purchases by big business.

16. *Washington Post*, May 4, 1993; *Wall Street Journal*, May 4, 5, 1993; *Arizona Republic*, May 4, 1993.

17. David S. Broder, "Senate's Master of 'Maybe': DeConcini Forces Clinton into Hard Bargaining," *Washington Post*, August 4, 1993. I first told George Mitchell, the majority leader, that I could not vote for the Reconciliation Act. Then I went to the White House and told President Clinton that I would vote for it if they did not have the votes. I knew that was like saying "yes."

18. Kyl had represented Arizona's congressional District Four since 1987.

19. *Washington Post,* August 4, 1993; *Arizona Republic,* August 4, 5, 1993; *Arizona Daily Star,* August 4, 5, 1993.

20. *Washington Post,* August 4, 1993; *Wall Street Journal,* August 5, 1993.

21. *Wall Street Journal,* August 5, 1993. Robert Reinhold of the *Wall Street Journal* assessed the political nuances surrounding my vote: "Mr. DeConcini was the only Senator mentioned by the President in his address Tuesday night. And Mr. DeConcini stayed in the political spotlight today with a trip to the Oval Office for a declaration from Mr. Clinton establishing the deficit fund, and with a news conference a few hours later announcing his support of the Clinton economic plan. It was a role the 56-year-old Senator has often relished as an unpredictable moderate Democrat who straddles political fences and delays his decision on close votes to gain leverage, sometimes voting with his party but often with the Republicans. This strategy has kept him in office even though Arizona has 40,000 more registered Republicans than Democrats. In 1988 he won 57 percent of the vote defeating Keith DeGreen, a little-known Republican opponent."

22. Warner had been ranking Republican on the Armed Services Committee, but had been usurped from that position by Strom Thurmond due to seniority. Because of the complexity of the rules, Warner had the problem of finding placement for about eleven staff people for this committee.

23. In a move for efficiency and bipartisanship, I decided to keep Brit Snyder, a Republican, as legal counsel to the committee. Under the previous Intelligence Committee administration, an office of legal counsel for the majority and minority existed. The majority counsel had left, and Snyder had taken over duties for the committee as a whole. I had worked with Brit for many years, knew he was bipartisan, and elected to keep him as the only legal counsel.

24. Asia Ayadintasbis, "The Midnight Ride of James Woolsey," *Salon* (December 21, 2001): 1–4.

25. In fact, Senator Warner and I, very early in our tenure, articulated our views that we were for more human intelligence first, then for other priorities. On a number of occasions prior to the markup of the intelligence bill, we investigated the budgets of the various agencies. In my opinion, we had one of the most extensive analyses of the CIA budget up to that time. The NSA, in fact, objected to our funding formula, and I went out

to its headquarters in Maryland, where I found computers scattered about, little security, leaking roofs, liquids destroying computers, and garbage cans punctuating the interior of buildings. Before I was going to authorize $250,000 for more computers, I wanted to see a plan that detailed the needs and uses of these computers. The NSA conformed, and it received the requested computers and space in the following year's budget.

26. Woolsey, after this budget skirmish, remarked that I cut the CIA's language capability when I was chairman of the Intelligence Committee. I did not give him the increases he requested because the committee's priorities and judgments—unanimous, by the way—were to increase human intelligence. In Iraq, Afghanistan, and other areas of conflict, this type of intelligence has proved crucial. Woolsey ultimately resigned—was unofficially fired—as CIA director after a little more than two years in office. He was unhappy with the Clinton administration and endorsed Bob Dole for president in 1996.

27. It is my longstanding contention that the American people will accept secret intelligence activity if certain conditions underpin the process. First, the acts must be consistent with policy goals; they must be carefully controlled under U.S. law; the operations should be consistent with basic American values and beliefs; and finally, when American intelligence agencies make errors, we must learn from them. In addition, because much of what the intelligence services do is secret, congressional oversight is crucial to proving to the American people that these conditions are being met.

28. The damage outlined here does not address the complexity or severity of Ames's deception. He identified CIA and other intelligence community personnel and provided details of technical collection and analytic techniques. During one "assignment," he delivered a stack of documents twenty feet high to the KGB.

29. It seems that Ames's sole motivation was greed; he was paid approximately $2.7 million for his activities.

30. For the sum and substance of these hearings on Ames, see U.S. Senate, *Statement of the Director of Central Intelligence on the Clandestine Services and the Damage Caused by Aldrich Ames*, 103rd Cong., 2d sess., December 7, 1995, 1–7.

31. *Wall Street Journal*, September 17, 1994.

32. See Jack L. August Jr., *Vision in the Desert: Carl Hayden and Hydro-*

politics in the American Southwest (Ft. Worth: Texas Christian University Press, 1999).

33. Dick Mahoney made an ill-fated and controversial run for governor of Arizona as an independent in 2002.

34. I am convinced William Mahoney would have been elected to the House had it not been for the right-to-work issue.

35. The Cracchiolos and DeConcinis have been Tucson-based friends for more than forty years. Andrea, Dan's younger brother, as mentioned earlier, went to school with me since the first grade and is a world-renowned orthopedic surgeon at the University of California, Los Angeles.

36. Dennis DeConcini, oral history interview by Jack L. August Jr., December 20, 2002, Tucson, Arizona.

37. *Arizona Republic,* September 17, 1993; *Washington Post,* September 17, 1993; *Roll Call,* September 20, 1993. As I left office, most newspapers mentioned the Keating scandal along with my committee assignments, including on the Senate Intelligence Committee, the Appropriations Committee, and the Subcommittee on Treasury, Postal Service, and Government. They also noted that in the Judiciary Committee, I headed up the panel on patents, copyrights, and trademarks. Senator David Durenberger (R–Minnesota) shared the media spotlight with me because he announced his retirement at the same time. His retirement was expected, whereas mine was "a surprise."

38. As it turned out, my chief of staff, Gene Karp, took vacation during the last two weeks of my term and thus was unavailable to help shut down, though Nancy Sutter, my executive assistant, was there each day helping me box items and store them or send them to the University of Arizona, where my congressional papers are housed.

39. Jack Valenti was a formidable lobbyist in his own right, and he employed the firm of Parry and Romani as soon as that partnership was formed.

40. Dick Bilby, my old friend from Tucson, and my mother counseled against pursuing a lobbyist role, but I decided to accept Romano's offer.

Chapter 11. Memories and Reflections

1. See *Arizona Republic,* February 16, 2004.

2. In fact, Campbell was a member of the 1964 U.S. Olympic Team in judo.

3. Pat Leahy also served with me on the Appropriations Committee.

4. Hatch filed his candidacy on the last day possible.

5. This trip lasted about two weeks, and Bob Maynes, my press secretary, met us in England and flew with the group to Helsinki. He was following up on several cases of Jewish Soviet Refuseniks who had applied for visas to leave the Soviet Union. Under the regime of Leonid Brezhnev, Refuseniks were often victims of police harassment, interrogation, and incarceration.

6. No wives were allowed for the photo sessions with Brezhnev or other Soviet leaders.

7. We also traveled to Minsk on this trip, the area of Belarus from which Senator Ribicoff's family emigrated. In a little village near Minsk, Ribicoff and his wife went searching for their roots. Unfortunately, the military had destroyed the village during World War II, but we did come across several people who knew his family, news that heartened the Connecticut senator.

8. In my view, the Palestinians set the stage for more meaningful negotiations.

9. The conditions in the townships were deplorable beyond description. Apartheid had bred a tremendous economic and cultural gap between whites and blacks.

10. These senators went to Kentucky to help with incorporation as a nonprofit, nongovernment organization at the behest of Senator Mitch McConnell; Dan Broughton, a nationally recognized physician; and Robbie Callaway, executive director of the Boys and Girls Clubs.

SELECTED BIBLIOGRAPHY

Although this account is autobiographical, much research in primary and secondary sources was conducted to validate, elucidate, and support factual information in the narrative. The items listed in the bibliography were especially valuable in preparing this book, but they do not represent all the sources consulted.

Archives and Manuscript Collections

Dennis DeConcini Congressional Papers Collection. Special Collections, University of Arizona Library, Tucson.

Ernest McFarland Papers. Ernest McFarland State Park, Florence, Arizona.

Personal and Political Papers of Barry M. Goldwater. Arizona Historical Foundation, Hayden Library, Arizona State University, Tempe.

Roy Elson Collection. Arizona Historical Foundation, Hayden Library, Arizona State University, Tempe.

Stephen Shadegg Collection. Arizona Historical Foundation, Hayden Library, Arizona State University, Tempe

Books

Abbott, Carl. *The New Urban America: Growth and Politics in Sunbelt Cities.* Chapel Hill: University of North Carolina Press, 1982.

Adams, James R. *The Big Fix: Inside the S&L Scandal: How an Unholy Alliance of Politics and Money Destroyed America's Banking System.* New York: John Wiley and Sons, 1990.

Arrington, Leonard, and David Bitton. *The Mormon Experience: A History of Latter Day Saints.* New York: Knopf, 1979.

August, Jack L., Jr. *Vision in the Desert: Carl Hayden and Hydropolitics in the American Southwest.* Ft. Worth: Texas Christian University Press, 1999.

Bacon, Donald, Roger Davidson, and Morton Keller, eds. *Encyclopedia of the United States Congress.* New York: Simon and Schuster, 1995.

Baker, Richard A. *First among Equals: Outstanding Senate Leaders of the Twentieth Century.* Washington, D.C.: Congressional Quarterly, 1991.

——. *The Senate of the United States: A Bicentennial History.* Melbourne, Fla.: Krieger, 1988.

Bowden, Charles, and Michael Binstein. *Trust Me: Charles Keating and the Missing Billions.* New York: Random House, 1993.

Brands, H. W. *TR: The Last Romantic.* New York: Basic Books, 1997.

Brock, David. *The Real Anita Hill: The Untold Story.* New York: Touchstone, 1997.

Calavita, Kathy, Henry N. Pontell, and Robert Tillman. *Big Money Game: Fraud and Politics in the S&L Crisis.* Berkeley: University of California Press, 1997.

Davidson, Osha Gray. *Under Fire: The NRA and the Battle for Gun Control.* Henry Holt: New York, 1993.

Day, Kathleen. *S&L Hell: The People and Politics behind the $1 Trillion Savings and Loan Scandal.* New York: W. W. Norton, 1993.

DeConcini, Evo. *Hey! It's Past 80: A Biography of a Busy Life.* Tucson: Sunrise Graphics, 1981.

Foskett, Ken. *Judging Thomas: The Life and Times of Clarence Thomas.* New York: William Morrow, 2004.

Garreau, Joel. *Edge City: Life on the New Frontier.* New York: Doubleday, 1990.

Gates, Paul W. *History of Public Land Law Development.* Washington, D.C.: Arno Press, 1979.

Goldberg, Robert Alan. *Goldwater.* New Haven, Conn.: Yale University Press, 1995.

Hill, Anita. *Speak Truth to Power.* New York: Doubleday, 1997.

Iverson, Peter. *The Navajo Nation.* Albuquerque: University of New Mexico Press, 1983.

——. *The Navajos.* New York: Chelsea House, 1990.

——. *The Navajos: A Critical Bibliography.* Bloomington: Indiana University Press, 1976.

Johnson, Rich. *The Central Arizona Project, 1918–1968.* Tucson: University of Arizona Press, 1977.

Mayer, Martin. *The Greatest Ever Bank Robbery: The Collapse of the Savings and Loan Industry.* New York: Charles Scribner and Sons, 1990.

McCain, John, and Robert Salter. *Faith of My Fathers: A Family Memoir.* New York: Random House, 1999.

McCulloch, David. *Path between the Seas: The Creation of the Panama Canal, 1870–1914.* New York: Simon and Schuster, 2002.

McMillan, James Elton. *Ernest W. McFarland: Majority Leader of the U.S. Senate.* Prescott, Ariz.: Sharlot Hall Museum Press, 2004.

Nash, Gerald. *The American West in the Twentieth Century: A Short History of an Urban Oasis.* Albuquerque: University of New Mexico Press, 1977.

——. *The American West Transformed: The Impact of World War Two.* Bloomington: Indian University Press, 1985.

——. *World War II and the West: Reshaping the Economy.* Lincoln: University of Nebraska Press, 1990.

Nugent, Walter. *Into the West: A Story of Its People.* New York: Vintage Books, 1999.

Pizzo, Stephen, Mary Fricker, and Paul Muolo. *Inside Job: The Looting of America's Savings and Loans.* New York: McGraw Hill, 1989.

Reisner, Marc. *Cadillac Desert: The American West and Its Disappearing Water.* New York: Viking, 1986.

Rhodes, John. *I Was There.* Salt Lake City: Northwest, 1995.

Richardson, Elmo. *Dams, Parks, and Politics: Resource Development in the Truman-Eisenhower Era.* Lexington: University Press of Kentucky, 1973.

Rudman, Warren B. *Combat: Twelve Years in the U.S. Senate.* New York: Random House, 1996.

Schweikert, Larry. *A History of Banking in Arizona.* Tucson: University of Arizona Press, 1982.

Sheridan, Thomas. *Arizona: A History.* Tucson: University of Arizona Press, 1995.

Sinclair, Barbara. *The Transformation of the U.S. Senate.* Baltimore: Johns Hopkins University Press, 1989.

Terrell, John Upton. *The Navajos: The Past and Present of a Great People.* New York: Harper and Row, 1970.

Thompson, Gerald. *The Army and the Navajo.* Tucson: University of Arizona Press, 1976.

Timberg, Robert. *The Nightingale's Song.* New York: Simon and Schuster, 1996.

Unger, Irwin. *These United States.* Vol. 2. Boston: Little Brown, 1978.

Watkins, Ronald J. *High Crimes and Misdemeanors: The Term and Trial of Former Governor Evan Mecham.* New York: William Morrow, 1990.

White, Richard. *It's Your Misfortune and None of My Own: A New History of the American West.* Norman: University of Oklahoma Press, 1993.

Wiley, Peter, and Robert Gottlieb. *Empires in the Sun: The Rise of the New American West.* New York: P. G. Putnam's Sons, 1982.

Government Documents

Arizona Secretary of State. *General Election, Official Canvass.* Phoenix: State of Arizona, November 2, 1976.

——. *General Election, Official Canvass.* Phoenix: State of Arizona, November 2, 1982.

——. *Primary Election, Official Canvass.* Phoenix: State of Arizona, September 7, 1976.

——. *Primary Election, Official Canvass.* Phoenix: State of Arizona, September 7, 1982.

U.S. Congress. *Congressional Quarterly Fact Sheet.* Washington, D.C.: Government Printing Office.

U.S. Congress. House of Representatives. Committee on Banking, Finance, and Urban Affairs. *Investigation of Lincoln Savings and Loan Association.* 101st Cong., 1st sess., 1989.

U.S. Congress. Senate. 95th Cong., 1st sess., 2d sess., 1977–79.

——. 96th Cong., 1st sess., 2d sess., 1979–81.

——. 97th Cong., 1st sess., 2d sess., 1981–83.

——. 98th Cong., 1st sess., 2d sess., 1983–85.

——. 99th Cong., 1st sess., 2d sess., 1985–87.

——. 100th Cong., 1st sess., 2d sess., 1987–89.

——. 101st Cong., 1st sess., 2d sess., 1989–91.

——. 102d Cong., 1st sess., 2d sess., 1991–93.

——. 103rd Cong., 1st sess., 2d sess., 1993–95.

——. Select Committee on Ethics. *Investigation of Lincoln Savings and Loan Association.* 101st Cong., 1st sess., 1989.

U.S. Department of the Interior and U.S. Congress, Senate. *Decisions of the Secretary of the Interior* and *Final Report and Legislative Recommendations: A Report of the Special Committee of Investigations of the Select Committee on Indian Affairs of the United States Senate,* 101st Cong., 1st sess. Washington, D.C.: Government Printing Office, 1989.

Newspapers and Periodicals

Albuquerque Journal
Arizona Blade Tribune (Florence)
Arizona Daily Star (Tucson)
Arizona Daily Sun (Flagstaff)
Arizona Range News (Wilcox)
Arizona Republic (Phoenix)
Daily Courier (Prescott)
Gallup Independent (New Mexico)
Los Angeles Times
Newsweek magazine
New Times (Phoenix)
New York Times
Phoenix Gazette
Regardie's (Washington, D.C.)
Roll Call (Washington, D.C.)
Sacramento Bee
Saturday Evening Post
Scottsdale Progress
Time magazine
Tucson Citizen
Washington Post
Washington Times
White Mountain Independent (St. Johns, Arizona)

Journal Articles

August, Jack L., Jr. "Old Arizona and the New Conservative Agenda: The Hayden-Mecham Senate Campaign of 1962." *Journal of Arizona History* 41 (winter 2000): 385–412.

Ayadintasbis, Asia. "The Midnight Ride of James Woolsey." *Salon* (December 21, 2001): 1–4.

Houghton, N. D. "Problems of the Colorado River as Reflected in Arizona Politics." *Western Political Quarterly* 4 (December 1951): 634–43.

Konig, Michael. "Phoenix in the 1950s: Urban Growth in the 'Sunbelt.'" *Arizona and the West* 24 (1982): 19–38.

Lamar, Howard R. "Persistent Frontier: The West in the Twentieth Century." *Western Historical Quarterly* 4 (January 1973): 5–26.

Lamb, Blaine. "A Many Checkered Toga: Arizona Senator Ralph Cameron, 1921–1927." *Arizona and the West* 19 (spring 1977): 47–64.

Luckingham, Bradford. "Urban Development in Arizona: The Rise of Phoenix." *Journal of Arizona History* 22 (summer 1981): 197–234.

Pomeroy, Earl. "Toward a Reorientation of Western History: Continuity and Environment." *Mississippi Valley Historical Review* 41 (March 1955): 579–600.

Ridge, Martin. "Ray Allen Billington, Western History, and American Exceptionalism." *Pacific Historical Review* 56 (November 1987): 495–512.

Robbins, William G. "The 'Plundered Province' Thesis and Recent Historiography of the American West." *Pacific Historical Review* 55 (November 1986): 577–98.

Worster, Donald. "New West, True West: Interpreting the Region's History." *Western Historical Quarterly* 18 (April 1987): 141–50.

Oral History Interviews

Ballen, Kenneth. "Dennis DeConcini and the Senate Select Committee on Indian Affairs." Interview by Jack L. August Jr. Dennis DeConcini Congressional Papers Collections, Special Collections, University of Arizona Library, Tucson, 2002.

DeConcini, Dennis. Oral history interviews by Jack L. August Jr. Dennis DeConcini Congressional Papers Collection, Special Collections, University of Arizona Library, Tucson, 2002, 2003, 2004.

DeConcini, Ora Webster. Oral history interviews by James F. McNulty. Evo DeConcini Oral History Project (EDOHP), Arizona Historical Society, Tucson, 1986.

Dill, Barry. "Dennis DeConcini Oral History Interviews." Interviewed by Jack L. August Jr. Dennis DeConcini Congressional Papers Collection, Special Collections, University of Arizona Library, Tucson, 2002, 2003.

Elson, Roy. "Dennis DeConcini and the Democrats." Oral history interview by Jack L. August Jr. Dennis DeConcini Congressional Papers Collection, Special Collections, University of Arizona Library, Tucson, 2004.

Hawkins, Michael. "Dennis DeConcini and His First Campaign." Oral history interview by Jack L. August Jr. Dennis DeConcini Congressional Papers Collection, Special Collections, University of Arizona Library, Tucson, 2003.

Murphy, Patrick. "Dennis DeConcini and Evan Mecham." Oral history interview by Jack L. August Jr. Dennis DeConcini Congressional Papers Collection, Special Collections, University of Arizona Library, Tucson, 2002.

Ober, Ron. "Dennis DeConcini Oral Histories." Oral history interviews by Jack L. August. Dennis DeConcini Congressional Papers Collection, Special Collections, University of Arizona Library, Tucson, 2002, 2003.

Pfister, Jack. "Dennis DeConcini and Phoenix Republicans." Oral history interview by Jack L. August Jr. Dennis DeConcini Congressional Papers Collection, Special Collections, University of Arizona Library, Tucson, 2004.

Rappaport, Michael. "Dennis DeConcini and the Central Arizona Project." Oral history interview by Jack L. August Jr. Dennis DeConcini Congressional Papers Collection, Special Collections, University of Arizona Library, Tucson, 2002.

Romani, Romano. "Dennis DeConcini Oral History." Oral history interview by Jack L. August Jr. Dennis DeConcini Congressional Papers Collection, Special Collections, University of Arizona Library, Tucson, 2003.

Sedlmayr, Laurie. "Dennis DeConcini and the Keating Five Scandal." Oral history interview by Jack L. August Jr. Dennis DeConcini Congressional Papers Collection, Special Collections, University of Arizona Library, Tucson, 2002.

Steiger, Sam. "My 1976 Campaign against Dennis DeConcini." Oral history interview by Jack L. August Jr. Dennis DeConcini Congressional Papers Collection, Special Collections, University of Arizona Library, Tucson, 2002.

Unpublished Manuscript

DeConcini, Ora. "Oscar and Ollie Webster." Unpublished manuscript, n.d., Dennis DeConcini Congressional Papers Collection, Special Collections, University of Arizona Library, Tucson.

INDEX

ABOUT THE AUTHORS

Dennis Webster DeConcini, born in Tucson, Arizona, May 8, 1937, served as a U.S. senator from the state of Arizona for three successive terms, 1977 to 1995. During his tenure, he served on the Senate Appropriations Committee (where he chaired the Subcommittee on Treasury, Postal Service, and General Government); the Subcommittee on Defense, Energy, and Water Development; the Subcommittee on Foreign Operations; the Senate Judiciary Committee; the Subcommittee on Antitrust, Monopolies, and Business Rights; the Subcommittee on the Constitution and the Courts; and the Select Intelligence Committee (for which he was the chair in 1993 and 1994). Senator DeConcini also chaired the Subcommittee on Patents, Copyrights, and Trademarks and the Commission on Security and Cooperation in Europe (Helsinki Commission). In February 1995, President Bill Clinton appointed Senator DeConcini to the board of directors of the Federal Home Loan Mortgage Corporation. In that year, Senator DeConcini joined the Washington, D.C., lobby firm of Parry, Romani, DeConcini, and Symms. Prior to his election to the Senate, he served one elected term as Pima County attorney (1972–76), where he acted as the chief prosecutor and civil attorney for the county and for the school districts within the county. He was also the legal counsel and administrative assistant to the governor of Arizona and founded the law firm of DeConcini, McDonald, Yetwin, and Lacy (where he is presently a partner with offices in Tucson, Phoenix, and the District of Columbia). He received his bachelor's degree from the University of Arizona in 1959 and his law degree from the University of Arizona in 1963.

Dr. Jack L. August Jr. serves as executive director of the Arizona Historical Foundation at Arizona State University, where he teaches graduate courses in water policy and management. He has taught at the University of Houston, the University of Northern British Columbia, Prescott College, and Northern Arizona University, where his courses focused on the history of the American West and environmental history. He is a former Fulbright scholar, National Endowment for the Humanities Research Fellow, and Pulitzer Prize nominee in the history category for his volume *Vision in the Desert: Carl Hayden and Hydropolitics in the American Southwest* (Ft. Worth: Texas Christian University Press, 1999). He served as historian and expert witness in the Natural Resources Section of the Arizona Attorney General's Office, where his work focused on Indian versus non-Indian water-rights issues and state trust lands. He has also worked in that capacity for Arizona State University, the city of Tempe, the city of Buckeye, the city of Tucson, and private law firms representing clients with land and water-rights claims. He has appeared on numerous television and radio programs, including *Horizon, Arizona Illustrated,* the KAET/PBS documentary *Arizona Memories from the 1960s,* and National Public Radio features. He is a frequent contributor to magazines and historical journals, including *Arizona Highways, Journal of Arizona History, Pacific Historical Review, Western Historical Quarterly,* and many others. He is working on the definitive biography of Mark Wilmer, who argued and won the legendary U.S. Supreme Court case *Arizona v. California* (1963). He received his bachelor's degree from Yale University in 1975, his master's degree from the University of Arizona in 1979, and his Ph.D. from the University of New Mexico in 1985.